THE TORSO MURDER

THE TORSO MURDER

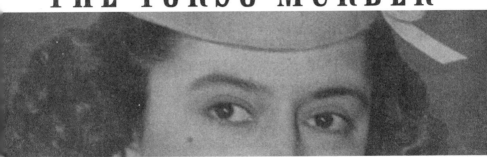

The Untold Story of Evelyn Dick

Brian Vallée

KEY PORTER ✒ BOOKS

National Library of Canada Cataloguing in Publication Data

Vallée, Brian
    The torso murder: the untold story of Evelyn Dick

Includes index.
ISBN 1-55263-340-3

1. Dick, Evelyn, 1920- . 2. Dick, Evelyn, 1920- – Trials, litigation, etc. 3. Dick, John, d. 1946. 4. Murder – Ontario – Hamilton. 5. Trials (Murder) – Ontario – Hamilton. 6. Murderers – Canada – Biography. I. Title.

HV6535.C33H35 2001   364.15'23'092   C00-9333327-4

THE CANADA COUNCIL | LE CONSEIL DES ARTS
FOR THE ARTS | DU CANADA
SINCE 1957 | DEPUIS 1957

ONTARIO ARTS COUNCIL
CONSEIL DES ARTS DE L'ONTARIO

The publisher gratefully acknowledges the support of the Canada Council for the Arts and the Ontario Arts Council for its publishing program.

We acknowledge the financial support of the Government of Canada through the Book Publishing Industry Development Program (BPIDP) for our publishing activities.

Key Porter Books Limited
70 The Esplanade
Toronto, Ontario
Canada M5E 1R2

www.keyporter.com

Electronic formatting: Heidi Palfrey

Printed and bound in Canada

01 02 03 04 05 06 6 5 4 3 2 1

For Mary Louise Lynch,
keeper of the secret and one tough woman

Acknowledgments

I would like to thank Anne Pick, of *Real to Reel*, for recommending that I write this book and for inviting me to work on her documentary *The Notorious Mrs. Dick*. Special thanks also to Sarah Jane Flynn for her tireless research help.

At Key Porter Books I would like to thank Anna Porter and Susan Renouf for taking on the project; editor Susan Folkins for her patience and advice; copy editor John Sweet; and Lyn Cadence and Alyssa Stuart in the publicity department.

Special thanks also to Linda Larsen, John Honderich, Andrea Hall and Jean Bradshaw for allowing me access to photographs and archives in the *Toronto Star* library; Margaret Houghton, archivist in Special Collections at the Hamilton Public Library; Sandra Guillaume and Corrado Santoro at the Archives of Ontario; and Jeanie Tummon, curator of the Ontario Provincial Police Museum.

When I embarked on this project I was determined to find out what I could about John Dick's personality and character. To that end, I contacted pastor Martin Friesen of the United Mennonite Church in Vineland, Ontario, and asked him to intercede on my behalf with Dick's Mennonite relatives. After contacting them, he told me the relatives didn't want to talk to me. I called one of Dick's nephews to make a personal appeal. He hung up on me. I thank Pastor Friesen for his efforts. Given the circumstances, I hope I have done justice to John Dick's memory.

contents

Sweet is the lore which nature brings;
Our meddling intellect
Misshapes the beauteous forms of things;
We murder to dissect.

—WILLIAM WORDSWORTH

Sooner murder an infant in its cradle
than nurse unacted desires

—WILLIAM BLAKE

Prologue

It was sometime in the fall of 1962 when Mary Louise Lynch strode into the lobby of Ottawa's Château Laurier. Tall and trim in a custom-cut black wool dress and jacket, she was as stately as the room itself. She had never met the woman she was to have lunch with, but she knew all about her and had studied her photos in the file. And the woman would recognize Lynch from the newspapers. Lynch had become a fixture in Ottawa's political and social life since her appointment to the new National Parole Board two years earlier. She was a successful fifty-year-old lawyer in Fredericton, New Brunswick, when Attorney General Davie Fulton, with the blessing of Prime Minister John Diefenbaker, asked her to take the ten-year appointment. They had wanted a woman on the board. That she was a lawyer and a lifelong Tory made her an inspired choice for Fulton.

The bust of the hotel's namesake, Sir Wilfrid Laurier, looked down on Lynch as she surveyed the lobby for her luncheon partner. A lot of famous people, from Winston Churchill to Marlene Dietrich, King George VI to Barbara Ann Scott had stayed at the Château since its opening in 1912. And its bars and restaurants had a regular clientele of business people, politicians, lobbyists, hangers-on and journalists. Lynch was certain no previous patron would match the notoriety of her luncheon guest.

The two women spotted each other almost simultaneously. Lynch thought her guest attractive, prettier than her photos. As she started towards her, she saw veteran CBC newsman Norman DePoe approaching. He had been heading for the hotel bar when he spotted Lynch. The other woman noticed DePoe and turned away. The gravel-voiced newsman was considered by many to be the best political broadcast reporter on Parliament Hill. Intelligent and hard-working, he was also a legendary drinker. "What's the first thing you do in the morning?" he was once asked. "I have a cigarette and I vomit—doesn't everybody?" replied DePoe. Lynch knew that DePoe was always on the lookout for a good story. But after a couple of minutes of agreeable small talk he continued towards the bar.

Lynch turned to see her guest approaching. She was short and slim, in a stylish suit and hat. Lynch noticed that her hands were small and lovely.

"You're Miss Lynch, right?"

"Yes, and I recognized you right away."

"Wasn't that Norman DePoe you were talking to?"

"Yes," said Lynch. "That's why I didn't go over right away."

"If Norman DePoe only knew the story that was right under his nose . . ." said the woman, smiling.

The two of them went into the Canadian Grill, where Lynch had booked a table in one of the small alcoves. As they sat down, she noticed John Turner and an associate at a nearby table. Turner was the recently elected Liberal Member of Parliament for the federal Quebec riding of St.-Laurent–St.-Georges. Lynch had known him since his teenage days, when his family had a summer place at the exclusive New Brunswick resort town of St. Andrews by-the-sea. Turner smiled and waved at Lynch, but when he came over to kiss her on the cheek and chat, she didn't introduce him to her guest.

After he left, the woman leaned into the table. "Do people ever ask you about me?"

"Yes," said Lynch, "particularly women, who say 'Never let her out.' And I say, 'Well, she's been out a long time under the old ticket-of-leave and she's leading a very productive life.' And they are rather surprised when I tell them that."

Her guest seemed pleased. After that they talked about politics and movies. During coffee and dessert the woman smoked a cigarette in an elegant holder. Lynch thought anybody observing her with this very presentable, well-dressed woman would surely think they must be old friends. Perhaps it was that image of the two of them that prompted Lynch to reveal her thoughts.

"You know, Evelyn," she said, "the thing that puzzles me is, I do believe that you killed that baby."

Evelyn Dick stared at her intently, took a long drag on her cigarette and exhaled a slow, steady stream of smoke, creating a diaphanous barrier between them.

Ash Wednesday

MARCH 6, 1946

It was about 9:30 a.m. on Ash Wednesday when John Dick and his cousin's wife, Ann Kammerer, left the house on Gertrude Street and hopped on the King streetcar heading uptown. John had been boarding with the Kammerers and their son for just over a month. He was dressed in a gray overcoat, a conductor's cap and the navy blue uniform of the Hamilton Street Railway—the HSR—which operated the city's buses and streetcars. Brass buttons gleamed from both the overcoat and uniform jacket, beneath which he wore a blue and white pinstripe shirt, a brown tie and a blue sleeveless wool sweater. The black oxfords were required HSR footwear. He had with him a small black leather satchel for carrying his driver's equipment: tin ticket box, transfer punch, cash and metal coin holder.

John Dick's shift didn't start until 4 p.m., but he had matters to attend to beforehand. Ann noticed the fleeting smile when he greeted his fellow driver. But as they moved back in the streetcar, the familiar furrowed brow and anxious look were firmly in place. She knew he was nervous about seeing Evelyn, his beautiful young estranged wife, who had called the day before to arrange a meeting. He had been subdued at breakfast, having only coffee instead of the usual bacon and eggs. Ann concluded he must have been thinking about Evelyn. He had lived with her for only two of the five months since their October wedding. Dick, solidly built, fair, just under six feet, was thirty-nine when he married Evelyn, a dark-eyed beauty, fourteen years younger than him. It was evident early on that the marriage was doomed, and Alex Kammerer was not surprised when his cousin showed up in a taxi with all his belongings on a Sunday morning in early February.

Ann had known John Dick for thirteen years, and in all that time she had never seen him so despondent. He had lost his appetite and his weight was down. Before his recent troubles she had always found him to be even-tempered, good-natured and usually hungry. He had skipped breakfast today, but last night he was at least talking about food.

"What are you having for supper tomorrow?" he had asked Ann.

"Why? What would you like?"

"I'd really like to have fish—salmon. You're going to be uptown tomorrow anyway, so why don't you go to the fish store on York Street and pick up some salmon?"

Ann agreed.

"I'll probably be home from work late," said Dick, "so just leave me some on the back of the stove."

Now, as the streetcar lumbered past the HSR car barns and offices on King Street East, John Dick moved towards the door.

"I'll see you tonight or tomorrow morning," he said to Ann as he stepped off the car at the Sanford Avenue stop. She watched him a moment as he began the half-block walk back to the HSR.

Dick had been a conductor with the company for three years—first on streetcars, then on buses, and for the past year on streetcars again. He replaced his conductor's cap with the brown fedora he had been carrying as he approached the inspector's office adjoining the car sheds. It was shortly after 10 a.m. when he entered. Inspector William Mottram was on duty. He had worked for the HSR for more than twenty-five years and had been promoted to inspector just before John Dick joined the company.

"Can I leave my cap and bag here for a while?" asked Dick.

"OK," replied Mottram. "Just put them on the desk."

Dick left the cap and bag on the desk and quickly left the office. About three hours later, just before 1 p.m., he returned to find that Mottram had left on his lunch break, replaced by Supervisor Harvey Walters. They talked a few minutes and then Dick picked up his satchel and conductor's cap, left his fedora on the desk and headed for the door. "I'll be back," he said.

The three-story red brick house at 32 Carrick Avenue, with its inviting white veranda across the front, was in a solid middle-class neighborhood. Evelyn Dick had purchased the house herself, closing the deal near the end of October 1945. Her new husband, John Dick, had moved in with her, but after three tumultuous months he was gone for good on February 3, when he picked up the last of his things and went to live with his cousin. Twenty-five-year-old Evelyn shared the house with her four-year-old daughter, Heather; her mother, Alexandra MacLean; and a border who had moved in the day after John Dick left.

Evelyn had been at the house all morning but after lunch she was readying to go out. She was wearing a stylish gray fur coat, gray overshoes and a black turban-style hat.

"Where are you going?" asked her mother.

"I'm just going uptown," said Evelyn. "I have to pick up a couple of things. I'll be back around five."

It was about 1:30 when she left the house.

William Landeg, owner of Grafton Garage, a sprawling single-story stone building at the northwest corner of King William and Catharine streets, knew exactly what Evelyn Dick wanted when she walked into his office at 2 p.m.

"You want to borrow the car, right?"

"Right," smiled Evelyn, her dark eyes fixing his.

"The car" was a 1938 eight-cylinder black Packard sedan. Evelyn had once owned it but four years ago had sold it to Landeg in lieu of $300 she owed him for repair and storage charges. It was a good deal for him—perhaps too good—and letting her borrow the car from time to time may have eased any guilt he felt. Besides, he genuinely liked Evelyn and had known her father for many years. In the last month she had borrowed the Packard four times. Before that, he hadn't seen her in two years.

"I'll get it back by five," she promised. She knew the Packard was his personal vehicle and that he needed it for the two-mile drive home for his supper break. Landeg wasn't worried; she'd always returned the Packard on time. As he handed her the keys, he warned her there were two outboard motors on the floor of the back seat.

Proprietor Joseph Visheau noticed that John Dick was wearing a crisp blue shirt when he showed up at the Windsor Hotel dining room at King William and John streets about 2:15 p.m. Lunchtime was over and the kitchen was closed. The place was empty, but Dick took a seat at one of the tables. Visheau's sister, Agnes Viola, was the waitress that day. "I'm sorry, but the kitchen closes at two," she said.

Not only was the kitchen closed but the restaurant had a policy of serving only full-course meals. However, Visheau liked John Dick; he called him Jack. Although Jack had been coming to the restaurant off and on for three years, Visheau didn't consider him a regular and he thought it unusual that this was the third day in a row he had showed up. Just the night before he had rushed in out of the rain.

"Can I order supper?" he had asked, swiping the rain from his coat.

"Sorry, Jack," said Visheau, "it's all closed up." Dick had to settle for a coffee at the bar.

The day before that—Monday—he'd made it in time for lunch. Visheau had allowed him a "short meal" of soup, pie and coffee, and he was quickly gone. "We never served short meals to anybody else," Visheau would say later.

Now here he was back again. Visheau went over to the table.

"Look, I'm in a hurry," said Dick. "And I have to go to work at four. Can't you just get me a bowl of soup?"

Visheau decided to bend the rules again. They served Dick his soup and complied when he asked to follow up with a sandwich and coffee. He ate quickly and didn't wait for his check. He went to the coffee bar, where Visheau told him he owed twenty-five cents. Dick dropped a nickel and a quarter on the counter and was gone. Always in a hurry, thought Visheau.

16

George Lawson, a stocky thirty-one-year-old detective with the Hamilton Police, was off duty on this day. He was downtown to do some mid-afternoon shopping when he noticed Bill Bohozuk in his two-tone Buick coupe in front of the Capitol Theatre.

"Standing there talking to him was Little Frances, the young girl who sold tickets at the Palace Theatre, which was only a block away," recalls Lawson, now eighty-seven. "He stood out like a sore thumb, you know—the way he dressed. And he was handsome and he had his beautiful big car."

Although Lawson and Bohozuk were both members of the Leander Boat Club, they had never been introduced and knew each other only by sight. Because of Bohozuk's reputation as a ladies' man, Lawson was feeling protective towards Frances. She was a favorite of the beat cops who regularly patrolled the downtown. They would often stop to chat with her or wave as they passed by. Frances didn't see Lawson as he walked by, but Bohozuk waved to him.

A while later Lawson was headed home after a disappointing trip to his favorite bakery for some "special cake." He'd forgotten it was closed on Wednesdays. "So I went to what they called the Polish Groceteria at the corner of Mary and King which was half a block down," says Lawson. "I did my business in there and walked back up to get the streetcar. And that's when I bumped into little Frances walking down to go to work at the Palace." He cornered her and kidded her about Bohozuk. "What are you doing talking to a fellow like that?" he asked.

"Which fellow?"

"The guy in the car I saw you talking with in front of the Capitol."

"Oh, we were just talking." Frances smiled. "He just comes into the show once in a while."

"Well you be careful," said Lawson.

Alexandra MacLean was preparing supper shortly before 6 p.m. when her daughter suddenly appeared at the back door off the kitchen and asked for the key to the garage. Behind

Evelyn, MacLean saw the large black car parked in the laneway in front of the garage.

"What are you doing with that car?" she asked, handing her daughter the key.

"I'm going to put it in the garage."

MacLean knew the garage was strewn with leftover lumber from a small second garage they had torn down when they moved in. "You're crazy," she said. "The car's too large, especially with all that old lumber in there."

"Just mind your own business."

Evelyn went to the garage, unlocked the large double doors and folded them against the front. She made several futile attempts to jockey the car into the garage. Her mother's anger grew as she watched from the kitchen window. She didn't want the car in their garage. She went outside with little Heather trailing behind. The narrow rear door to the garage was open. MacLean entered, but as she stepped around some of the loose lumber, she noticed the dirt floor was muddy and retreated outside to the laneway. It had started snowing and she noticed it was getting heavier.

"Get that car off the place altogether," she ordered. "You have no right to bring other men's cars around here."

"I told you to mind your own business," said Evelyn, her voice rising. "This is my house and this is a friend's car I have the use of, so I can do what I like." By this time she was out of the car checking damage to the right running board, which had struck the garage doorway. As she argued with her daughter, MacLean glanced at Heather standing near the back door of the house. They had recently installed a new lock and she was afraid the girl would push the door closed and they would be locked out.

From his room on the second floor of the house, boarder Robert Corbett, a student at Hamilton's Canadian Army Trade School, could see his landlady attempting to maneuver the car into the garage. He had never seen Evelyn with a car, although she once told him she owned a big Chrysler that was in storage downtown. Corbett didn't drive but thought he could help. He went downstairs, through the kitchen and out the back door.

MacLean was relieved to see him. "Would you please take Heather into the house," she said. "And keep an eye on the potatoes on the stove."

"You know," said Corbett, "if Mrs. Dick would back up on the other drive, she could get the car into the garage. It looks too big, but maybe I can help her."

"No, don't trouble yourself," said MacLean. "She is separated from John Dick and she mustn't be driving other men's cars. Just take Heather into the house if you would."

"Are you sure I couldn't help her?"

"No, it's OK. Don't bother."

Corbett shrugged, picked up the little girl and took her inside. In the kitchen, he stirred the potatoes that were boiling on the stove.

Outside, MacLean returned to her confrontation with Evelyn. "Get that car out of here," she ordered.

"I have the use of the car. You mind your own business."

"You'll never get it into the garage, so get it out of here."

Seeing the damage to the running board and realizing her mother was probably right, Evelyn jumped into the car, slammed the door and backed up the laneway. A few minutes later MacLean came in, washed her hands and served supper to Heather and Corbett.

It was about 7:30 p.m. when the passenger-side wheels of Bill Landeg's Packard mounted the curb across from the Grafton Garage show windows on Catharine Street as Evelyn Dick parked it half on the road and half on the sidewalk. Mechanic Roy Graham was reading a newspaper when she entered the office with the keys. He didn't know much about women's fashions, but he noticed her smart fur coat. Graham wasn't officially on duty. He was always on days, but tonight he was working on a friend's car as a favor.

"I need a piece of paper and an envelope," said Evelyn, handing him the keys. "I have to leave a note for Mr. Landeg. My little girl had an accident and I had to take her to the hospital. I'll see Mr. Landeg about it later."

Graham handed her a sheet of paper and she wrote a

message. "I'll just leave it here for Mr. Landeg," she said, sealing the envelope and dropping it on the office desk.

"I'll see he gets it," said Graham.

Bill Landeg arrived half an hour later, still a bit peeved that he had had to use another car to get home for his dinner break. But he was relieved when he saw the Packard parked on the street.

"She left you this," said Graham, handing him Evelyn's message. Landeg ripped open the envelope and read the note:

I am sorry I was late Mr. Landeg but my little girl cut her face and I had to take her to the hospital for stitches. She got blood on your seat cover and your cushion. I will replace them later.

Evelyn G. Dick

Crumpling the note, Landeg dropped it into the wastebasket.

About 8:30 p.m., Alexandra MacLean was on her way to the kitchen when her daughter returned home, looking grim and annoyed.

"Where were you?" she asked. Evelyn didn't reply. "Do you want any supper?"

"No," said Evelyn sharply. She went to the front hall closet, where she removed her overshoes and hung up her fur coat. Her mother, smarting from her daughter's snub, went up to bed. Following a few minutes later, Evelyn undressed and got in beside her. Neither of them spoke.

William Landeg brought the Packard into the garage from the street about 9:30 p.m. As it was wheeled in, he noticed it was splattered with mud—on the fenders, hood, windshield, even the roof. And the right running board was bent at the front near the fender. Landeg decided to put the car on the wash rack. Opening the door, he noticed that the blanket he used to cover the front seat was missing. Also missing was the caning-type seat cover with the red vinyl trim. And when his right palm landed on the middle of the seat as he was shifting his weight behind the wheel, it felt damp. When he got out after centering the car on the rack, he saw blood on his hand.

"The little girl," he thought.

Missing

THURSDAY, MARCH 7

Alexander and Ann Kammerer weren't overly concerned when they awoke to discover that John Dick had not returned from work the night before, even though he had asked that the salmon be left on the stove for him. In the past, if he was later than usual leaving work, he sometimes slept in the HSR offices and returned home the next day. They didn't think he was in any sort of trouble. "He always minded his own business," Alex Kammerer would say later. "He never had parties or anything like that, and wasn't mixed up with the wrong kind of friends. I'm positive."

The Kammerers thought he must have made up with his wife. In a previous attempt at reconciliation, John Dick hadn't bothered to inform his cousin that he had checked into the Royal Connaught Hotel. He had the room for three days but Evelyn spent only an afternoon with him.

It was 8 a.m. and William Rushton and George Meharg had already been on the job an hour with the Hamilton works department. They were in a good mood. It was crisp and sunny, and it was payday. Their job was to patrol Hamilton Mountain's main roads in a city truck, looking for potholes and potential landslides. Rushton was driving as they headed to the top of the escarpment to do some repair work. They were on Mountain Boulevard, on the face of the escarpment, heading for Flock Road, which snaked up to Mountain Brow Road along the summit.

About three or four hundred feet from the junction with Flock Road, Meharg spotted a clump of clothing in the middle of the road. "It looks like a shirt," he said.

Rushton pulled over and they got out of the truck. They could see it was a bloodstained man's shirt. There had been an overnight frost, but the early morning sun had thawed the blood.

"It looks fresh," said Meharg.

They thought it odd that the shirt was buttoned and the arms seemed to have been cut, or ripped off, below the shoulders. And there was a lot of blood around the collar, which was intact.

"Maybe there was an accident," said Rushton. But there was no evidence of tire tracks on the shirt.

Meharg kicked the shirt towards the shallow ditch at the side of the road. It came to rest near the base of the sign indicating the Flock Road junction ahead. "We'll just leave it here, and if we hear of anything, we'll report it," he said. "It will be easy enough to find."

Car dealer Alex Feilde arrived at midday to see William Landeg at the Grafton Garage. Over the years Feilde had sent a lot of vehicles to Landeg for bodywork and paint jobs, but today he was in the market for an outboard motor. Landeg had two of them in the back seat of his Packard. Which motor was he interested in? "Whichever one I could talk him out of," he said later. The motors had been in the car for more than a week now, and if Feilde wasn't interested, Landeg planned to take them to the cottage. Surely somebody at the lake would be interested.

The Packard was still on the wash rack in the back of the garage. Landeg opened the rear doors so Feilde could examine the motors on the floor. As they looked at the motors, Landeg spotted something between the back of the front seat and one of the propeller shafts. He leaned in and retrieved a blue wool sweater with dark, damp stains.

"Who in the hell does this belong to?" he said, holding it up in front of him. "It certainly doesn't belong to me."

Feilde thought the dark spots might be oil stains and he also noticed a couple of holes or tears in the sweater. Landeg shrugged and tossed it on the hood of a rusting Chrysler Air-Flow in the corner of the garage.

Feilde carefully examined both motors but left without making a purchase.

FRIDAY, MARCH 8

Alexandra MacLean was almost recovered from a five-week cold. It was a sunny day, so in the afternoon she decided to take Heather for a walk. They could both use the fresh air. As they had often done, they walked to the corner of Sherman Avenue and King Street, arriving about the time John Dick usually passed with his streetcar. Whatever problems he had with Evelyn didn't detract from the fondness he felt for Heather. She had her mother's dark hair and eyes, and he found her delightful. Whenever she walked up with her grandmother to meet him, he would sound the streetcar's gong and she would laugh and wave wildly. Today the little girl was on her toes with anticipation as the car approached but was disappointed when she didn't see John Dick in the driver's seat. "I guess he's not on today," said MacLean.

Evelyn was at home when they returned.

"John was not working," said MacLean. "He wasn't on his usual car."

"Well, you will never see him on a streetcar again," said Evelyn, "and it's not likely he'll bother me again."

The words were disturbing enough, but the coldness with which they were delivered startled her mother. "What do you mean?" she asked.

Evelyn's face flushed. "Shut your damn mouth and keep your nose out of my business."

SATURDAY, MARCH 9

Alex and Ann Kammerer couldn't understand why John Dick hadn't at least called to let them know where he was. They had telephoned his mother and two sisters in nearby Vineland, but none of them had seen him or heard from him.

He must know they would be worried by now.

"He's probably back with his wife," said Alex.

"That's what I thought too, but he would have called by now," said Ann.

Ann decided to call Evelyn Dick. When Evelyn answered, Ann asked if John was with her or if she'd heard from him.

"No," said Evelyn, "but I would like to know where he is. Have you called his home—his mother's house—in Vineland?"

"Yes, I did, but he wasn't there."

"Well, I'd like to get hold of him," said Evelyn. "I'm sending the police down to Vineland because there's money and bills that he owes and I'm liable for them. I'm sending the Provincial Police out to his mother's place to have him arrested."

"I don't know anything about that," said Ann, shocked at what she was hearing.

"Well there's a woman suing him for seventy-five dollars. I've got the notice right here. And John told me your husband borrowed some money from him—money that I gave John—and I need it back."

"I can't believe he owes all this money," said Ann. "But if he does, he will be caught eventually."

"I hope you're not angry with me for telling you this over the phone," said Evelyn. "I don't want to cause trouble between your husband and John Dick."

"I just don't believe it's true."

"Well, anyway," said Evelyn, "if you hear from him, please let me know."

Alex Kammerer was speechless when Ann told him what Evelyn had said. "I certainly didn't borrow money from him," he said. "Maybe John was having financial problems we weren't aware of. Maybe that's why he has disappeared."

SUNDAY, MARCH 10

Alexandra MacLean tried as best she could to push to the back of her mind the possibility that John Dick was dead—had been killed. She had never liked him, but that didn't mean he deserved to be dead. Just having him out of her life was enough for her. She loved her daughter—her only child—and if they had problems, it was because they were so much alike: stubborn, with sharp tongues and quick tempers. They had fought a lot more when John Dick was around. Since his departure it had been much more pleasant around the house—until the past few days. Now she was worried. If something awful had happened to John Dick, who was responsible?

After their blow-up over the car and the nasty words of two days ago, nothing more had been said of John Dick, and Evelyn seemed more cheerful than she had been in weeks.

"It's another nice day," said Evelyn in the early afternoon. "Your cold seems to be gone. Wouldn't you like to go out for a walk with Heather?"

"Oh yes, I would," said her mother. "It's a lovely day."

Evelyn dressed Heather but stayed behind when they left the house. They were gone about two hours.

Around 8:30 that evening Evelyn Dick showed up at Grafton Garage. She had delivered a new set of seat covers the day before, and Landeg had already installed them in the Packard. She didn't say why she needed the car but asked if she could borrow it for an hour. "I won't be late this time," she promised.

"No problem," said Landeg, fetching the keys.

Evelyn returned the car at 9:30. Landeg said he was about to close and she accepted his offer of a ride home. He didn't ask why she had needed the car and she didn't tell him.

TUESDAY, MARCH 12

Detective John Freeborn was working in the afternoon when Evelyn Dick came into the detectives' office at the Central Police Station. He had never seen her before.

"Is there something I can do for you?" he asked.

"Yes, could you tell me if Dick has been arrested?"

"Dick who?"

"John Dick, my husband."

"Just a moment, I'll check the records." Freeborn flipped through the files and shook his head. "There is no one named

Dick under arrest. If there had been an arrest or a warrant issued, would it be for non-support?"

"No, for running away with tickets and money belonging to the company," said Evelyn.

"What company?"

"The Hamilton Street Railway Company."

Freeborn shrugged and Evelyn Dick left the police station.

WEDNESDAY, MARCH 13

The source of heat for the house at 32 Carrick, as in most homes of that era, was a coal furnace in the basement. Evelyn Dick had always tended the furnace even when John Dick lived in the house. To make the job easier, Evelyn's father, Donald MacLean, who had been living apart from his wife since July 1945, had arranged for a young man from the HSR to put the ashes into cans for removal by the city on Saturday mornings. MacLean was a long-time worker at the HSR, first as a conductor and in recent years in the offices.

It was only Wednesday and Alexandra MacLean, in the basement to do some laundry, was surprised when her daughter came down and began struggling with the metal rocker used to sift ashes from the furnace. There were more ashes in a garbage can beside the rocker.

"What are you doing with the ashes?" she asked her daughter. "The young man will put them out on Friday night."

"I'm going to put them over the mud in front of the garage," said Evelyn, annoyed.

Her mother noticed that the rocker was about two-thirds full. She thought it would be too heavy for Evelyn to manage on her own. There were handles on each side of the container. "Well, I'll take one side of the can with you."

"No, I'll take care of the ashes. You just go ahead with the washing."

Evelyn gripped the rocker by its handles, struggled up the stairs and carried it through the backyard to the laneway. There she spread the ashes in the ruts and mud in front of the garage's double doors. Then she returned and repeated the process with the garbage can.

three

Torso

Faith Reed usually went along with her older brother, and she was all for it when he suggested they join the Weaver boys for an outing to Albion Falls, a few miles east of the city's center on Hamilton Mountain. Besides, Faith considered nine-year-old Fred Weaver to be her boyfriend. She was eight years old and her brother David, eleven. The Reeds lived at Dundurn and Herkimer, about two blocks from the Weavers at 400 Herkimer. They made up their own little gang with the oldest, Jimmie Weaver, twelve, the self-appointed leader. The third Weaver brother was ten-year-old Robert. The five of them were usually together around the neighborhood, where they played games like Red Light Green Light on the street.

Today, the plan was to take a city bus to the top of Hamilton Mountain, hike around a bit, and then have a picnic lunch with hot dogs as the main course and jelly rolls for dessert. The Reeds took along their collie, Teddy. They got off the bus at Mountain Drive Park and began the trek along Mountain Brow Road—known to the locals as Scenic Drive—to Albion Falls. Hamilton's much-loved "Mountain" is really a heavily wooded hillside, part of the horseshoe-shaped Niagara Escarpment that sweeps west, in a wide curve, to the town of Grimsby.

The band of children left the road and were walking through a clearing about a half-mile from the Silver Spur Riding School when Robert and Jimmie Weaver began arguing over a small telescope. It was Robert's, but Jimmie wanted to use it. The argument intensified and the older boy threw a punch at his brother. It landed on Robert's nose and he ran off across the road and down the hill, with Fred, the youngest Weaver, right behind him. The others continued across the clearing but stopped when the boys climbed back up the hill and began screaming at them.

"They were yelling that they had found something," Faith Reed recalls fifty-five years later. She, her brother and Jimmie Weaver were anxious to get to the Falls to eat their lunch, but the panic in the boys' voices convinced them to investigate. "They said it was a pig or part of a dead man."

As Robert and Fred pointed, the others looked down at what they thought was a dead pig nestled in the underbrush about twenty feet below the brow of the hill. It was a steep incline and they had to grab the underbrush to keep from slipping or tumbling down. When they saw what appeared to be a T-shirt and shorts, they knew it was a human torso and not a pig.

The children scrambled back to the road, where they formed a human chain to block traffic. "Several cars went almost through us," says Faith Reed. "And then one stopped quite a ways back. Then my brother—not Jimmie—went up to the car with the dog."[1]

The car had a male driver and a female passenger. The children explained that it wasn't a prank, and the man pulled the car to the side of the road and went down to investigate. He was quickly back up on the road. "I don't know if the woman with him was his girlfriend or his wife, but he sent her off to get the police and he stayed with us," says Reed. "It seems like we waited an awfully long time for the police to come."

Now that the police were involved, Faith Reed was suddenly scared and began to cry. "I can't remember the boys being upset," she says. "It was just me, because I was thinking, what's my mommy going to say, now that the police were involved." She also remembers that it was March and quite cold on the Mountain, and there were still some patches of snow visible in secluded ravines. "And then the police came and I remember this one officer—I don't know what his name was—but he loaned me his gloves and his hat. I'll never forget that."

Ontario Provincial Police sergeant Carl Farrow and constable Leonard Mattick arrived at the scene just before 11 a.m. They jotted in their notepads that a human body, discovered about a half-mile north of Albion Falls, was missing its head, arms and legs. They figured they were about two miles from the intersection of Flock Road and Mountain Boulevard. The torso was on a wooded slope about twenty feet from the brow, which dropped at a forty-five-degree angle. Only a narrow flat spot, where the body had come to rest, prevented it from tumbling another two hundred feet to the bottom. Because it was March, the underbrush was sparse and there were no leaves on the handful of elm saplings near the torso. One of the elms, "an inch or two in diameter" had been snapped off by the weight and momentum of the falling torso, which was resting stomach down, the shoulders facing the bottom of the gully "as if it had been pushed straight over the brow."

The only clothing was a form-fitting, one-piece underwear garment, put on by stretching and stepping through the elasticized neck. The legs and arms of the underwear had been crudely torn off. The label, still intact, read: Harvey Woods P.D.Q. size 44. Sergeant Farrow removed the label. Most of the blood on the underwear was around the neck. There was no evidence of the torso sliding until ten or twelve feet below the brow, indicating it had been thrown with some force, flipped end over end, or both. The policemen saw a four-foot "noticeable skid mark" on the dried leaves immediately above the torso.

Mattick left the body in the care of Sergeant Farrow and went off to fetch OPP photographer William Pinch. On their return Pinch took photos of the torso, and then a Brown Brothers' ambulance and an undertaker were called to remove the body to the morgue at the General Hospital.

When the police officers helped the undertaker turn the body over, they noticed what appeared to be two bullet holes through the right breast of the underwear and a large bloodstain, the result of a deep gash across the stomach. They concluded that someone had tried to cut the torso in half. Despite the massive cut, there was no trace of blood on the ground, convincing Mattick and Farrow that the killing and cutting had been done elsewhere and the torso dumped in the ravine. The body was placed in a special carrying basket, but the slope was so steep that ropes had to be attached so two officers at the top of the hill could help pull it up.

It was an emotional and exciting day for Faith Reed, her brother and the Weaver boys, but when the police offered them a ride home, they refused. "We still hadn't had our hot dogs yet," says Reed. "I mean, we carted these hot dogs all that way, and we had worked delivering papers to get our money to buy all this stuff. So after the hearse and everybody left, we went over to the field and roasted our weenies."

When the word got out about the torso found on the Mountain, the Reed and Weaver children became instant celebrities. "All the newspaper people came and we had to go up to the spot with them," recalls Faith Reed. "Every newspaper carried the story. So they would take us for lunch; even the dog went, and he had lunch too. And at school we were heroes. It was neat, I'll tell you. I mean, this was stardom to us."

Twenty years earlier, in October 1925, another group of children, on a school outing, found the body of a young woman on Hamilton Mountain.[2] She had been shot in the head. The crime was never solved and the victim never identified even though more than ten thousand people viewed her body in a Hamilton funeral home.

Hamilton was a rough, raw blue-collar town with its steel mills, factories and belching smokestacks. It was a sports-mad place, boasting horse racing, two football teams and a senior hockey team. Its proximity to the U.S. border ensured that, like Windsor, Ontario, it was a center for rum-running during Prohibition. And there was still a strong Mafia presence in the city's north end. The bars were thriving and the bookies, bootleggers and prostitutes had not packed up and left town.

The discovery of the torso brought an avalanche of theories about the identity of the victim. It might be a gangland slaying, suggested the *Hamilton Spectator*. In all, Hamilton Police had five missing persons on their books over the previous two years, including reputed mobster Rocco Perri, missing since April 1944. Fourteen years earlier he was with his wife, Bessie, in the garage of their home when gunmen shot her dead. Police were suspicious that he was unhurt, but the killers were never found. Later, Perri escaped two attempts on his life—first his house was bombed, then his car—only to disappear while taking a walk to get rid of a headache. Rumors quickly spread that the torso was Perri, known to some as King of the Bootleggers, but police scoffed. The torso was that of a husky man. Perri was slight, and if he had lain on Hamilton Mountain for almost two years, decomposition would have left no more than a few bones. Besides, underworld informants had already told police that Perri was at the bottom of Hamilton harbor in a slab of concrete.[3]

The public had not yet heard of John Dick, and few people knew he was missing.

John

John Dyck, born May 25, 1906, in Russia, was a descendant of Dutch Mennonites who, in the sixteenth century, fled religious persecution in Holland, settling in Silesia, part of German-speaking Poland, where noblemen welcomed their expertise at reclaiming swampland through an intricate system of dikes and canals. The Mennonites—named for Menno Simons, a Dutch Catholic priest who left the Church—grew out of the radical Anabaptist movement during the Reformation. They became conscientious objectors who favored separation of church and state and rejected infant baptism and other basic Catholic doctrine and ritual.

For more than two hundred years the Mennonites prospered in Prussia, where the Dutch language was gradually replaced by, or incorporated into, their own form of *Platdeutsch*—Low German. By the late 1700s, faced with increasing civil and religious restrictions from the ruling Prussian and German autocrats, the Mennonites were on the move again. This time it was to the Russian Ukraine at the invitation of Catherine the Great, who offered them religious freedom, land grants and exemption from military service. By 1835 the largest Mennonite colony in Russia—on the Molotschna River—boasted fifty-eight villages, including New Halbstadt, where John Dyck was born. Besides their thriving farms, they raised cattle, horses and sheep and built successful mills and factories. But beginning in 1874 the special privileges granted by Catherine were gradually withdrawn and about eighteen thousand Mennonites decided to pack up and leave Russia for North America. Those who stayed behind, including John Dyck's family, faced war and the end of the Romanov dynasty.

John Dyck was eighteen when he arrived in Ontario in 1924 with a thousand German-speaking Mennonites, part of a wave immigrating to Canada in the chaos following the Russian Revolution. They were fleeing the Communists, roaming bandits and famine. In all, about twenty-one thousand Mennonites came to Canada between 1922 and 1930 before the Russian government put an end to emigration.[4] The new Ontario arrivals dispersed into mini colonies around Markham and Kitchener-Waterloo.

About three hundred of them, attracted by the rich soil, settled in the Vineland/Beamsville area near Hamilton. They built their own church, and by 1936 the congregation received its charter and became known as the United Mennonite Church. They were hard-working and religious but did not follow the isolated, strict way of life of the Old Order Mennonites.

To emigrate to Canada, the Mennonites had to organize into families. Dyck's group included his two sisters; his mother, Emilia Dyck; grandmother Rosine Kammerer; and brother-in-law John Wahl, whose passport covered all of them. Dyck's father, John, had died in the famine that swept the Soviet Ukraine and Russia in 1921.

Dyck went first to Markham and then to Kingsville, Ontario, where he worked as a farmhand. Eventually his family moved to the Vineland area. The strong anti-German sentiment that had led Berlin, Ontario, to change its name to Kitchener during World War I would intensify during World War II and prompt many of the newcomers to anglicize their names. John Dyck became John Dick, and some of the Wahls became Walls, although John Wahl's family roots were also Dutch. John Dick's second sister, Helen (Lena), married one of John Wahl's brothers, Jacob (Jake), and they all settled in the Vineland and Beamsville area. The two Wall brothers became successful fruit farmers, and a third brother, Peter, ran a thriving canning company in Niagara-on-the-Lake. After Kingsville, however, John Dick had had his fill of farming. He opted to live in Hamilton, where he found a job as a truck driver for a construction company. He maintained close family ties and visited Vineland on his day off—usually Sunday.

Dick worked for a time at the Frost Wire and Steel Company and then a few months with F.W. Fearman, a meat packing company. There he met and befriended Dominic Pollice, who remembered him as a good worker and "a good-natured fellow who was always the same—happy and pleasant and never down in the dumps." They worked together until mid-1943, when Dick found secure employment as a motorman with the Hamilton Street Railway.

On his application Dick said he was living in a housekeeping room at 148 Emerald Street. The bottom of the HSR application form stated:

> *(Will employ for train service only men of pleasing address, healthy and intelligent; free from any bodily defect; with good sight, hearing and speech; with a good record for honesty and sobriety; able to write and speak English intelligibly.)*

In legible, neat handwriting Dick stated that he was five feet eleven inches tall, weighed 180 pounds and had two dependents—his mother and grandmother. He was issued badge No. 277 and began work as a driver for the HSR on June 15, 1943. The starting pay was 58 cents an hour. To the question "Do you use any intoxicating liquors?" Dick responded "No." Like most applicants he lied.

John Dick had his roots in the Mennonite culture and religion, but it was wartime and he was living and working in a rough-and-tumble labor town. He was a blond, clean-cut, thirty-seven-year-old bachelor, and was soon comfortable straddling both worlds—living a bachelor life in the city and visiting his Mennonite family in the country. He liked to drink with his friends and had an eye for women, although he was somewhat shy and naive.

John Dick had known Anna Wolski and her husband since 1934, and often visited them after their marriage in 1935. But when Anna's husband drowned in 1941, Dick stopped coming around. He didn't see Anna for about two years. Then one day she stepped onto the streetcar he was operating. They talked about old times and he asked about her children. Everything was fine.

"Are you married yet?" she asked.

"No," said Dick. Then he asked if it would be all right if he came to visit her and the children. Wolski thought it a wonderful idea. Not long afterwards he took her and the children out in his car to a restaurant. It went well and the outing was repeated a week or two later. Wolski considered him a good friend. She was also attracted to him.

Soon Anna Wolski asked Dick to marry her. He told her he had a ninety-two-year-old grandmother and a seventy-two-year-old mother to look after. That was in August 1945. Later the same month Anna asked him again. This time he said he was already married but hadn't told her because he wanted to continue being friends. "Go to your wife," she ordered. "Your wife comes first." For a long time after that she stayed away from the streetcars.

John Dick had lied to Anna. He wouldn't marry until two months later.

Evelyn

Evelyn Dick was raised in an often dysfunctional household filled with contradictions. Her God-fearing, domineering mother had an explosive temper and was dissatisfied with the family's social status. Through her beautiful daughter, Alexandra MacLean thought they might climb a notch or two. Evelyn's loutish father was subject to violent mood swings—from charming to very nasty—and was often drunk and verbally abusive. He was also a thief. As an only child, Evelyn was either doted on to excess or used as a pawn in her parents' bitter confrontations that resulted in seven separations during their thirty-five-year marriage. A psychiatrist would say years later that the battles and separations profoundly affected young Evelyn—a lovely child with dancing dark eyes and rich black hair. Her mother considered her "delicate" and restricted her contact with other children. All of this would arrest Evelyn's socialization skills, increase her dependency on imagination and fantasy as escape mechanisms, and create a consuming need for acceptance and approval.

Alexandra Grant was twenty-six when she married Donald MacLean, seven years her senior, in Scotland in 1911. The following year, they emigrated from the Highlands to try fruit farming in Beamsville, Ontario. Farming life was difficult, and, in 1918, Donald was forced to find outside work to supplement their income. Dominion Power and Transmission hired him as "third man on freight" on its radial railways running from Hamilton to outlying centers like Brantford, Oakville, Beamsville and Dundas. His starting pay was $1,400 per year.

They were still living in Beamsville, on East Avenue, when Evelyn was born on October 13, 1920—delivered at home by

Dr. C.W. Elmore. "The baby was a hard feeding case," he recalled more than a quarter of a century later. "This, I thought was perhaps due to the fact that the mother was not very young and this was her first child."[5]

The following year they moved to Hamilton, where Donald continued to work as a freight handler for Dominion, which also owned the Hamilton Street Railway. In 1924, MacLean was laid off "owing to reduction of staff," but six weeks later the company re-hired him as a motorman with the HSR, at a time when the streetcars required two men. The references on his application form were James H. Boyle, manager of Aylmer Canning Co., and Major Armand Smith of Winona.[6]

The MacLeans bought a small, comfortable brick house at 214 Rosslyn Avenue South, near the base of Hamilton Mountain. The only drawback, in Alexandra's view, was that it was in the city's south end—the wrong side of the tracks. The rich and powerful lived in mansions in the gentrified west end. Hamilton's population when Evelyn was growing up in the 1920s and 1930s was about 150,000, of which forty or so families were considered wealthy. Most of them were members of the Royal Hamilton Yacht Club and the exclusive Hamilton Club.

Initially, Evelyn was enrolled in Memorial High School, in Hamilton's east end. When she didn't do well there, her parents pulled her out and sent her to Canada Business College in downtown Hamilton, where, until dropping out around Christmas 1936, she sat in the sixth row in front of Muriel Leslie. "Evelyn was always a very friendly person," Leslie told *Hamilton Spectator* "Street Beat" columnist Paul Wilson in 1998.[7] "Evelyn often went away on the weekends. She'd go shopping and come back with lots of clothes. We all waited for her to come into class. One day she came in with a fur coat." In February 1937, Muriel received a postcard from Evelyn. In neat handwriting the message said:

> *Thought I would drop a card to you, just after arriving in Buffalo on my way to New York. Weather is very cold, plenty of snow. Suppose you are as smart in school as ever. Give my regards to Mary. Will see you in the near future.*

But they never saw each other again.

Alexandra MacLean decided the best place for her daughter was the prestigious Loretto Academy, a private school attended by many of the daughters of Hamilton's elite. It would be the ideal place for Evelyn to meet the right people. But the school was expensive; where would the money come from? One theory, advanced years later, was that her schooling was paid for by her father. This would be absurd if one considered only Donald MacLean's annual income from the HSR, which at that time was about $1,700. But he was taking home a lot more from the Hamilton Street Railway than anybody knew.

In December, 1926, after less than two years as a conductor and motorman, forty-nine-year-old MacLean was considered a trusted employee and was moved inside, to the office, as a messenger and assistant to the cashier. Each night, the fare boxes from all of the buses and streetcars were locked in a large vault in the cashier's office. MacLean was first in each morning, and after cashier Percy Bristol arrived and opened the vault, he carried the fare boxes out to a table where Bristol opened them with special keys. The contents—coins and tickets—were dumped into a large sorting and counting machine. What his employer didn't know was that MacLean had stolen the combination to the company vault and had his own set of keys that could open any fare box in the place. He was able to enter the vault and rifle the fare boxes before Bristol arrived.

MacLean was off between 9 a.m. and 1 p.m. In the afternoon he worked as a messenger, until his day ended at 4 p.m. By the time he was caught in 1946, his total take of HSR proceeds over twenty years in the office was estimated at $200,000 to $250,000—a fortune at that time.

There had been claims that Bristol knew about Donald MacLean's stealing from the company, but the accusation was never officially raised, investigated or proven. Bristol was obviously considered clean, because he was subsequently put in charge of the books of another company owned by one of the principals of the HSR.

Donald MacLean was no miserly cartoon Scot. He always left generous tips and did little to hide the source of his largess. He was often seen at the Balmoral House hotel, near the HSR barns, plunking down a pile of coins to buy a round of beer. And Ross Hough remembers working after school at Wentworth Meat Store and making deliveries to the MacLean house. "I was about sixteen then. He would come in and order meat or a case of Campbell's soup and I would deliver it to his house. And gosh, he'd give me a buck as a tip! He was a great old fella. He'd go up the street and he'd give streetcar tickets to people on the corner."

Hough is seventy-two and now retired from a long career with Amtrak and Via Rail. He says MacLean was often called Scotty or Old Scotty, and he remembers him walking behind an oversized wagon pulled by the HSR cashier as they took the company's receipts to the bank at Sanford and King.

"Old Scotty would walk behind it, and he wore a smock and he had this old gun under it. I think it was more or less for show. If somebody had the idea that they were going to snatch and grab or whatever, they wouldn't have bothered him at all when they saw that revolver."

In court, his lawyer would describe MacLean as "a kindly old man with an expensive daughter." But others had a different view of him. Ivan McTaggart, who lived on Rosslyn Avenue, near the MacLeans, and worked as a streetcar driver for the HSR in the early forties, told his family before he died that Donald MacLean had a cruel streak. McTaggart's grandson, Ernest Abel, said that during a lunch break at work one day his grandfather, MacLean and others watched a stray cat approach. "My grandfather said Donald MacLean picked up the cat and wrung its neck. Then he went back to finishing his lunch."

Frank Cooke, who started in the cashier's office at the HSR in 1946, just after MacLean left the company, says fellow workers who knew "Scotty" well described him as "a blowsy, bluff sort of a guy who liked to pull practical jokes. One guy told me he would do things like put a lighted piece of scrap on a windowsill and let the smoke blow into the shop."

Cooke, now eighty-six, went on to become general manager of the HSR for a decade before retiring in 1981. He believes MacLean's long-time thievery from the HSR was the result of "sloppy administration—sloppy security. You know, an old and trusted employee who'd been there for a long, long time. People were very closemouthed about what went on, because nobody wanted to disclose that they had intimate knowledge of MacLean's machinations."

Cooke says a lot of old-timers worked for the HSR in those days because there was no pension plan. "There were people that were up in their seventies. There was one guy in the shop who was eighty-four, and I replaced a man, in purchasing and stores, who was seventy-four."

In retrospect, it was obvious that Hamilton's transit-riding public financed Evelyn MacLean's education through her father's fleecing of the HSR. Back then, however, Alexandra MacLean bristled at the thought. She once told the *Toronto Daily Star*'s Marjorie Earl that Evelyn's grandmother and a rich aunt, both in Scotland, had paid for her education at Loretto. She said the family in the old country was "well off" and that it was her mother who had initially suggested Evelyn be sent to a private school.

Independent sources were never able to prove or disprove the existence of Alexandra's "well-off" family. But if they did exist and were so affluent, why did they let Alexandra struggle for several years to scratch out a living on a fruit farm in Ontario? More likely, Alexandra created the story in an attempt to preserve some of the cash in her bank accounts after her husband was arrested for stealing from the HSR.

Whatever the source of the income, Alexandra MacLean believed that her daughter was now on the stage where she belonged, where she would be noticed. But even though the dark-eyed beauty with the full lips and the perfect figure purchased all the latest fashions, it didn't do her much good at Loretto, where all the girls were required to wear uniforms. And because of her cloistered upbringing, Evelyn was awkward in her attempts at establishing normal friendships. She simply didn't know how, and therefore wasn't being invited to the society parties she so coveted. She and her mother decided they could buy her way in.

Evelyn was particularly fond of one girl at Loretto, and for her birthday she gave her expensive lingerie.[8] The recipient thought the gift too personal and too extravagant. If a group of students went to a restaurant for coffee, Evelyn would insist on picking up the tab. She wanted to be popular, but her desperation was palpable and so she was politely avoided.

Wilma Keeber, now an eighty-one-year-old widow living in Burlington, Ontario, attended Loretto Academy at the same time as Evelyn. "I wasn't a Catholic, nor was she," she recalls. "I would say about one-third of the girls were Protestant. It was a very nice building and nice grounds, and of course the teachers were nuns. Mother Loyola was the head nun. Some of them were brutal at times. In religion classes, first thing in the morning, Protestant girls just read books or whatever while the Catholics went through their religious routine. But they didn't try to pressure us or influence us in any way. Mind you, just by being there I learned a lot about the Catholic religion."

To this day Keeber clearly remembers Loretto's strict dress requirements. "Our uniforms were navy blue jumpers with boxed pleats and white blouses. They were quite nice. I always liked wearing them. But I do remember that Evelyn had a gray coat with gray Persian lamb lapels, and she also had a gray kid coat. We were all so impressed to think that someone at our age could afford to have fur coats."

Keeber would later learn that the coats were paid for by the coins stolen from the HSR by Evelyn's father. "Her coat pockets were always full of nickels and dimes. We couldn't figure out where they came from. She used to give them out to the girls. My impression, even at that time, was that she was trying to buy friends."

On at least two occasions when boys asked Evelyn on a date, they were rewarded the next day with sterling silver cigarette cases. The other girls thought the gifts puzzling, if not somewhat bizarre. Evelyn also threw intimate parties for several couples at a time at the Royal Connaught Hotel and at Burlington's Brant

Inn, handing out sterling silver compacts and cigarette cases as favors.[9] Alexandra MacLean would later say that her daughter attended such parties but certainly didn't pay for them. She agreed that Evelyn purchased a couple of cigarette cases for dates, but that was it. "She would have to be a Vanderbilt to pay for something like that [hotel parties]," she said.

Wilma Keeber says she went to at least three such parties and that Evelyn personally invited her and the other girls. "There were at least two dinner dances that she had at the Brant Inn, which is long gone. It was really a landmark in Burlington. The other one, at the Crystal Ballroom in the Royal Connaught Hotel, is where she gave all the boys silver cigarette cases. And I think the girls got compacts, but I don't have mine any more. I would say there were ten or twelve couples. She invited us by word of mouth, but as far as I can remember only the Protestant girls in the class were invited. She never seemed to include the Catholic girls. She just said come along and bring a boyfriend. Of course we were pretty naive in those days. It was in the thirties—Depression years and so on—so we really didn't realize exactly what was going on.

"I just know that she was buying her friends by having these dances and giving these gifts and so on. I think she was very insecure. Nobody really wanted to be friendly with her, and she was trying so hard to make friends. I didn't see her car, but I heard about it—her yellow convertible. And the fur coats stick out in my mind.

"I've since read where they refer to her as a femme fatale. Believe me, she was no femme fatale. She was kind of a shifty person. She never looked you straight in the eye and she certainly didn't have any personality as far as I was concerned. Of course, we weren't aware of all the emotional turmoil Evelyn was going through at home at that time because she wasn't very communicative. She would never tell us anything about what was going on at home or talk about her mother and father."

Frances Simpson, who grew up a few doors from Evelyn and also attended Loretto Academy, had a different memory of Evelyn.[10] "She was lovely. The rest of us showed up to school in kids' clothes, but she had a fur coat and a fur hat. She was always dressed up." And Simpson remembered Donald MacLean allowing Evelyn and her classmates to ride across the city at the back of the bus. "She was such a sweet, nice girl."

When it was reported in the media years later that a check had been written to Birks Jewelers for $2,187, Alexandra said it didn't go to purchase favors for a lavish high school party but to pay for Evelyn's own expensive jewelry, which included a large square-cut diamond surrounded by several smaller diamonds.

Her classmates may have shunned her, but from the age of fourteen or fifteen, men were taking notice of Evelyn MacLean and she of them. By the time she left high school, rumors and whispers about her abounded. Her wardrobe now included expensive furs to go with the jewelry. She drove a fancy car, frequented the racetrack and Toronto dances, and was often seen in the company of prominent gentlemen. Her mother encouraged her to seek out wealthy men: Who knew where it might lead? Evelyn complied, but she also enjoyed the company of men of her own class and age. She was particularly attracted to athletic types; football players were favored. When the war came, men in uniform caught her eye.

Charles Foster, a seventy-seven-year-old writer and newspaper editor now living in New Brunswick, knew Evelyn when he was posted to an air base on the outskirts of Hamilton for a few weeks in 1943. He was among the thousands of men Britain's Royal Air Force sent to Canada for pilot training. "We all knew her," says Foster. "I never dreamed she was like she was according to the final story that came out. I didn't think of her that way at all. She was a very pleasant person."

Perhaps it was the uniforms or the excitement of wartime that prompted Evelyn MacLean to pretend she was a driver with the Red Cross in Hamilton. She was able to procure a cap, jacket and khaki skirt of a Red Cross worker. She sewed phony insignia on the shirt and embroidered her name on the waistband of the skirt. Then she had her photograph taken in full uniform. The uniform seldom left her closet at the Rosslyn Avenue house, but the photos were always at the ready.

Ontario Provincial Police inspector Charlie Wood would later describe Evelyn's outfit as "an elaborate bluff which she put up so she would be in the swim like other girls.[11] She wanted to have a natty uniform and swank around as though she belonged to the Red Cross." The Red Cross has no record of Evelyn MacLean.

George Lawson, now eighty-six, remembers that Evelyn even had an eye for men in police uniforms. "I used to see her around town and around the marketplace on a market day. There was one officer—Basil Brown—I think he's dead now. She was trying to get close to him. She was quite taken up with Basil, but of course he was an astute Englishman. He wouldn't have anything to do with her. She had quite a repu-tation around. If she knew you were a policeman, her eyes would follow you all the way up the block."

Ross Hough says that before working in the meat store he had a paper route, "and I always had extras that I used to sell right on the corner of Wentworth and King Street in front of Leggett's drugstore." He remembers Evelyn waiting to meet her father when he got off work. "And she'd sit on the corner in her car and she'd buy a paper. That's when they were only two cents. Gosh, it was nothing for her to give me a quarter. Boy, I was really doing good."

Hough's favorite memories of Evelyn are of the summers when she drove a pale yellow Pontiac convertible with leopard skin seat covers. "Oh man, it was a beautiful car and she was a beautiful woman—a real knockout. She'd just pull around the corner on King Street and she'd sit there in the convertible. Everybody used to go by and just look at her. She was such a nice-looking woman. It was exciting. I'd never seen anyone like her at the time. She'd wear some of the nicest outfits— lots of flimsy outfits, and very well kept. I didn't see her in a bathing suit, but I saw her in a lot of things close to it. She looked like a woman who wore expensive clothing and was used to it. You'd swear she was a movie star."

When high school graduate Evelyn MacLean was twenty-one, she had never held a job. She was living the life of a courtesan—in today's parlance, a high-priced escort. Whether she was a prostitute or not is open to question. She dated a lot of men, and of those that are known about, she certainly wasn't charging a fee for her company. In fact there are documented incidents of her offering her dates financial help. It may be that she simply craved attention and a lot of men were there to provide it. If they gave her expensive gifts to show their appreciation, so much the better.

Evelyn MacLean had a list, a *black book*, in which she kept a record of her lovers. Whether this was a business tool, a list of her conquests or simply the names of her paramours will probably never be known. What is known is that her list contained the names of some very prominent Hamiltonians, including two lawyers, a financier, a merchant, a magistrate's son, a druggist, a furrier and the sons of two important families.

It was rumored that Evelyn's dalliances had led to one or two pregnancies that ended in abortions. Whatever the truth, on July 10, 1942, a daughter was born. Hospital records list the baby's name as Heather Maria White. Evelyn had created a husband for herself. He was from a wealthy Cleveland family, his name was Norman White and he was in the navy, on duty at sea. Evelyn MacLean was now Evelyn White, although her Norman White didn't exist. Having a husband helped her avoid the stigma—considerable in those days—of bearing an illegitimate child.

A second daughter was stillborn on June 20, 1943, and on May 4, 1944, Evelyn went to see obstetrician Dr. Douglas Adamson at the Medical Arts Building. He confirmed she was again pregnant. She told him she was married to J.N. White, who was on active service with the Royal Canadian Navy.

When Donald MacLean found out about the impending birth, he ranted about one child around the house being more than enough. He vented his verbal wrath on Alexandra when she defended her daughter.

Evelyn decided she needed a quiet place of her own to escape the bickering and entertain her male friends. She vowed it would have a more upscale address than Rosslyn Avenue. Her search led to the exclusive Henson Park Apartments at 316 James Street South, where she discovered there would be a vacancy as of October 1. It wasn't a large apartment, but the location was right. Introducing herself as Evelyn White, she arranged a meeting in August with Samuel Henson, who owned several apartment buildings around Hamilton.

"You probably noticed I am in a certain condition," said Evelyn.

"What do you mean?" asked Henson.

"I'm going to have a child," she explained. "But medical examinations have shown the baby is dead and I have to go to the hospital to have it removed."

Henson said he was sorry about her losing the baby.

"I have a three-year-old daughter," said Evelyn. "I am very anxious to get this apartment, and I thought you might be worried about there being too many children."

Henson felt sorry for her and understood her reasons for telling him about her pregnancy. "I couldn't blame her for doing that, because I knew the difficulty there is in securing apartments," he said later.

He agreed to rent the apartment to Evelyn, and they negotiated a lease.

At 9 a.m. on September 4, 1944, Dr. Adamson accompanied Evelyn to Mountain General Hospital for the birth of her third child. The baby, a boy just over nine pounds, was not born until 2:40 the next morning. The child was registered as Peter David White. Evelyn told Norma Gowland, supervisor at the hospital's nursery, that her husband was in the navy and had been lost at sea. She was now a widow with two children.

Child care specialist Dr. Frank Boone checked the baby over and declared it was in excellent health, although the mother was unable to nurse it and formula would have to be prescribed.

Alexandra MacLean came to visit her new grandson about a week after the delivery. She brought with her a large beige suitcase for Evelyn's things, and for the baby, a white dress, a pink and white woolen jacket, bootees, and a slip and vest. On September 14, the day before she left the hospital, Dr. Adamson circumcised the baby and applied a dressing that he told Evelyn was to stay in place for two days. He thought she displayed normal love for her child and scheduled the first of three postnatal checkups for October 5.

It was Dr. Boone's practice to see a baby on the day it left the hospital and give the mother final feeding instructions, but nurse Gowland telephoned him on the morning of September 15 to tell him that Evelyn was preparing to leave.

"He's on his way," Gowland told Evelyn, "and he would like to see the baby."

"Oh, it's not necessary that I see him," said Evelyn.

She left a forwarding address in Port Nelson, near Burlington, Ontario. Before leaving, she signed a hospital form certifying that she had cut a temporary necklace from the baby. The necklaces were used by the hospital to ensure that babies weren't accidentally switched. When Dr. Boone arrived at noon, Evelyn was gone. He prescribed a feeding formula that he mailed to the address left by Evelyn, but it was returned undelivered a few days later.

With suitcase in hand, Evelyn arrived home by taxi three hours after leaving the hospital, but her child wasn't with her. "Where's your baby?" asked her mother.

"Oh, the Children's Aid Society took it to put up for adoption," replied Evelyn calmly.

Her mother was silent but no doubt relieved that there would be no protracted battles with Donald MacLean over a second child in the house. Eighteen months would pass before the name Peter David White was mentioned within the family again.

On the first day of October, two weeks after leaving the hospital, Evelyn took possession of her new apartment on James Street South. However, after tastefully furnishing and decorating it, she did not move in. For the next eight months, while she continued to live at home, the apartment was used as a private hideaway where her male companions could be entertained. Evelyn soon reverted to a busy social schedule, but she managed to keep her three postnatal checkups with Dr. Adamson. He noted in his records that she was in good spirits and that she reported her baby was fine.

Bill

Like many young men of his era, William "Bill" Bohozuk was enticed by the good money and the security a factory job offered. It was the rapid route to a new car and a snappy wardrobe—sure to attract the opposite sex. It provided instant gratification as opposed to dedicating four years to the pursuit of *that piece of paper*—a university degree. Also, there was a war on, and in June 1940 the National Resources Mobilization Act became law. Its purpose was to identify anyone over sixteen, male or female, who could contribute to the war effort. The government decreed that registration under the new act would take place during the month of August 1940. It was a sure ticket into military service for healthy young men not working in industries essential to the war effort. On August 1, the first day of the registration process, Bill Bohozuk, twenty-one and healthy, landed a permanent job at Dominion Foundry, one of the most war-essential plants in industrial Hamilton.

Bohozuk, a former Anglican altar boy at Christ's Church Cathedral, lived with his family at 21 Picton Street. With a secure job, home-cooked meals and a roof over his head, he had extra dollars in his pocket to pursue passions outside work. He liked cars and clothes and women, but he had other interests too, notably horses and rowing. Bohozuk was a fine physical specimen, carrying 220 pounds on a solid six-foot athletic frame, and he was an accomplished oarsman with the Leander Boat Club in Hamilton. Others at the club liked the brash young man. He was a member of the "heavy eight" sculling crew and was dedicated to his rowing. Year after year his boat would be in the water as soon as the ice broke up in the spring. Whenever he could, he rowed Saturday afternoons, twice on Sundays, and three hours each evening during the week, maintaining that schedule until Labor Day.

Olympic oarsman Claude "Sandy" Saunders,[12] a rowing legend in Canada, witnessed Bohozuk's dedication first-hand. "I only wish I'd had more rowers like him," says Saunders, now in his early nineties.

Saunders's association with the Leander Boat Club goes back to 1932, and he was for many years the driving force behind the Royal Canadian Henley Regatta, an annual event he chaired for forty years until 1998. For his efforts he was awarded the Order of Canada in 1992.

"I knew Bill Bohozuk very well because I rowed with him for three or four years," recalls Saunders. "He was very congenial and as easy a chap to get along with as I've ever met. He was very straightforward." Saunders says that when waiting for rough water to calm, some of the rowers would sit around the club playing cards or engaging in impromptu wrestling matches, but Bill Bohozuk would find something else to do. "Bill would go out and maybe wash the coach's car. And we used to kid him and say 'That's how you got on the team.' But it wasn't. He was a good athlete, a good oarsman—a non-violent, gentle man."

Retired Hamilton detective George Lawson also remembers Bohozuk from the boat club and attests to his non-violent nature. "Even the guys he worked with at the foundry said, 'Christ, the guy wouldn't even pick up a shovel and hit a rat running across the dirt floor of the open hearth pit.'" And Lawson confirms the young rower's image as a charming Lothario. "Bohozuk was a handsome-looking bugger—a real ladies' man. He looked a lot like Joe Louis, only better-looking. And he was a pretty well-built fellow, too. And of course he was a very nice dresser. He kept himself well."

Besides his life as a rower, Bohozuk had an interest in a couple of horses as a hobby, and he sometimes traveled with them. It was on the Canadian racing circuit that he met Helen Kleean Mitchell in 1944. She was a widow whose parents lived in Hamilton. Her husband had been in the horse-racing business before his death. She met Bohozuk at a racetrack and they began dating.

They were in downtown Hamilton in late June of 1944 when they saw a woman Helen had known for eight years. Her name was Evelyn MacLean, said Helen, and she too was a widow. Bohozuk found the woman attractive.

Bohozuk's active bachelor life seemed to be over when he and Helen married at St. Patrick's Church in Hamilton a month or so after the chance meeting with Evelyn. The couple decided to live for a time at the home of Bohozuk's parents, but in the third week of October 1944, three months after the wedding, Helen suddenly packed up and left. She later explained that she had received a telegram urging her to go to a sick friend in Ohio. She nursed the friend until his death and then moved to California, where she found a job and settled permanently. Bohozuk seemed to shrug off her departure and resumed his former lifestyle.

Bohozuk saw Evelyn driving around town a few times after his wife pointed her out to him, but they had never been introduced. Then, in the spring of 1945, several months after Helen left, he was returning to his car after lunch at a downtown grill when he noticed a black coupe double-parked beside his car. It was the same car he had seen Evelyn driving, and she was behind the wheel. They smiled at each other. She was writing down his license number on the back of a telephone bill.

"Why are you taking my number?" he asked.

"Wait until I pull over," she said.

When she parked at the curb, Bohozuk got into her car on the passenger side.

"What's the idea?" he asked.

"That's the same car Helen Mitchell was in last summer," said Evelyn.

"That's right, and we got married right after that."

Bohozuk explained that his wife had moved to the U.S. They talked for a while and then Evelyn handed him her phone number.

"Call me sometime," she said.

Bohozuk telephoned several times over the next three weeks, but there was no answer, so he stopped calling.

seven

Till Death Do Us Part

By the spring of 1945, Alexandra MacLean had decided that living with her husband was unbearable. There had been six previous separations, but this time it would be final. It was painful to think about happier times early in the marriage—arriving from Scotland and settling on the Beamsville farm before moving to Hamilton after Evelyn was born. "We moved into the city because the work was too heavy for me on the farm," she would tell a reporter in 1947.[13] "I think perhaps things would have been very different for us if we had just stayed there."

Her loving husband of those early days was now an abusive, full-blown alcoholic. And hadn't his ranting against "another little bastard running around the house" driven Evelyn to give up her son to the Children's Aid? It just wasn't right. The arguments were fierce. Until alcohol turned Donald MacLean's anger into uncontrollable rage, Alexandra had been a formidable opponent, even though she was only five foot three and 125 pounds. In photos from that period, wearing wire-rimmed glasses and with her gray hair in a tight bun, she resembles Anthony Perkins dressed up as the depraved Norman Bates's mother in the Alfred Hitchcock movie *Psycho*.

She despised MacLean's foul language and drunkenness, and she told him so—often and loudly. But now she was sixty and she had had enough. Alexandra's circumstances were much improved compared with previous separations. For all of his faults, Donald MacLean had been a good provider, even if she knew very well that most of the money was stolen from the HSR. The security of that income had been a deciding factor in many past reconciliations. But since 1938, Evelyn had been giving her mother money. At first it was $100 here, $50 there, but after Heather's birth in 1942 the payments came more frequently and now added up to several thousand dollars overall. Evelyn had never held a job, so Alexandra had to know the money was coming from one or more of the men her daughter was seeing. The timing suggested it was probably from the man who fathered Heather. Whatever the source of Evelyn's new-found wealth, Alexandra no longer had to depend on Donald MacLean for survival. And she didn't have to look far for a new place to live: Evelyn invited her to move to the exclusive Henson Park apartment that she had been using as a love nest for several months.

On June 7, 1945, Evelyn, her mother and her daughter moved from the Rosslyn Avenue house to James Street South. The apartment was one of several in a converted nineteenth century mansion on an expansive estate in the shadow of Hamilton Mountain. It was like a private park for Heather's walks and playtime. Its relative isolation had made it ideal for Evelyn's romantic trysts, but they would be curtailed now that her mother and daughter were living with her. She therefore looked on the arrangement as temporary—a necessary disruption to escape the raving Donald MacLean. Her long-term plan was to buy a house and use the apartment for its intended purpose.

As far as Samuel Henson was concerned, Evelyn and her family were excellent tenants. In his weekly inspection of the building he often saw Heather playing on the grounds, usually in the company of her grandmother.

It's likely that Evelyn MacLean, calling herself Evelyn White, first met John Dick in late August 1945 on his streetcar run. They were soon dating. The question persistently put later on was what did she see in this immigrant streetcar driver? One implausible answer, provided by Evelyn herself,[14] was that John Dick helped with the dishes from time to time and was able to obtain rationed items, such as soap chips, which had been hard to come by because of the war. A more likely scenario is that he misled Evelyn about his personal wealth, hinting that he held shares in his in-laws' successful fruit farming and canning factory operations. His brother-in-law John Wall later confirmed that John Dick didn't own a single share.

Evelyn might also have been concerned that the story of her fictitious husband could unravel now that the war was over. Under the laws at that time, if it was discovered that her daughter was illegitimate, Children's Aid had the power to step in and remove her to a foster home. Her daughter needed a father; John Dick was convenient and reliable. It may have been as simple as that. Whatever the motivation, neither John nor Evelyn were getting what they thought they were getting when, within two or three weeks of meeting, they decided to get married.

On October 1, 1945, Dominic Pollice boarded a streetcar operated by John Dick. The two had been friends when they worked together at the Fearman meat packing company before Dick took the job with the HSR. "You're just the man I want to see," said Dick. "I'm getting married."

"Congratulations," said Pollice. "Where do I come in?"

"I want you to stand up for me at the wedding," said Dick.

Pollice was flattered, but he was taken aback when he learned the wedding was to be in three days. He hadn't seen his friend in more than two years and wondered why John wanted him as best man on such short notice. The answer was simple: John and Evelyn had no real friends.

When Pollice told him he too was in a serious relationship, Dick said: "Maybe you can get your girl to stand up for Evelyn."

"John was very enthusiastic about Evelyn," Pollice would say later. "He told me he was marrying a beautiful girl who had been married to a naval officer who had been killed—a man who was a peacetime stockbroker who had left her a lot of money."[15]

Evelyn had been impressed enough by Bill Bohozuk that she had mentioned him to her mother three or four times since their meeting in the spring. But Alexandra MacLean didn't hear about John Dick until two weeks before the wedding. She was extremely upset. "It's just not proper that you take out a marriage license without me knowing the man," she complained. And when Evelyn introduced him to her just days before the wedding, she was even less impressed. He looked fine, but he was a foreigner and a streetcar operator with a paltry income—not the big catch her mother had been dreaming of. Alexandra's low opinion of John Dick was confirmed before the wedding when Dick tried to borrow money from her. And the day before the wedding, Evelyn and her mother had a terrible argument.

"Don't marry him!" screamed Alexandra.

"It's none of your damn business who I marry!"

Back and forth they went until Evelyn stormed out of the house. Alexandra was so incensed, she refused to attend the wedding. "Suit yourself," said Evelyn.

In the afternoon of Thursday, October 4, Evelyn and John met for drinks with Dominic Pollice and his girlfriend, Dorothy Jackson, at the Royal Connaught Hotel. Evelyn was dressed in a fashionable short dress and was wearing a cloth coat trimmed with Persian lamb. Dorothy, who had never met Evelyn, thought the bride looked very happy and noticed a ring with several diamonds on her right hand. She was impressed.

"Did John give you that?" she asked.

"No, it was my mother's ring."

From the hotel the foursome moved on to the Church of the Ascension, where Archdeacon W.F. Wallace married John and Evelyn to the uplifting strains of Wagner's "Bridal Chorus" from *Lohengrin*. Dominic Pollice was best man and Dorothy Jackson maid of honor. It was the only time either of them would see Evelyn and John together. The only others in the church were two women from the boarding house where John Dick lived at 148 Emerald Street North. The marriage certificate listed the groom as John Dick, bachelor; Mennonite; age 39; born in New Halbstadt, Russia; father, John Dick; and mother's maiden name, Emilia Kammerer. Evelyn listed herself as Evelyn White, widow; Anglican; age 24; born in St. Catharines, Ontario; mother's maiden name, Alexandra Grant.

There was no crowd, no confetti and no reception. Instead, the four of them went out to dinner at a quiet restaurant. During the meal, Evelyn presented John with an engraved gold penknife on a gold chain and he gave her a pair of expensive earrings. Dorothy had to work the next day, so she and Dominic left by taxi before 11 p.m.

John Dick had assumed he would be going home with Evelyn on their wedding night, but it was not to be. The place was too small, she told him. There was only enough room for her and her mother and daughter. They would have to get a house with room for all of them before they could move in together.

At 12:15 a.m. on her wedding night, Evelyn returned to her apartment and, as usual, crawled into bed beside her mother.

Deadly Triangle

Bill Bohozuk had a busy rowing season with the Leander Boat Club in the summer of 1945, and he hadn't thought much about Evelyn Dick after failing to reach her in the spring. But in early October he was downtown when they met by chance as she was getting out of her car. She seemed glad to see him and he asked her for a date. Making no mention of her recent marriage, Evelyn agreed.

They drove to a hotel in nearby Dundas for a couple of glasses of beer and then he drove her home. Evelyn told him her naval officer husband had been killed in action and she was going back to her maiden name—MacLean. She accepted when he asked her for a date the following Sunday.

Little Heather came along on their second date. They went for a leisurely drive, stopping at a city park. Bohozuk had brought along a camera and they took pictures of each other. During the drive home, Evelyn told Bohozuk her car had been stolen. The truth was that her father was so angry at her for marrying John Dick, he had cut her off from using his Chrysler, which sat in the garage on Rosslyn. [MacLean often paid a fellow HSR employee to chauffeur him around in the car].

"Well I'm working days," said Bohozuk. "I can give you my extra set of keys if you need a car during the day. You could pick it up at the Dominion Foundry, providing you get it back to the parking lot by five o'clock."

It was mid-morning, Thursday, October 17, when Evelyn Dick approached the security shack at the Dominion Foundries where Bill Bohozuk worked in the open hearth. Robert Morrison was the watchman on duty. She told him she had permission to borrow Bohozuk's car while he was at work. She produced the keys as proof and he allowed her to drive off. Returning to the parking lot about 3:30 p.m., she waited in the car until Bohozuk's shift was finished at four. Morrison watched as they drove off together.

That night Bohozuk took Evelyn to the Tivoli Theatre. His sister, Lillian, and her girlfriend went along with them. Afterwards they went to a coffee shop, where Bohozuk gave Evelyn snapshots and enlargements of the pictures he had taken on their second date. Once again she made no mention of her marriage to John Dick and went to Bohozuk's home where they had sex. On the drive back to her place Evelyn told Bohozuk she liked him a lot. She said she was well off financially and if he ever needed financial help, he could come to her.

Early the next morning a tearful John Dick, who had been spying on his new wife, approached Robert Morrison at the Dominion Foundry parking lot and explained that he was Evelyn's husband. "I know she's been driving Bill Bohozuk's car. It's not right that she goes out with him when she's married to me. We were just married on October fourth. I don't want you to give her the car again."

Morrison agreed. He didn't think it proper for a married woman to be seeing other men. He said he would not give her the car voluntarily.

At 8 a.m. Dick watched from the security shelter as Bohozuk drove into the lot, parked his car and headed for the plant. As he crossed the railway tracks, Dick ran from the shelter and caught up to him. Bohozuk could see he was upset.

"Did you loan your car to a woman yesterday?" asked Dick.

"Yes, I did."

"Did you know she is my wife?"

"No . . . no, I didn't," said Bohozuk, confused and surprised.

Morrison couldn't hear their conversation, but he watched as they walked up the roadway to the plant for more than a hundred yards. "I didn't know what they were talking about, but I seen Bohozuk waving Dick off, as much as to say he didn't want to listen to his conversation."

Dick followed Bohozuk all the way to the time office and employees' entrance on Depew Street. There they smoked and talked a few minutes before Dick returned to the security shack. Bohozuk went up to the employment office, where he telephoned Evelyn to ask for his keys back. She wasn't in. He told her mother he would call back later.

Morrison noticed Dick "was still crying quite a bit" when he returned to the shanty after confronting Bohozuk. Then he left.

A couple of hours later Morrison looked up to see Evelyn Dick approaching.

"I'd like to borrow Bill Bohozuk's car again."

"I'm sorry, it's against company policy. I can't let you have it unless you have a written statement from the owner or from the Chief of Security."

She smiled. "That's perfectly all right. I won't bother."

Morrison watched her walk the short distance to the streetcar stop and, minutes later, board a westbound car. The soap opera continued for Morrison when a subdued John Dick returned in the afternoon, followed shortly by Evelyn. She was headed for Bohozuk's car when her husband intercepted her. Morrison watched as they argued animatedly. He couldn't hear them, but he could see they were both angry. Dick took Evelyn by the arm and they boarded a westbound streetcar together. A few minutes later Bill Bohozuk came out of the plant for his car.

"That woman from yesterday was down for the car," said Morrison. "I didn't give it to her. She's a married woman, you know. I think you should lay off her. Her husband was by this morning. They've only been married three weeks, and she won't let him live with her."

"I didn't know she was married," said an embarrassed Bohozuk. "I don't really know her. She's just testing the car as a business proposition in a deal to sell it."

Bohozuk was able to retrieve his second set of keys from Evelyn later that day and resolved not to ask her out again. He didn't date her again, but it wouldn't be their final meeting. He later swore under oath that the next time he saw her was in November or December as he came out of the liquor store.

"What are you doing?" he asked.

"I'm just getting a bottle of liquor," she replied.

It was mid-morning. He offered to drive her home and she accepted.

In the latter part of January 1946, Bohozuk damaged his car in an accident. He remembered Evelyn's offer of financial help and on impulse called and asked her if he could borrow $200. She agreed. Two weeks later he took out a bank loan and paid off Evelyn and several other creditors. The loan was arranged through the personnel manager's office at the foundry. The bank sent out checks directly to his large creditors, and separate checks were sent to him with the amounts and names of the smaller creditors, including Evelyn, already filled in.

Bohozuk telephoned Evelyn to tell her he had her money, but she had just had a tooth extracted and didn't want to come out. "You sign my name on the check and bring me the cash," she said.

Bohozuk's sister, Lillian, endorsed the check with Evelyn's name and he cashed it at the post office. In the company of a neighbor's son, twelve-year-old Rocky Cupido, Bohozuk delivered the cash to Evelyn. She was with Heather when she opened the door.

"I handed her the money; thanked her for her kindness; and left," Bohozuk would later testify in court.

John Dick was smitten, and on occasion Evelyn did share the bed in his Emerald Street room, but he was convinced he needed his own house to truly win her over. The problem was, he was virtually penniless. When his rooming house went on the market for $3,000, Dick went to Evelyn for the down payment. Both she and her mother refused him the money. The first time Alexandra met John Dick—before the wedding—she had asked him about his financial situation. "I have $2,500 in the bank," he replied. Now he was after her for $1,200.

"Well, it's peculiar how you have to approach me for $1,200 if you have $2,500 in the bank," she told him. When Dick didn't respond, Alexandra pounced. "That is positive proof that you haven't even got a bank book."

Dick was despondent. Without the down payment there would be no house and perhaps no Evelyn.

Evelyn, however, had enough for a down payment of her own, and soon afterwards she went out and purchased the house at 32 Carrick Avenue for $6,300, with $2,500 down.

On October 31, 1945, Evelyn, her mother and Heather moved from the Henson Park apartment to the three-story brick house. John Dick was there to meet them. Alexandra MacLean wasn't happy about it, but Evelyn allowed him to move in. John and Evelyn shared the large front bedroom on the second floor, installing a cot for Heather. Alexandra had her own bedroom in the rear on the same floor, and a third bedroom was used for sewing and storage. John Dick would later falsely claim to others that he had put up $1,300 towards the down payment, but his name did not appear on the mortgage or other documents related to the house.

His hopes for a happy home life with Evelyn were quickly dashed. His impromptu best man, Dominic Pollice, learned of the newlyweds' troubled life when he called Evelyn soon after the wedding. He had heard she and her mother were moving to a new home on Carrick, and he and his bride-to-be were looking for rental accommodation. He hoped she might offer them space at the new house. No offer was forthcoming.

"How are you getting along?" he asked.

"Oh, as well as can be expected," said Evelyn.

Shortly after the move to the Carrick Avenue house, Pollice saw John Dick on a streetcar, "and he talked of nothing but his domestic difficulties. That was the last time I saw him. He seemed really stirred up and said that either his mother-in-law had to leave Carrick Avenue or he would." In his first ten days at the Carrick house Dick helped a lot with cleaning, repairs and maintenance, but that ended when he learned he was excluded from the mortgage. He told HSR co-workers, relatives, and even casual acquaintances and shopkeepers that the house was rightly his but he was being unjustly frozen out. If Evelyn didn't relent and include him, he threatened, he would give her "a hell of a life."

On Saturday November 3, 1945, three days after they moved into the Carrick Avenue house, Alexandra heard her daughter arguing over money in the dining room with her new husband. He didn't have the $75 advance, or bond, the HSR provided to all its drivers to purchase tickets and make change. Inspectors routinely made spot checks to ensure they had the money.

"Give me $100 or I'll slit your throat," Dick threatened.

"I'm not giving you anything," said Evelyn, leaving the room.

"Then I'll get it from your mother," Dick shouted after her. He went into the kitchen.

"What's the trouble?" asked Alexandra.

"She won't give me any money. I've only got $20 of my bond, and I'm not going to work without it. I need $100."

Alexandra reluctantly wrote him a check for $100. In all, he would borrow more than $300 from her over several weeks. She never got it back.

The bickering between John Dick and her daughter was relentless. If they were arguing downstairs, Alexandra would go up to her bedroom and close the door. If she was upstairs and they were arguing in their bedroom, she would go downstairs. Soon Dick was threatening to leave, and began staying away two or three days at a time. "And then," Alexandra would say later, "he would come back and they would make up, and then they would have a fight in another few days."

"What are you always arguing about, Evelyn?" she asked after one heated exchange.

"Women and money," said Evelyn.

Their tumultuous relationship would have made an interesting psychiatric case study. Evelyn seemed to have no qualms about seeing other men, but she harped on at John Dick when he reacted in kind. What probably galled her most was that he was carrying out his trysts while living under *her* roof, without sharing in the chores or the financial upkeep. Had Dick been wealthy, his relationship with Evelyn might not have been so emotionally destructive; no doubt she would at least have pretended to care about him. But if there was any romance in this relationship, it was one-sided. He cared—or thought he did—but she didn't care at all. John Dick simply wasn't her type. She probably found him too straight and boring. It was the wallets—not the hearts—of men like John Dick that interested her. And when she discovered he had no wallet, she wanted him out. The all-consuming quest for cash and the finer things in life had turned greed into a virtue for Evelyn and her parents. Alexandra MacLean, with thousands in the bank from her estranged husband's thefts and Evelyn's sexual philandering, loathed the fact that John Dick seemed incapable even of supporting himself, let alone of contributing to the household.

Evelyn realized she had made a mistake even before moving to the Carrick house. Two or three weeks after the wedding she went to a lawyer seeking a separation agreement. The lawyer drew it up and Evelyn signed it. But whenever she approached John Dick for his signature, he refused. He was putting his "make-her-life-hell" strategy into action.

A few weeks after the move to Carrick, Alexandra overheard yet another argument between Evelyn and John. "I can go with all the women I like," he said loudly. "It was a mistake marrying you. I should have married somebody else."

It wasn't the first time Alexandra had heard him talk about other women. "One morning at breakfast time he was telling us how he used to have women in the streetcars running with him at night," she claimed in court later. "He would pick them up about eight o'clock and they would be with him on his runs until midnight." He mentioned his friend Anna Wolski as one of the women. Furthermore, Alexandra said, "foreign women used to be calling the house." When she answered, the women asked for John Dick. Evelyn argued with him over those calls.

During lunch one Saturday in November, Evelyn answered a different kind of call. "John, you are wanted on the phone," she said.

Dick was on the phone about ten minutes, and when he returned to the table, according to Alexandra, he "was just shaking like a leaf on a tree—shaking—he couldn't hold a knife or fork in his hand." Dick didn't respond when they asked him who it was on the phone. Later, Alexandra heard him and Evelyn arguing, and when he left for work in mid-afternoon she approached her daughter.

"What's wrong?" she asked. "Who was the telephone call from?"

"Well," said Evelyn, "it was from Bill Bohozuk, but when I answered the phone I didn't take it to be his voice at all. He changed his voice because I had answered. And when John came on, he told him he was going to get him."

Bohozuk, who was slightly taller and thirty pounds heavier than John Dick, had heard that Dick was still telling people he was seeing Evelyn, when in fact he wasn't. Anna Wolski had told John Dick that a friend of hers, Sonia Anilowski, had seen Evelyn in Bill Bohozuk's car. Then Evelyn heard the same story and phoned Bohozuk. "Anna Wolski is going around saying she saw me in your car," she said.

Bohozuk was so upset that he went to Anilowski's home on Barton Street East to confront her. She was there with her sister and two male friends.

"Why did you say you saw me with John Dick's wife?"

"I saw you with her at King and James streets in your car," she said.

"It's not true, because my car was in the garage for three days. You better tell John that it's not true or he'll be after me with a shotgun."

The November phone call from Bohozuk was probably a pre-emptive strike because he feared Dick was becoming increasingly unstable and might come after him. Bohozuk was so afraid that sometime in February he purchased a .32-caliber Ivor Johnson revolver from a friend, Roger Fonger.

John Dick had spurned Anna Wolski's marriage offer, but within two weeks of his marriage he showed up at her home appearing "worried and sad." He told her about his woes with his new wife and she agreed to help him determine whether or not Evelyn was seeing Bohozuk. She went to Bohozuk's Picton Street neighborhood and to the Carrick Avenue house, but she didn't see the two together. The trip to Carrick was made just before Christmas 1945. Wolski knocked on the door and when Evelyn answered, Wolski asked if she had an apartment to rent. "No, you're mistaken," said Evelyn.

By December, John Dick's absences from the Carrick house grew more frequent and he told Alexandra he had taken an apartment on Main Street where he now stayed on his nights away. He was at the Carrick house for Christmas and New Year's, but on Sunday, February 3, he was gone for good.

Moving in with his cousin Alex Kammerer brought no peace of mind to John Dick. So strong was his obsession with Evelyn that he admitted to the Kammerers he often staked out her house from ten in the morning until his shift started at four in the afternoon.

With Evelyn Dick's volcanic father working at the HSR, his place of employment provided no sanctuary for John Dick. Donald MacLean hated him and made no secret of it. He had been in full rage since learning about the marriage from fellow workers a week after the fact.

Long-time employee John Walker had known Donald MacLean for more than twenty years and John Dick for three. On February 21, on his way to pick up his pay, he heard Dick arguing with MacLean in front of the HSR office in the rail yards.

"Damn you, Dick, you are trying to break up my home," said MacLean, his florid face more flushed than usual. Walker noticed that Dick was quite pale.

MacLean had complained to Raymond Castle, superintendent of transportation, that John Dick was constantly borrowing money from Evelyn and her mother. "My daughter has to keep giving money to that damn Russian, because he never has a dime," said MacLean. "She's given him so much, I have to give her money."

Castle received several third-party reports about MacLean and Dick squabbling over the marriage and he noticed that Dick's work had begun to suffer. In November and December, Dick was involved in four minor accidents while operating his streetcar. Castle warned him he would be fired if the situation didn't improve.

MacLean and Dick weren't the only family members Castle had to deal with. In the third week of November, Evelyn stormed into his office.

"Where is Van Every?" she demanded.

"What do you want with him?"

"He sent this anonymous letter to my husband about me." She handed the letter to him. It read:

> *I am just writing you this note so as you can get wise to your so-called husband. He certainly uses you as a sucker. There isn't a night but he has some woman standing behind him. The guys was talking about him Saturday in the ticket office how good you are to be buying him tickets more than he could ever buy. He certainly doesn't appreciate you for all the kindness you do for him. There was a brown-haired foreigner asking about John the other night when I was cashing in. She wanted to know what he was on as she had to see him. So don't say you haven't been told. Even your Dad knows. So he can't give you much money when he carries on with women. He don't give two hoots for you, all he took you for was so he could always have bond money, but one of these days, he will leave you flat, he is such a miserable, dirty foreigner. I sure feel sorry for you.*

"How can it be anonymous if you know who wrote it?" asked Castle. "I think you wrote it yourself."

"I didn't write it," protested Evelyn. "I'll show you." She wrote out a couple of sentences as a sample of her handwriting.

"There is already sufficient trouble between your father and your husband without having more," said Castle.

Evelyn insisted she wanted to confront Van Every.

Castle was becoming increasingly irritated. "If you want to see Van Every, you'll have to see him outside company time. There will have to be a settlement of these domestic troubles or everyone concerned will be dismissed." He told her he was tired of the ongoing arguments between Dick and MacLean. For three or four weeks he had put up with the bickering, with each of them coming separately to his office to complain about the other. Dick moaned about his marriage and how he was being treated at home, while MacLean was angry that his daughter had married a scrounger and a scoundrel.

In addition, a woman named Betty Fontaine had phoned Castle requesting that John Dick call at her house with money he owed her. "I loaned him $75 to make up his bond money, but I've since married and I need the money," she said.

Castle told Evelyn her husband had always been a good worker, but in recent weeks his performance had fallen off and he had had four minor accidents. "If these accidents continue, he'll be fired."

As she was leaving, Evelyn eyed Castle for a moment. "You know," she said, "my father is making a good thing out of the company. He is stealing from the company and Mr. Bristol knows it."

"You're crazy," said Castle.

"He is!"

"I don't believe it."

"Come to my house then."

"I wouldn't be so foolish," said Castle. "I know your husband is out working and isn't at home."

"Come when my husband is there."

"I don't want any part of your domestic problems, except to stay as far away as possible."

After summoning Dick and MacLean to his office and warning them they faced dismissal, Castle heard no more and presumed their differences had been resolved. What Castle didn't know was that during one of their confrontations, John Dick foolishly told MacLean that he knew all about his stealing cash and tickets from the company. MacLean was furious and threatened to shoot Dick. Dick took the threat seriously enough to contact the Hamilton Police.

Towards the end of January 1946, Castle received a call from Hamilton Police inspector Eric Howell. He said John Dick had told the police he was afraid of Donald MacLean and that MacLean was carrying a gun. MacLean was summoned to Castle's office, but he denied carrying or even owning a gun.

With John Dick gone from the Carrick Avenue house, there was now a boarder in the back bedroom and Alexandra MacLean was again sharing Evelyn's bed in the front bedroom, with Heather in her cot nearby. Donald MacLean was now allowed to come over for meals once or twice a week for the first time since his estrangement from the family the previous summer.

On Monday, March 4, 1946, John Dick failed to show up for work. The next day he said he had been ill the day before. Even though he still wasn't feeling well, he completed his shift. On that day he also called Alexandra MacLean and asked for a loan. She turned him down. That was the last she would ever hear from him.

He failed to show up for work the next day—Ash Wednesday.

A couple of days later, Raymond Castle approached MacLean. "Do you know where we can get a hold of John Dick?" he asked.

"I don't know a thing about him," said MacLean.

When the newspapers ran the story about the discovery of the torso, Alexandra mentioned it to her daughter. "I see they found a body on the Mountain," she said. Evelyn was silent.

Later, when the body was identified, Evelyn said to her mother, "It might not be his body. Look at how many people are missing."

Investigation

The day before John Dick's torso was found on Hamilton Mountain, Raymond Castle telephoned Hamilton Police to report the streetcar operator missing. And on the morning of Ash Wednesday he approached Donald MacLean in the cashier's office. "I had to send the police down to 32 Carrick Avenue to look for Dick because it's one of his last addresses," he said.

"For God's sake, don't send the police down there," said MacLean, panic in his voice. "I'll find out where he is."

About 2:30 that afternoon MacLean called Castle and gave him the Gertrude Street address where he said Dick could be found. Castle sent an HSR inspector to the address, but Dick's cousin said Dick hadn't been there since March 6 and he didn't know where he was.

Castle then called the Ontario Provincial Police to report John Dick missing. He gave them the Carrick Avenue address and said there were also relatives in the Beamsville area. Dick had reported he wasn't feeling well the day before his disappearance and Castle thought he might be recuperating with his relatives. He also told police Dick's $75 in bond money was missing.

"You should take out a warrant if there is money missing," Castle was told.

"But he might be ill, and I would like that verified before taking any action," he replied. The OPP told Castle to inform Hamilton Police that John Dick was missing.

SUNDAY, MARCH 17

When city worker George Meharg heard about a torso being discovered by a group of children, he remembered the bloody shirt he and William Rushton had found on Mountain Boulevard ten days earlier. Immediately, he telephoned the Hamilton Police and in the company of Detective Albert Chinery returned to the site and recovered the shirt.

MONDAY, MARCH 18

John Dick's as yet unidentified torso had been removed to the city morgue on Saturday, but it would be two days before the provincial pathologist, with the unlikely name of Dr. William J. Deadman, would get to perform a post mortem examination. He had been practicing medicine for thirty-three years and was the pathologist for Hamilton General Hospital as well as for the province. He conducted the examination in the presence of Inspector Charles "Charlie" Wood of the Ontario Provincial Police, Criminal Investigation Department, and Clarence Preston, a detective sergeant with the Hamilton Police Department. The torso had been found so close to the city boundary that jurisdiction over the investigation was in question; so it became a joint investigation, with Wood as the lead investigator. Wood, a seasoned cop with twenty-two years' experience, had traded shots with rum-runners on the Niagara River during Prohibition. Preston too was a veteran with twenty-five years' service on the Hamilton force.

Deadman accurately estimated the victim's weight at 185 pounds, his height at five ten or five eleven, and his age at forty to forty-five. He said that "given the state of the body, having in mind the time of year and the temperature," death had occurred from ten to fourteen days earlier. Again, he was spot-on. He was able to conclude, by studying genital and armpit hair, that the victim was fair-skinned. He estimated the torso weighed 125 pounds. "The genitals were of good size," Deadman noted, "but the right testicle was up in the groin and not down in the scrotum, as the left one was." He said undescended testicles were unusual but he was seeing them more and more in his practice.

As to marks of the horrendous external violence, he said the neck had been severed "just at the level of the voice box or larynx" and "the lacerations of the flesh of the neck had the appearance of having been made with a saw rather than with a keen cutting instrument."

The right arm had been severed by a slightly diagonal cut, four and a half inches below the shoulder. "It was consistent with having been caused by sawing almost through the bone and then bending it so that the last unsawn part splintered." The left arm had been sawed cleanly off, about seven inches below the shoulder. Both legs had also been sawed off—the left about six inches below the hip and the right about fourteen inches below. There was a foot-long saw cut just above the belly button that was so deep it had perforated the bowel in three places. "It had the appearance of a saw cut which had been begun and then abandoned," Deadman said later.

There were several scratches on the torso's shoulders and back, and two gunshot wounds—one entry and one exit—caused by the same bullet, about three and a half inches apart in a line about an inch above the right nipple. The .32-caliber bullet had entered the breast on a flat angle near the center and exited out the side. The wound was superficial and the bullet had not penetrated the chest wall or damaged the ribs. Deadman concluded the chest wound occurred before death and the scratches after death.

In his internal examination Deadman found six ounces of undigested meat and vegetables, and chemical analysis of urine showed a reading of .16 percent alcohol. "He certainly at some time had at least that percentage in his blood . . . and experience shows that eighty percent of people will be intoxicated at that level," the pathologist wrote in his notes.

In his conclusion Deadman wrote: "The cause of death cannot be determined by the post-mortem examination, but may have been caused by injury to the missing head." He said in court later that it would take a person of some strength at least half an hour of continuous sawing to sever the limbs and head from the torso.

John Wall had known John Dick for more than thirty years, stretching back to their years together in Russia. Like Donald

MacLean, Wall hadn't learned of his brother-in-law's marriage to Evelyn until Dick told him a week after the ceremony. He had complained to Wall that Evelyn had "put one over on him" by falsely claiming to be a widow and he said this had led to a lot of arguments. He also told Wall how Evelyn's family mistreated him and that he often heard her and her mother whispering behind his back.

Wall, married to John's sister Anna, had been home just a day from a month-long Florida vacation. He had not seen his brother-in-law since early February and didn't know he had been missing until he received a telephone call from Evelyn Dick about three in the afternoon.

"This is Evelyn, John's wife," she said. Wall was silent. "Are you Jake Wall, Lena's husband?"

"No, I'm John Wall, Anna's husband."

"Mr. Wall, where's John?" she asked. "He owes $500 to different people, and a lady who he owes $75 has sued him. He was supposed to appear in court for that, the week before last on Thursday, but he didn't show up. So the judge gave the order to lock him up, and the police searched the whole of Hamilton but couldn't find him. He even took the company's money along with him. Now they are trying to collect the money from me, and I haven't got any money to pay."

"I know what kind of a gang you got John into," said Wall. "You made a sucker out of him and now you're trying to make him into a crook. How much money do you owe him?"

"I don't owe him anything, Mr. Wall. In fact when John needed money, we helped him out. He was always borrowing from me. He even borrowed money from my mother and said he would pay it back by selling shares in the canning factory."

Wall was upset. Dick had no shares in the factory, located at Niagara-on-the-Lake and owned by a company headed by another Wall brother, Peter. John Wall himself owned "just a few shares."

Evelyn continued: "John told me his mother had claimed his shares in the company and she wouldn't let him sell them. Mr. Wall, does John's mother have any shares in the canning factory?"

"No," said Wall, his voice rising. "John's mother never had any shares, and John doesn't have any shares either."

"Well, we will see," said Evelyn, hanging up.

Wall was livid as he related the story to his wife. He was also worried about John Dick. "Why don't they know where he is?" he asked.

His daughter Melitta was in the room. She told him that while he was away in Florida on the previous Saturday, Aunt "Annie" Kammerer had called and asked if John Dick had been home since March 6. "I said, no," she told her father.

That afternoon Jake Wall and his family arrived for a visit. John Wall told his brother about the unsettling call and they decided to go into Hamilton to see Dick's cousin, Alex Kammerer. They planned to set out the next morning but John Wall was so concerned that he called Kammerer late that night. By that time Kammerer had already called the police, concerned that the torso might be his cousin. Police had come to his house and, when he described John Dick to them, they said Kammerer was probably right. They had asked him to go to the morgue with them the next morning.

"I have bad news for you," Kammerer told John Wall when he called. "They found a body on Hamilton Mountain. The detectives were here tonight and they said it looks like it might be John. Try to come in as early as you can in the morning."

TUESDAY, MARCH 19

John and Jake Wall arrived at Alex Kammerer's house on Gertrude around 9 a.m. Together they went to the Ontario Provincial Police station, where they met Inspector Woods, Detective Preston and Dr. Deadman. From there they went to the city morgue to view the torso.

Despite the missing head and limbs, John Wall immediately recognized the torso as the dismembered body of his brother-in-law. They had swum together many times in Lake Ontario, and for years John Dick had visited his mother in the Vineland area once a week. "I saw John quite often shirtless," Wall would testify later, "and at the first view of the body I was positive it was John's body." He recognized the hairless chest and the stubs of one arm and one leg. The sight of the torso on the floor of the morgue was too grotesque for John Wall's brother. Jake took one look and quickly turned away and went out the door.

The identification of the torso was a major break in the case for Wood and Preston. After listening to Alex Kammerer and the Wall brothers talk about John Dick's woes with Evelyn and her family, they knew where their investigation would take them next.

It was lunchtime when Charlie Wood and Clarence Preston arrived with a search warrant at Evelyn Dick's Carrick Avenue house. With them were OPP officers Sergeant Carl Farrow and Constable Leonard Mattick. Inside, Evelyn, her parents and her daughter had just sat down for lunch.

Evelyn answered the door when Preston knocked. She invited him in, with Wood and the others following. Preston, like most other senior Hamilton policemen, had known MacLean from his years with the HSR. While they talked, Wood went into the living room with Evelyn.

"Are you Mrs. Dick, the wife of John Dick?" he asked.

"Yes, I am."

"When did you see your husband last?"

"March 4," said Evelyn.

"Do you drive a car?"

"No," said Evelyn.

Wood hesitated a moment. "You have probably read in the paper about the finding of a torso on the Mountainside," he said. Evelyn was silent and there was no visible reaction. "That torso has been identified as the body of your husband."

"Don't look at me, I don't know anything about it," said Evelyn.

No horror. No grief. No sorrow. Wood was taken aback. "Well, you better put your coat on and come to police headquarters with me so we can talk this over." He went to the hall and told Preston they would be taking Evelyn in for questioning.

"Can I go down to the station with my daughter?" Donald MacLean asked Preston.

"Wait here a second," said Preston. He went into the living room, where Wood was waiting for Evelyn. "Is it all right if her father comes along too?" asked Preston.

"Yeah, sure," said Wood.

Only Alexandra MacLean and Heather were left with Farrow and Mattick, who stayed behind to execute the search warrant. They looked first in the main-floor clothes closet, where Mattick found a conductor's ticket punch in the pocket of a fur coat. He had the punch in his hand and was rifling through the coat when Alexandra MacLean came into the hall.

"That is my fur coat," she said sternly.

"Oh, is it?" said Mattick.

"Yes."

Alexandra left for a moment to let four-year-old Heather into the house from the backyard where she had been playing. When she returned, Mattick had the coat upside down and was trying to run his hand between the lining and the fur.

"Don't handle my coat like that," she said.

Mattick ignored her and she went into the kitchen. He followed a few minutes later, still carrying the coat. "Can you tell me what kind of fur this coat is?" he asked.

"Seal," she said coldly.

Later, in one of the two rooms in the third-floor attic, Mattick and Farrow unlocked a trunk, using a key found in Evelyn's bedroom, and discovered a streetcar conductor's money-changer among the clothing and letters. They also found a tin box used by conductors to carry streetcar tickets; inside was $43.75 worth of unused tickets. Farrow seized from Evelyn Dick's purse, found in her bedroom, a snapshot of Bill Bohozuk, and from a dresser drawer, two bankbooks from the Bank of Commerce. Both were in Evelyn's name. One had a balance of $720 and the other $10,128.

Talk, talk, talk . . .

At police headquarters Evelyn was taken to the small interview room at the rear of the detectives' section. Preston went off to find a court reporter to take down Evelyn's interview in shorthand, leaving her and Wood alone in the room. Wood began questioning her, recording the conversation in his notebook.

"When did you last drive a car?" he asked.

"March 4, 1946."

"Have you been driving a car recently?"

"No, absolutely."

"What were the relations between your husband and your dad?"

"Not friendly," said Evelyn, "but since we separated they have been all right."

"When was the last time you borrowed Bill Landeg's car?"

"Well, it was not this week, it was a week Monday."

"I suggest you had Bill Landeg's car on Wednesday the sixth."

Evelyn said she was in the house all morning on that day but had picked up the car about 1:30 p.m. She said she was alone, went shopping for enamel paint and shoes, dropped off the paint at home and then returned the car to Landeg's garage.

"Did you leave a note?" asked Wood.

"Yes?"

"What did it say?"

"There was blood in the car . . . The little girl had a bleeding." Evelyn said there was blood on the seat and that she had removed the front seat cover; thrown it out; and replaced it later.

"Is that the last time you had the car?"

"Yes," Evelyn lied. She didn't tell Wood about borrowing the car for an hour on the evening of March 10, when Landeg drove her home. She also said she returned the car at 6:30 p.m. on the sixth, but the garage employee on duty at the time would later say it was returned at 7:30 p.m.

Evelyn also told Wood that she had borrowed the Packard on Monday, March 4, and had driven over to the Astor Hotel, where she saw John Dick. She said he asked her what she was doing there and told her to "get the hell out of here."

"I drove around the block, and when I came back I went into the hotel and John had gone," said Evelyn.

Up to that point in their conversation Evelyn had not been charged or given any warning. But when Preston and court reporter William David Torry arrived at the interview room, Wood informed her that she was being detained in connection with the death of John Dick. She was not obliged to say anything, but if she did, it could be used against her. There was still no formal charge.

Once at the police station Evelyn and her father had been separated, and she did not get to see him before he left to go home. Without her father or a lawyer present, Evelyn agreed to be interviewed by Wood, with Torry recording the questions and answers in shorthand.

"I have already told you that the torso found on the Mountainside has been identified as that of your husband," said Wood.

"Yes."

"What can you tell me about that?"

"Well," said Evelyn, "I have known he was running around with women and in one instance he had broken up a man's home in the city. I had seen him myself with other women." She told of a Ukrainian woman coming to her house in December pretending she was interested in renting an apartment. The woman was Anna Wolski, who had asked John Dick to marry her the previous summer. "I said there was no apartment on Carrick Avenue. Well, she said in her broken English, 'I think I made a mistake,' and turned on her heel and went away." She said the woman later saw John Dick on the streetcar and told him, "I found your wife at the house, you really are married."

"How do you know that?" asked Wood.

"He told me when he came home from work that night."

A well-dressed man she "took to be Italian" came to her door looking for her husband that same week in December, Evelyn said. He told her John Dick had been seeing his wife while he was at work and he was there "to straighten matters out." "He said he [John] was breaking up his home and he would like him to lay off visiting his wife or he would *fix* him, and I said, what do you mean? He said, 'You know what we mean by fix him—we fix him all right, one way or another we get them sooner or later.'"

She said the Italian wasn't the husband of the woman who had come to the door. Wood asked Evelyn to describe the woman. "Her husband was drowned in Lake Ontario or the Bay six years ago," said Evelyn. "All I know is her first name is Annie . . . She is taller than myself, and the night she came to my home it was starting to snow. She had on a green coat, a light fur collar—they call it platinum—and a pink fascinator."

"A kind of crocheted headgear?" Wood asked.

"Yes, and brown hair, and broken English. I understand he had been quite friendly with her and one night she was getting off the Cannon Street bus at City Hall and she said, 'Boy, would I like to drive a bullet through your head after the way you have treated me.'"

"Who did she say that to?"

"To John as she was getting off the front door of the Cannon Street bus."

"How do you know that?"

"Because John told me."

Evelyn said she never saw John Dick after their meeting on Monday at the Astor, but he called her mother the next day and asked to borrow $50. "And my mother said she had helped him out enough. Well, he said he had to go and show his bond money and he had only $26, but he was supposed to have $75."

Evelyn repeated that she had borrowed William Landeg's

Packard on the afternoon of Ash Wednesday. She said she had had shopping to do and that she went to Garvin's Hardware, Eaton's, Bronx Shoe Store, "and then I stopped at the smaller places like Woolworth's and Tamblyn's Drug Store." She said she was home by 4:45 p.m.

Half an hour later Evelyn said there was a telephone call from "a member of a gang from Windsor." She told Wood that the gangster said, "We caught up with your husband. He was warned to lay off a friend of mine's wife and he has left her in the family way. Now she is expecting a baby, so he paid us to put John out of business."

"He said this to you over the phone?" asked Wood.

"Yes, officer, he did."

Evelyn said the gangster instructed her to drive Landeg's Packard to a rendezvous at the old James Street incline, where he arrived with another man in a 1941 or '42 black Oldsmobile. "It was a beautiful car, parked in the dark." One man stayed in the car and the other got out.

"And he approached you?"

"Yes, that's right."

"Was it the same man who came to the house that night?"

"No, it wasn't," said Evelyn. She said the man was dragging a heavy sack as he approached her. "He said he wanted to get rid of this, quick. I said, 'You had better not use this car.'" But he ignored her and put the sack on the front seat of the Packard, telling her they were short a car because "part of the gang had gone to Windsor, as there is a big load of alcohol coming in, and the rest of the gang had gone to Toronto." Pushing the sack over the top of the seat and into the back, the gangster got in the front beside her. Evelyn said she was scared the whole time.

"And what did he say?" asked Wood.

"He said, 'Come on, I haven't got much time. I am losing out on this job in Windsor.'"

"Did he tell you what was in the sack?"

"Yes, he said 'part of John.'" Following the gangster's directions, Evelyn said she headed to Concession Street and out towards Albion Falls on Hamilton Mountain. "He said hurry up, drive faster, and he kept putting his foot over top of mine because he didn't like the way I drove. I drove too slow." When they reached Mountain Brow, he took the wheel and, after driving a short distance, pulled over to the side of the road.

"Then when you got along there, what happened?"

"He pulled him out."

"And what did he do with him?" asked Wood.

"Rolled him down the bank," said Evelyn.

"Still in the bag?"

"No, he took the bag off him." She said he threw the bag out of the car on the way back to town, where she dropped him at the Connaught Hotel.

Wood had interrogated hundreds of suspects in more than two decades of police work; his skepticism was palpable. "So that was it," he said; "just a matter of driving out there, meeting this man and letting him put the bag in the car with part of John in it, driving along to a bend in the road before you get to Albion Falls, and he throws it over the hill after he took the bag off it, and you drive back down the Mountain, down Ottawa Street and leave him off at the Connaught Hotel?"

"He had to meet other people," explained Evelyn. "He had to meet somebody."

"Why would this man call you up to get you to drive him up with part of a body in your car when he already had it in his car?" asked Wood. "It would be a simple matter for him to throw it out of the car instead of bringing it up to you."

"They had something else to do."

"Do you know what they had to do?"

"No, I don't."

"How did you feel when he told you it was part of John in the bag?"

"Well, I just can't express how I felt."

"Were you glad that your husband was being done away with?"

"Well, no, but it was a pretty mean trick to break up a home."

"But he was your husband."

"Yes, but he had so many enemies."

Evelyn denied conspiring to have her husband murdered but told Wood that the gangster said he was going to give her two hundred dollars for driving the car.

"Mrs. Dick, did you take any actual part in the murder of your husband?" asked Wood.

"No, no. I know nothing about where his legs, arms or hands are."

"But you do know they are missing?"

"Yes."

When Wood asked her if the gangster had a gun, she said she didn't see one but "they always carry them."

"You are always referring to them as 'they.' Who are the others?"

"I don't know. I know there were about a half-dozen in the gang."

"What nationality are they?"

"Well, I would say Italian."

Evelyn said that on the way downtown from the Mountain, besides throwing out the bloody sack, the gangster also threw out John Dick's shirt and the front seat covers.

"What happened to the blanket?" asked Wood.

Evelyn said it had been cleaned and was now in the spare bedroom at her house.

"Who cleaned it?"

"The washing machine," said Evelyn.

In response to Wood, Evelyn said that her mother didn't know about what had happened up on the Mountain.

"Does she know the torso found on the Mountainside was your husband?"

"She thought it might be when she saw it in the paper today. She knew his days were numbered."

After relating this detailed account of what had happened to her husband, Evelyn told Wood she was afraid to say anything more.

"What are you scared of?"

"It is all right to talk, but look at the way those foreigners get back at you. Suppose they put a time bomb under my veranda or back porch. Where would I be?"

Wood was more skeptical than ever. "It is pretty hard for me to believe that this 'gang,' as your refer to them, would cut him up and get the body halfway up the Mountain in a car and then call you to drive them the rest of the way. Why bring you into it at all?"

But Evelyn stuck to her story. "They had a job to do in Toronto and alcohol to get in Windsor."

"But if they had the torso in the car up on the Mountain, in the time they waited for you to get there they could have driven along and dumped it over the embankment."

"Well, the boys had something else to do."

Exasperated, Wood asked if there was anything further she could tell him about the death of her husband. "I am afraid to say too much. I will get a knife in my back or a bomb under my house."

Evelyn had chain-smoked throughout the interview, while Inspector Wood puffed continuously on his pipe. Clarence Preston, a non-smoker, had sat quietly, listening to Wood and Evelyn. Now he asked her if she would be able to recognize the gangsters if she saw their mug shots.

"Yes, I could," said Evelyn. She said the one who had come to her house had "dark Italian features" and wore a bowler hat, a dark overcoat, and "a flashy tie." She said he had beautiful pearl teeth, with a gold filling in one and a gold cap on another. The man who dumped John Dick's torso up on the Mountain was described as short and stocky, with Italian features and a slight foreign accent. Evelyn didn't overburden her imagination when she described his clothing. His shoes were oxblood brown oxfords "exactly the same" as Wood's. Remarkably, their suits were also exactly alike.

"A brown suit with stripes in it?" asked Preston.

"Yes," Evelyn said, and no cuffs, just like Wood's suit.

"Did he have an overcoat?" asked Preston.

"Like what you are wearing yourself today," said Evelyn without hesitation. "A raincoat—gabardine." When she told the policemen the gangster's hair was black, Preston asked her if it was straight or wavy. "Not so very wavy, more like the inspector's."

"How was it combed?"

"Back like the inspector's, and he had a ring something like you have on your right hand. It was silver."

When she accompanied the gangster to the Mountain, Evelyn said she was wearing her gray fur coat, a black hat and a coral dress. "Did you get any blood on your fur coat?" asked Preston.

"No, I got it on the front of my dress. There was a drop . . . but I had brought a supply of handkerchiefs with me."

As soon as word got out that a human torso had been found on Hamilton Mountain, media from around the country began descending on the city. The three competing Toronto newspapers—the *Star*, the *Telegram* and the *Globe and Mail*—all sent representatives. The *Star* and the *Telegram* were bitter rivals engaged in a circulation war going back to 1892, when the *Star* was founded by two dozen striking printers from the *Telegram*. The traditionally conservative *Telegram* considered the upstart *Star* and its owner, Joseph E. "Holy Joe" Atkinson, to be not only liberal but even Bolshevik.[16]

The much-despised Harry C. Hindmarsh, Atkinson's son-in-law, was a powerful force at the *Star*. Over six feet tall and heavy-set, with close-cropped hair, Hindmarsh was brutal with his reporters, especially those exhibiting talent or independence.

"Old man Hindmarsh always worked on the theory that any reporter who got a scoop was too big for his britches, and so he'd tell the desk to give him some obituaries to write," says eighty-seven-year-old Gwyn "Jocko" Thomas who covered the torso murder for the *Star*. "I tell the story about Bill Stephenson, who wrote the book *A Man Called Intrepid*. He was over in Europe for the *Star* and he got a great big scoop that even the *New York Times* picked up. And he came back to the office and a few reporters came around to congratulate him. And all of a sudden I hear Jimmy Nichol from the desk yell out, 'Bill Stevenson—take an obit!' And Stephenson looked around to see if there was another Bill Stephenson; surely they wouldn't ask a senior reporter from London to write an obituary. And then Nichol yells louder and goes running over, chewing copy paper as he always did. 'I told you to take an obit,' he growled. And that was the way they rewarded you. They did that to Gordon Sinclair too a couple of times when he came back from his trips. So you could never figure you were stepping up."

At the time of the torso murder case, Jocko Thomas himself had just stepped up to the position of senior crime writer, replacing Athol Gow. "He retired that year," says Thomas. "Old man Atkinson loved him for the great stories he got for the *Star* in his time." But Gow was a heavy drinker and he'd sometimes miss a week at a time, leaving Thomas and others to cover for him. "He was sort of immune from being fired," says Thomas. "But I was never immune. I always felt I'd get fired one day, but I stayed on for sixty years." In that time he became a legend as the *Star*'s police reporter, winning three National Newspaper Awards for his work.

Arriving in Hamilton, Thomas met a blue wall of silence. "It was a torso murder, a good-looking girl involved, and the police weren't giving any information. That heightened the intrigue and the interest in it. It took a while before the police charged anybody. There were all kinds of rumors that Mrs. Dick was involved with socially prominent people in Hamilton and that's why it was being suppressed. You couldn't even guess what was going on."

Police in those days didn't hold press conferences to detail their progress on an investigation. "The police and the press worked pretty well separate," says Thomas. "The police just hoped that we wouldn't tread on their toes, but sometimes we did. Today there is more co-operation between the police and the press, but there was none in the Dick case."

Thomas says that the only information initially released by police was the identification of the torso as the remains of John Dick, a Hamilton streetcar operator. "After that there was nothing. They weren't progressing too much until they got Evelyn Dick to talk, and then she talked her head off—talked herself into almost getting hanged."

March 19 was a crucial day for the police. They had identified the torso and, in John Dick's room at his cousin's house, found Bill Bohozuk's name written on a scrap of paper. From the Kammerers they learned that Evelyn and her family despised Dick. And in the search of Evelyn's house they found the snapshot of Bohozuk and John Dick's ticket punch, tickets and money-changer. Now Evelyn's statement triggered more police action.

In the early afternoon Bill Landeg's Packard was impounded and brought to the Central Police Station garage. Police went back to Evelyn's house, where they picked up the blanket she had laundered, a gold watch-chain belonging to John Dick, and the dress she said she was wearing in the car with the torso. At Donald MacLean's house at 214 Rosslyn Avenue police found a .32-caliber Harrington & Richardson nickel-plated revolver wrapped in cloth in a dresser drawer in a rear bedroom off the kitchen. The gun was registered to MacLean, who was at the house when police conducted the search. In the same drawer, they found a large quantity of rifle ammunition, shotgun shells and a box of .32-caliber ammunition.

Meanwhile, Evelyn Dick sat quietly munching chocolate between drags on her cigarette after giving her statement to police in the "back detective room," formerly the Crown attorney's room, overlooking King William Street at the Central Police Station. Inspector Wood left the room for a time. On his return he asked Evelyn if she would be willing to take a drive up the Mountain to point out locations "where certain articles were thrown out of the car." She agreed, and in a police cruiser with two uniformed officers in the front seat and Wood, Evelyn and Preston in the rear, they set off from the police station.

As they drove along Mountain Brow Road near the intersection with Flock Road, Evelyn said, "Right here he threw the cap out the right window over the top of the car to the left towards the Mountain brow. The satchel was also thrown out here."

Preston wrote in his report later: "The car was stopped and I got out with Constable William Melody, the driver, and we took a look over the brow of the Mountain, but discovered nothing." As they traveled east about a half-mile past the Silver Spur Riding Club, Evelyn told the driver to slow down and "pull up here. This is where the torso was tossed over the Mountain." In this account of what happened, Evelyn had a name for the gangster who dumped the torso: Romanelli. She said he told her: "Give me a hand with this, it is heavy." But when he pulled the sack off to reveal the torso, Evelyn said she became ill and vomited. She said Romanelli then picked up the torso, ran across the road and tossed it over the mountainside. He returned to the car with John Dick's bloody shirt, which he threw into the back seat.

On the return trip, a few car lengths past the intersection of Flock Road and Mountain Drive Road, Evelyn said, "It was right along here that the shirt or bag was thrown out. I'm not sure which it was." But police found nothing there or at two other locations where she said pieces of the seat cover had been thrown out.

Preston later said that Evelyn Dick "was in her usual good mood" when they returned to the police station shortly after 5 p.m. But that evening she was charged with vagrancy, a catch-all offense often used by police in those days to hold suspects while more serious charges against them were being investigated. "If you're investigating a case and you suspected somebody, you charged them under section 'A' of the Vagrancy Act," says Jocko Thomas, "in other words, to keep them in custody." That practice was eventually eliminated, largely because of the torso murder case.

Evelyn was held overnight in a police cell and the next morning was arraigned on the vagrancy charge before Magistrate Henry A. Burbidge. Orville Walsh, the lawyer representing Evelyn, asked for bail. "My client has lived with her family in Hamilton all her life," he said, "and I don't know of any previous—"

"I am objecting," interjected Crown Attorney Harvey McCulloch. "Due to the exigencies of the situation, she should be required to be in custody at least one week. If necessary, I can give the details as alleged, and the investigation to date."

But Burbidge said he could accept the assurance of the crown that "it was a proper case. A lot can be behind a vagrancy charge." He turned down the request for bail. Evelyn stood in the prisoners' box wearing a chic black pillbox hat and a black and gray checked suit, with her gray kidskin coat over her shoulders. Her head was bowed, but she glanced under her dark lashes at the packed courtroom.

Denied bail, Evelyn Dick was remanded one week, to March 27, and taken to a cell in the dingy Barton Street jail.

My Boyfriend's Back

On March 21, the day after Evelyn's arraignment, police officers Wood, Preston, Farrow and Mattick were at Bill Bohozuk's house at 21 Picton Street where he lived with his father and sister. From a bedroom drawer they seized the .32-caliber Ivor Johnson revolver, purchased by Bohozuk from his friend Robert Fonger a month before. Unfortunately for Fonger—who was still owed money for the gun—Bohozuk had failed to change the registration. Police later detained Fonger while his story was verified. Bohozuk said he had purchased the gun for his own protection but didn't even know how to load or fire it. Subsequent forensic tests determined that the gun had not been fired for some time. Also seized at the Picton house were photographs of Bohozuk and Evelyn Dick, shot the day they took Heather to the park.

Bohozuk was escorted to the police station for questioning. It happened that Evelyn Dick was also at the station. She had been brought over from the jail to sign her statement made the day before, and she heard that Bohozuk had been picked up. She spotted Clarence Preston in the hallway.

"I understand you have brought Bill in," she said.

"Yes."

"Well, there are certain things I wish to put in the statement I made yesterday. Will you see the inspector?"

Preston went to Charlie Wood and they met with Evelyn in the back detective room. Also in the room was court reporter Douglas Ewing, from the magistrate's office. He would take down her statement in shorthand. The interview began at 3:55 p.m. Once again the room quickly filled with smoke as Evelyn lit cigarette after cigarette and Wood puffed on his pipe. Preston would testify later that Evelyn "was in a very good mood, quite contented, and appeared to want to talk freely." Once again it was Wood who did the questioning.

"Now, Mrs. Dick, I understand you have been talking to Detective Sergeant Preston and have some further information you want to give us in connection with the death of John Dick," said Wood.

"Well, as you know, Bill Bohozuk detested my husband," said Evelyn. "They were bitter, bitter enemies and John seemed to be causing Bill quite a lot of trouble. He had gone down to the Dominion Foundries and Bill had nearly lost his job." She explained that her husband had gone there "to tell Bill to stop seeing me . . . not to come near me and mind his own business and get some other woman instead of bothering his wife."

"Was Bill seeing you frequently then?"

"No, he had just seen me once, to be exact . . . it was on Tuesday and John went down to the foundries on Wednesday morning."

Evelyn said her husband was convinced Bohozuk was continuing to see her and complained about it to anyone who would listen. She said Bohozuk grumbled to her that every time John Dick saw his two-tone Buick driving along King Street or Main Street, "he accused him of coming down to my home." She said Bohozuk told her before Christmas 1945 that he was "just watching his chance to get even with John." And then, in late January, she said Bohozuk asked her for a loan of two hundred dollars. [That was the two-week loan that Bohozuk used, with others, to repair his damaged car.]

"Did he say what he wanted the money for?" asked Wood.

"Yes, he was expecting a job to be done and they had to have two hundred dollars as down payment."

"What kind of a job?"

"John to be fixed," said Evelyn.

"In what way?"

"Put out of business . . ."

Wood interrupted her. "What do you mean by that—'put out of business'?"

"Well, murdered I guess." She said Bohozuk was going to give the two hundred dollars "to the gang that had come through Windsor."

"Bill was going to pay somebody two hundred dollars to murder your husband? Is that it?"

"It was going to be more than two hundred," explained Evelyn.

"How much more was it going to be?"

"That I did not know. There were going to be four involved and they each had to have fifty dollars down payment."

"You gave Bill the two hundred dollars?"

"Yes, made up of five twenties and ten tens, to be exact— in a white letter envelope."

"Now," asked Wood, "were you paying him that money to have your husband murdered or was he borrowing it from you for that purpose?"

"He was borrowing it from me because he was in a tight corner himself." But, said Evelyn, the two hundred dollars was returned by Bohozuk a week or so later because, for the moment, "the gang" was too busy to go after John Dick. "He said that he might have to borrow it later on, when they would not be so busy." She said he informed her later that the gang was now asking one thousand to twelve hundred dollars to eliminate John Dick, "and I told him I did not have that much in the bank."

In her rambling statement Evelyn intimated that John Dick was jealous of others besides Bill Bohozuk. "John had also accused one of the inspectors at the Hamilton Street Railway of coming down too often. He said on one occasion, he had seen him leaving the house."

In a further expansion of her statement from the day before, Evelyn said the Italian gangster, Tony Romanelli, had threatened her "with a nickel-plated revolver in one pocket and a scalping knife in the other" to force her to make the trip to dispose of the torso. "I did not want to take the torso in the car, as I was afraid of getting caught."

During the drive up the Mountain, she said Romanelli told her he and an accomplice had met John Dick at the King

George Hotel about 1:30 p.m. on Ash Wednesday. After consuming eight or nine beers, the three of them went up the Mountain to continue drinking. "They had a bottle of Jamaica rum, gin and ginger ale and dago red wine," said Evelyn. "They later went on as far as Glanford and went down a deserted road, where they finished the bottle of rum and some of the wine. John had got suspicious of going away out there and when he looked at his watch, it was nearly three-thirty. He was due to go to work at 4:11 p.m." When the car got stuck on a muddy concession road, she said John got angry and accused them of purposely making him late for work. "And another argument started and John said, 'I won't come again with you wops,' and with that, Romanelli let him have it."

"What do you mean?" asked Wood.

"One shot in the back of the neck and one through the right eyeball." She said the gangsters then drove to a house in Hamilton's north end, where they began cutting up the body.

"Now, were you in the car with these men when this happened?" asked Wood.

"No, officer."

Evelyn said that Romanelli told her Bill Bohozuk was paying him to dispose of John Dick.

"Did Romanelli tell you how much he was being paid?"

"No, officer . . . I understood it was on the installment plan. He said, 'We are getting a little now and then.'"

"Do you know where the limbs are from your husband's body?"

"I understand they were burned in a furnace."

"How did you come to understand that?"

"Romanelli had told me that they had—the head and arms and legs were all burned."

"Do you know where?"

"All I know is, in a furnace in the north end."

"In a house or factory?"

"In a house."

Wood asked Evelyn if there was any part of her husband's body in the Packard when she attempted to park it in the garage behind her house on March 6. "No," she replied.

"Is there anything else you would care to tell us at this point?"

"I think that covers everything."

While Evelyn Dick was giving her statement to the police, Francis John Evans, a lawyer representing Bill Bohozuk, arrived at the station to see his client. He also asked to see Evelyn Dick on behalf of her lawyer, Orville Walsh, who was a partner in the same law firm. Walsh had instructed Evans to tell Evelyn not to sign any statements or make any statements to police. Clarence Preston heard that Evans was looking for Evelyn, and he came out of the interview room determined to keep the lawyer away from her until after the statement was signed. Evans and Preston met in the detectives' office.

"I am here to see Bill Bohozuk and Mrs. Dick," said Evans.

"It would be better if you saw Bohozuk first," said Preston. "He's down in the cells in the station duty room."

When Evans went there, he was told he couldn't see Bohozuk. He said later it was obvious he was getting the runaround. Alarmed when he saw a court reporter walk by with what appeared to be a statement, Evans went back to Preston and demanded to see Evelyn Dick. He rightly concluded that the statement was for her to sign. But Preston told him Evelyn was speaking to her mother on the telephone and he would have to wait until the conversation was completed.

Preston admitted later in testimony that he purposely "stalled around for time, and Mr. Evans got a little hot under the collar. He followed me around and we had a little bit of an argument. I did not give him any satisfaction as to where this woman was."

By the time Evans got to see Evelyn, she had signed the statement.

twelve

Ashes and Cement

THURSDAY, MARCH 21

Charlie Wood and Clarence Preston arrived at Evelyn Dick's house on Carrick Avenue about 10:30 a.m. Alexandra MacLean was alone and Wood sat with her in the living room as Preston searched the house. He went first to the attic and worked his way down to the basement, where he saw a bushel basket and a steel rocker containing ashes as well as a small pile of ashes on the floor. He noticed dark stains on the basket that he thought might be blood. He carried the basket out to the garage, dumped the ashes on the cinder floor and began sifting through them. When he discovered what looked like pieces of bone, he went into the house and showed Wood what he had found.

The policemen went to the garage, opened the main double doors to allow more light in, and picked through the ashes, placing what they thought were bone fragments in a box. Expanding the search to the rutted driveway in front of the garage, Wood discovered the stump of a human tooth. In the basement again, they shoveled the small pile of ashes from the floor into the rocker and carried it out to the garage. More small pieces of bone were found when they sifted through these ashes. Examining the garage itself, Wood noticed red stains on the south wall that he thought might be blood. Using his penknife, he sliced several slivers of the wood from the wall.

They locked up the garage, kept the keys and left. Later that afternoon they returned to the garage with pathologist Dr. Deadman and his assistant. The ashes were checked once more and the recovered items were boxed and individually marked. All of the ashes, including those from the ruts in front of the garage, were removed to the police station. Three days later they were taken to the city hospital morgue, where they were sifted, washed and sorted. Wood, Preston, and Deadman and his assistant carefully examined each fragment and came up with several more pieces of bone material and seven tooth roots. Deadman was convinced he recognized parts of "leg bones, parts of thigh bones, parts of upper arm bones, and parts of skull bones." Wood later took all of the recovered material to bone and teeth experts at the University of Toronto. Deadman, meanwhile, tested the stains Preston had seen on the bushel basket and confirmed they were human blood, type O—the same as John Dick's.

Before sifting through the ashes, Clarence Preston, in his search of the attic, had noticed a lock broken off a large steamer trunk. When he asked Alexandra MacLean about it, she said her husband Donald was responsible. The day before he had arrived "the worse of drink" and asked her if the police had been around. She told him they had searched the house, including the attic, that morning. "The detectives couldn't open the cabin trunk," she had told her husband.

"Get me something to smash the lock," he ordered. Alexandra reluctantly complied, handing him a hammer and screwdriver. "I'll open the goddamn thing," he said. He rushed up the stairs and she could hear him banging at the trunk. Then the pounding stopped. "Get me a stronger hammer," he yelled.

Alexandra found a heavier hammer and brought it up to him. "It's my trunk and you're damaging it," she protested.

When he started smashing at the lock, he was annoyed that she was watching him. "Get the fuck out of here," he said, raising the hammer in a threatening manner.

She retreated downstairs to the kitchen, wondering what was in the trunk that he didn't want her to see.

When the pounding stopped, Alexandra knew the trunk was open. She was cooking supper. Her husband was supposed to stay and have dinner with her and Heather and their border, Robert Corbett. However, just as MacLean reached the ground floor hall, Sergeant Farrow and Constable Mattick arrived at the front door in search of the blanket from the Packard and the dress Evelyn wore the night the torso was dumped on the Mountain. The policemen left after a few minutes, but when Alexandra called her husband to supper, there was no response. She checked the cellar. He wasn't there, "but the side door was open and he was not to be seen." He had slipped out while the police were there.

After securing the ashes at the police station, Preston told Wood he had seen bath towels, books, and a few odds and ends—nothing of significance—in the trunk with the smashed lock, but they wondered what Donald MacLean might have removed. It was decided that a further search of the Carrick house and of Donald MacLean's house would be conducted the next day.

FRIDAY, MARCH 22

Detective John Freeborn was the officer Evelyn Dick had seen at the police station on March 12 when she complained that her husband had run out on his debts, leaving her stuck with them. Now, the twenty-six-year veteran had been assigned to accompany OPP officers Farrow and Mattick for the morning search of Evelyn's house. It would be an experience none of them would soon forget. What they found would shock the city and the country, and intensify the already white-hot media spotlight.

Returning to the attic where Preston had found the trunk with the broken lock, the policemen found a locked beige suitcase—the one Evelyn Dick had brought home from the hospital after the birth of her last child. Alexandra MacLean told the officers the key had been lost. She said she last saw the suitcase open in January and it was filled mostly with books. Freeborn testified later that the lock was pried open with a screwdriver "and a strong odor came from it." Inside was a burlap bag covering a small wicker basket, and inside that was a cement-filled cardboard box, with pieces of clothing protruding through the cement. The suitcase was immediately closed and removed from the attic. It weighed about seventy-five pounds. On the way out of the house Freeborn asked Alexandra who owned the suitcase. "Evelyn," she replied.

The suitcase was taken to the Central Police Station where, in the presence of Dr. Deadman, the cement was chiseled away, revealing a zippered shopping bag wrapped in a brown skirt with the name *Evelyn Dick* written on the inside band. Inside the shopping bag, which measured thirteen by five by eight inches, was the partially mummified body of a newborn baby. "The baby was doubled up and forced into the bag," said Deadman.

Describing the baby's clothing, he said there was a diaper held by two rusty safety pins; a cotton shirt; and over that "an infant's dress, lacework, and a sweater of knitted wool." Decomposition was so advanced that the left foot and ankle were missing. A knotted piece of heavy string was looped around the baby's neck.

Leaving that grisly scene, Freeborn, Farrow and Mattick returned to the Carrick house, picked up Donald MacLean and went to his house on Rosslyn for a second search. The policemen went first to the attic, which included two finished rooms: a bedroom in front and a storage room in back. Some of MacLean's clothing, including his HSR uniform, was hanging in the storage room, which also housed a gun locker. MacLean had lost his key to the locker, he had told police on their first visit. This time he produced the key when they threatened to force the lock. MacLean, who had told HSR management he didn't own a gun, watched as police opened the locker and found two shotguns, a deer rifle, a .22 rifle and a hunting knife. Freeborn examined the guns and concluded they had never been fired. "They were greased and wrapped up very carefully and placed in the gun locker," he said.

At the bottom of the locker, in a brown haversack, was $4,440 in bills—twenties, tens and fives. Freeborn described the bills as "all flattened out nicely with leather bands around them." And filling the pockets of MacLean's uniform and of other clothing hanging in the storage room, police found loose streetcar tickets. They were used tickets stolen from bus and streetcar fare boxes. Since they had no cancellation marks, they were as valuable as new tickets. Throughout the house, police found thousands more tickets stuffed in dresser drawers, in clothing—even in teacups on a plate rail.

The overhead electric light in MacLean's cellar was quite dim, and police had made only a cursory inspection during their first visit to the house. This time they had brought along flashlights and a bright bulb on an extension cord. Snug against the rafters and the stone wallhead they found three large paper bags stuffed with thousands more streetcar tickets.

Beneath a work bench on the south side of the cellar was a large wooden box. Inside were a pair of muddy black oxfords, identified in court later as belonging to John Dick. Using the extension light, the police carefully examined the shoes. On the side of one and the soles of both were spots "which looked like blood to us," said Freeborn. The shoes were seized, along with a butcher knife with a fifteen-inch blade and a small carpenter's strip saw.

In a dresser drawer in the front bedroom of the house the police found a ring with five keys, four of which were capable of opening the fare box of any streetcar or bus operated by the HSR. (The combination to the HSR vault was later found on a piece paper in the house.)

One of the most intriguing finds was an August 5, 1944, edition of *Famous Detective Stories*, discovered by Farrow in an upstairs bedroom. He paid particular attention to a story in which the victim of a failed abortion is dismembered and the body parts are burned in a furnace. It was a blueprint for cutting up a human body:

> *The old doctor lost no time in going to his gory chore.*
> *One by one he cut away the arms, the legs, the head.*
> *He worked like a butcher—first the knife, then the saw.*
> *The floor was wet with blood when he finally finished.*
> *The dull sun of a new day had routed the night of horror*
> *before the bloody job was completed . . .*

Evelyn MacLean, at age ten, with her mother, Alexandra. (*Toronto Star*)

Evelyn MacLean as a teenager. (*Hamilton Spectator*)

Evelyn with the family dog. (*Hamilton Spectator*)

Evelyn with her daughter
Heather. (*Hamilton Spectator*)

Evelyn Dick in her fake Red
Cross driver's uniform. The skirt
was later used to hold crumbling
cement in place around her dead
infant. (Archives of Ontario)

Alexandra MacLean, at age sixty. (*Toronto Star*)

Donald MacLean, at age sixty-nine. (*Toronto Star*)

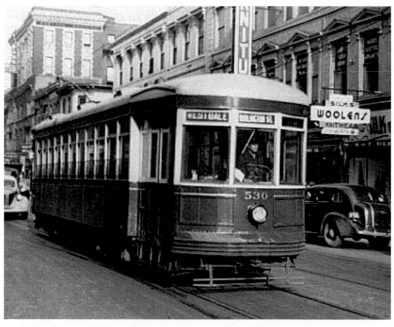

The type of Hamilton Streetcar operated by John Dick in the 1940s. (HSR Archives)

Basement entrance to 214 Rosslyn Street South were John Dick was likely dismembered. (Courtesy Ontario Provincial Police)

This photo of John Dick was the only one released to the media. (*Toronto Star*)

Young Hamilton steelworker and accomplished rower, William "Bill" Bohozuk. (*Toronto Star*)

The house Evelyn purchased at 32 Carrick Avenue. Her infant was found encased in cement in the attic. (*Hamilton Spectator*)

The 1938 Packard that carried John Dick's torso to Hamilton Mountain. (Courtesy Ontario Provincial Police)

The Reed and Weaver children who found the torso on Hamilton Mountain. (*Hamilton Spectator*)

John Dick's torso, as it was discovered by the children on Hamilton Mountain. (Courtesy Ontario Provincial Police)

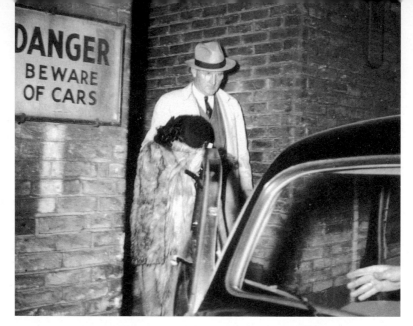

Evelyn Dick leaving Hamilton police station with Detective Clarence Preston. (*Hamilton Spectator*)

John Dick's sisters, Helen (Lena) and Anna with their husbands, brothers Jake and John Wall. John and Anna are on the right. (*Hamilton Spectator*)

The story went on to describe a peculiar odor in the air:

It was the odor of burning human flesh. For this was the funeral pyre of Gladys Lawson, cremated that March morning in the gloomy shadows of an abortionist's abattoir.

In all, police seized $4,800 in cash and more than twenty-six thousand bus and streetcar tickets, valued at $1,704. It was later discovered that MacLean and his wife had accounts at several branches of the Dominion Bank and the Canadian Bank of Commerce, with balances totaling about $60,000. When he was arrested at his home that evening, MacLean was carrying $882.62 in cash, about $25 of it in coins, and $11.14 in HSR tickets. He was charged with the theft of streetcar tickets and cash, and remanded in custody overnight.

Earlier this same day, Evelyn Dick was brought from the Barton Street jail to the police station. After finding bones in the ashes in her house and in front of her garage, Charlie Wood and Clarence Preston wanted to question her once again. The *Toronto Daily Star* reported that she was "dressed in a sleek, gray fur coat" as she entered the station about 9 a.m. While Charlie Wood was briefing the officers who would conduct the searches of the Carrick and Rosslyn houses, Clarence Preston met with Evelyn. He told her about finding pieces of human bones in the ashes. "Is there any explanation you wish to make?" he asked.

"I will tell you the whole story," said Evelyn.

Preston found Wood and told him that Evelyn wanted to talk. They searched for a court reporter, but none was available. It was decided that Preston himself would record the interview in longhand. In the interview room, Evelyn, still charged with vagrancy, was given the usual police warning. Once again she and Wood filled the small room with smoke.

At the start of the interview, Preston asked Evelyn if she had ever had sex with Bill Bohozuk. After a long preamble she got around to answering. "October 9, 1945, was the first time I had sex relations with Bohozuk at his home after the show." Leading to that answer, she had explained: "I was married to

Dick on October 4, 1945, and on Tuesday, October 9, I went to the Tivoli Theatre with Bohozuk. We came home at midnight and as I went to the door John bounced out from the bushes and demanded to know what this was all about. That day I had Bohozuk's car all day, getting it from the plant. On Wednesday I was to get it again."

Evelyn then recounted the confrontation between Bohozuk and John Dick at the Dofasco plant. Later that day Dick happened to see Bohozuk driving to her apartment on James Street South to pick up the extra set of car keys he had loaned her. She said Dick called her and complained: "I see Bohozuk didn't lose any time seeing you." Bohozuk had vowed he wouldn't date Evelyn again, and she said that when he took his keys from her he said of Dick: "By God, he's a bad-acting son of a bitch."

She repeated much of what she had said in her earlier statement about Bohozuk hiring a gang to "fix" John Dick. Using language straight out of potboilers, she said that around Christmas, Bohozuk stopped his car downtown, told her to get in and, before dropping her off in front of a jewelry store, told her she would be hearing from him shortly about John. "He told me that he would fix John—the gang is coming through Hamilton next week from Toronto."

The story began to differ from her earlier statement when she said that sometime in February, Bohozuk "enticed John to get into his car and they sat and talked for a long time but nobody showed up." Presumably, she was referring to the gang members who were supposed to show up to 'fix' her husband.

"On Monday, March 4, I met John uptown by accident and he accused me of being out with Bill and having spent the past weekend with him," said Evelyn. And before that she said her husband accused her of "being in the family way to Bill Bohozuk."

In the early afternoon of Wednesday, March 6, the day John Dick disappeared, Evelyn said she had seen him come out of the King George Hotel with two men, "one being Tony Romanelli, and the other man I didn't know. I had seen Bohozuk's car parked on James St. near Virginia Dare's facing north. John and the two men were walking east . . . I figured this was what Bill had been leading up to. The last week in February, John's grandmother had died, and Bill called me by telephone and said when they got Bill they intended doping his drink."

After arriving home about 4 p.m., Evelyn said she received a telephone call from Bohozuk telling her, "We've got him at last." She said he urged her to meet him at the Royal Connaught as soon as possible. "I went to the Royal Connaught and was met there by Romanelli, who gave me John's watch-chain and some car tickets and a small tin box with some more tickets. 'These were in a paper bag,' he said. 'Here's some stuff that Bill thought you would like to have.' He asked me for a loan of Bill Landeg's Packard, and I didn't like the idea, but I allowed him to take it. He told me he had something to do. He drove me home, left me there, and drove away."

Romanelli called later to tell her he was returning the car, she said. "I remarked that there was a lot of blood on the car and he said, 'That will come off all right.' There was a blanket in the back of the car and it was covered with blood. Wrapped up in a piece of cloth was a part of the face, which was all smashed, and some other parts which he said they had tried to burn and were not able to succeed in. Romanelli removed the parts from the car and put them into the garage. He told me I was too bloody slow and was very mad because he wanted to get back uptown. He was cleaning a gun and a knife, and he used some 'It' cleaning fluid to remove blood from his gabardine coat. After he had cleaned himself up, he locked the door to the garage. The parts of the body removed from the car were placed inside a bushel hamper."

Evelyn said she and Romanelli then drove to the Royal Connaught, where he got out and she returned the Packard to the Grafton Garage. "I walked up to the Royal Connaught alley and took a taxi home," she said. "I told my mother that John had been fixed, put out of business, and she said, 'Well, they've tried long enough,' or words to that effect. She did know that Bohozuk was after him."

Evelyn said her mother asked, "Is there anything out there?"

"A couple of pieces that they couldn't dispose of."

"Well, you had better get them out of there."

But, said Evelyn, nothing was done. "I was expecting Bill or Romanelli to come and clean up the garage, but they didn't show up."

It was apparent to Wood and Preston that Evelyn was about to conclude her story by admitting she had no choice but to burn what was left of John Dick's remains, but she didn't get to finish her story. A telephone call came for Charlie Wood and he left Preston alone with Evelyn. She was silent a moment and then asked Preston, "Have you gotten John Dick's uniform and shoes out of the trunk upstairs?"

"Who put them there?"

"I did."

Just then, Wood returned to the room. He had learned from one of his officers on the telephone that a baby encased in cement had been found in a suitcase in Evelyn's house with her skirt wrapped around it.

"I heard about it," Evelyn said coolly, "but my lawyer told me not to talk."

Wood once again left the room and Evelyn leaned in towards Preston. "I have something to say, but you must not tell my lawyer."

Preston nodded.

"In September 1944, I gave birth to a baby boy, the spit of Bohozuk. It had dark hair. It was fat—weighed nine pounds and two ounces. It was born at the Mountain General Hospital. Dr. Adamson attended. The day I left the hospital, I met Bohozuk at the Royal Connaught. I got into the car and Bohozuk said, 'I will get rid of the little bastard,' and he strangled it by knotting a blanket around its neck."

Evelyn claimed Bohozuk forced the baby's body into a small zippered bag. She said she knew nothing more of the baby until February 1946, whcn he returned her $200 loan and along with it a cardboard carton. "Here's the brat," she said he told her. "I can't get rid of it until we start rowing."

"How do you explain the presence of your Red Cross uniform?" asked Preston.

"The cement started to crumble, so I wrapped the skirt around the package, mixed up more cement and poured it on."

In the corridor outside the interview room, lawyer Walter Tuchtie, who said he was Evelyn Dick's new lawyer and was looking for his client, approached Wood, who directed him to the interview room. Tuchtie informed Preston he had replaced Orville Walsh. Immediately, he instructed Evelyn to say nothing further.

The pattern of Evelyn's statements to date must have been clear to Wood and Preston. Whenever new evidence was uncovered, she tailored her story to fit, always ensuring she was painted as an innocent forced to go along. But now there were so many glaring inconsistencies that they had no doubt she had played a major role in the demise of John Dick. First she knew nothing; then she put herself in the car when the torso was dumped over the Mountain; now she wasn't in the car. There is no doubt that if she had remained silent, it would have taken the police a lot longer to unravel the truth. Perhaps they would never have found the ashes with John Dick's bone fragments, but there was plenty of other evidence right out in the open.

"Every confession she gave was the true confession, but it was always different than the last one," says Peter Preston, who was a small boy when his father, Clarence Preston, was investigating John Dick's murder. "And the point is, she did confess. She confessed half a dozen times, and gave half a dozen different stories. She said she was going to keep telling and telling and telling until nobody really knew what happened."

Preston, whose father died in 1964, two years after retiring, says the John Dick investigation was "slow and grueling. A lot of paperwork and a lot of searching, searching, searching. My father would come home and say, 'Well, we found a bullet' and 'We found the knives.' And when he found something, he would talk to my mother about it—kind of let go all the tensions of the day.

"What is really confusing is that there was no attempt made to really hide any evidence. Just to throw the body over the Mountain, and to leave the Packard there, with all the bloodstains on it . . .and the ashes full of bones from the cadaver . . . No serious attempt to hide anything. And then the baby in the attic—I mean, what kind of a keepsake is that? It has baffled a lot of people."

About the time the police and pathologist William Deadman were reviewing details of the discovery of the newborn baby encased in cement, what was left of John Dick's remains was being buried in a graveyard in the small community of Vineland. "The little United Mennonite Church at Vineland was packed with sorrowing relatives and friends yesterday afternoon for the funeral service of John Dick," reported the *Hamilton Spectator*.[17]

> *A simple quiet dignity graced the short service in which both the German and English languages were used. Encased in a simple gray casket, almost hidden beneath sprays of wreaths of flowers, the body of the torso-murder victim was placed before the altar in the church from which he had helped to carry the remains of his ninety-two-year-old grandmother, Mrs. Rosine Kammerer, on February 28 [six days before his own death].*
>
> *Very touching was the final scene in the church as the grief-stricken seventy-two-year-old mother of the murdered man, his two sisters, and other relatives, gathered around the casket while the congregation softly sang a beautiful German hymn.*
>
> *Mennonite Bishop John J. Wichert said in English, before his main address in German, that grieving relatives must "lift their eyes unto the hills" for comfort. "These words from the Psalms were written by John Dick in the last letter he sent to his mother after the death of his grandmother," he said. "In circumstances under which this beloved had to leave the world—a death shrouded in mystery—we can turn our hearts to the hills from whence comes our help and sometime we'll understand. We know there is a just Judge. We know not why He planned these things in the way they*

have occurred, but, in the words of the hymn, sometime we'll understand. This is our prayer. May the Lord grant him an everlasting entrance into heaven.

John Dick's cousin Alex Kammerer and his brother-in-law John Wall were among the casket-bearers at the funeral. Earlier in the day Preston had informed Evelyn about John Dick's funeral. "Do you want to go?" he asked. "Members of the press have been asking me. What do you want me to tell them, if anything?"

Evelyn thought for a moment. "Tell them that I'm too sick to go to the funeral."

But she hadn't been too sick to sit down and give Wood and Preston another statement.

As Evelyn Dick was escorted back to the Barton Street jail, the *Toronto Daily Star* reported she was "noticeably nervous when she left headquarters." The story also revealed that Evelyn's fate was now in the hands of Walter Tuchtie. "Mr. Tuchtie was nine years with the late C.W. Bell, K.C., one of Canada's most famous criminal lawyers. Mr. Tuchtie said he had spoken to Mrs. Dick who was 'quite ill and upset.'"

Charges

SATURDAY, MARCH 23

Bill Landeg's 1938 Packard, once owned by Evelyn Dick, was waiting at Hamilton's Central Police Station when pathologist William Deadman arrived to examine it for blood traces and whatever else he might find. The two outboard motors that were lying on the floor in the back when Evelyn borrowed the car on March 6 were still there.

"And in the examination of that car," Deadman testified later, "I found a stain on the inside handle of the left rear door which looked like blood." He also saw the stain on the front seat that had bloodied Bill Landeg's palm after Evelyn returned the car. And he found what appeared to be blood on the handle of one of the outboard motors. "And testing of those stains—the laboratory examination of them showed them to be human blood of type O. I also found in the corner of the back seat of the car a necktie, still tied, which was very much blood-stained." He said the stains on the tie also proved to be Type O.

On this day he also examined the shirt that city workers William Rushton and George Meharg had found the day after John Dick disappeared, and the stained sweater Bill Landeg had found in the Packard's rear seat. The stains on both were human blood—type O, the same as John Dick's.

While Dr. Deadman was checking out Bill Landeg's Packard, sixty-eight-year-old Donald MacLean, the once-trusted long-time employee of the Hamilton Street Railway, was appearing before Magistrate James MacKay charged with theft from his employer. MacLean was represented by the busy Walter

Tuchtie. MacKay remanded him to March 29 on bail of two thousand dollars. Half an hour later MacLean was back before the magistrate to hear Tuchtie ask if "two thousand of the five thousand dollars the police now have in their possession" could be accepted as payment for his client's bail.

MacLean made bail and that afternoon became the only one of his family to obtain a legitimate membership in the Canadian Red Cross Society. His daughter had purchased a phony Red Cross uniform and paid to have her picture taken, but he didn't have to spend nearly as much. He was home from court when a Red Cross canvasser came to his door. For a one-dollar donation he was given official receipt No. E 035527, which gave him automatic membership in the Society.

MONDAY, MARCH 25

The police decided not to release any information to the press about the dead baby found encased in cement in Evelyn Dick's attic. It was through sheer happenstance that the story became one of the great scoops in the long career of the *Toronto Daily Star*'s Jocko Thomas. Despite all that was happening in the investigation, the police were keeping a tight lid on the story, so much so that Thomas had headed back to Toronto for the weekend of March 23/24. Although he was back home, it was still his story and he was instructed to stay on top of it.[18] "But the police continued to say nothing and I had plenty of other work to do," recalls Thomas. "Then at city hall I ran into Art Keay, a Toronto detective and former Olympic runner, who was also just back from Hamilton." The two knew each other well and Keay was aware that Thomas was covering the torso story.

"That's a great case they got over in Hamilton," said Keay. "I was over there to pick up a car thief and they brought in the body of a baby encased in cement in a suitcase they found in Mrs. Dick's closet."

Thomas, fearing the wrath of Joe Atkinson and Harry Hindmarsh, thought he had been scooped and rushed across the street to get a copy of the first edition of the *Telegram*.

"But they didn't have it," he says. "So then I got on the phone to the deputy attorney general, Cecil Snyder, who knew I was getting reports, and I asked him about the baby in the suitcase. Of course he thought I knew a lot about it and he started telling me more. He must have assumed I knew a lot more because he started reading me the report about bone fragments—presumably the remains of John Dick's head, arms and legs—being found in the ashes in the driveway of Evelyn Dick's home. He said, 'Oh we've got a great case against her. We've got the body of that baby encased in cement.'"

The sensational story hit the *Star*'s headlines the same day, scooping all the competition, including the local *Hamilton Spectator*. "Simply by being in the right place at the right time, I had come up with a clean scoop," Thomas says. "The story even took prominence over the trial of Fred Rose, unmasked as a Soviet spy by Igor Gouzenko. And from what Snyder had told me, I was also able to predict that the police were about to make an arrest."

As important as the scoop was, Thomas received no public credit. "It appeared in the paper, but they didn't give you bylines in those days. If you were out of town they put 'Special to the *Star*,' that's all—no byline. They never gave you credit for anything. Mr. Atkinson, who owned the *Star*, had given orders that bylines were to come off the papers. The idea was that newspapermen who were given bylines got too big for their britches. It was just an old-fashioned idea. I didn't complain about it. I had lots of bylines afterwards, and a few before."

With a torso, a baby in cement and bone fragments in ashes, the media descended on Hamilton in greater numbers than ever.

"And of course, when they found the baby encased in cement and tied it in with the torso case, it added great excitement," says Thomas. "The case had been dead for about two weeks before I sprung that story. And when the opposition gets scooped like that, they've got to get their forces out and catch up. I think the reason the story got so much publicity was because the people had been reading war news for years, and here was something with lots of rumors, intrigue and sex."

TUESDAY, MARCH 26

Hamilton detective John Freeborn was back at Donald MacLean's house at 214 Rosslyn Avenue with OPP sergeant Carl Farrow and constable Leonard Mattick. This time they brought a powerful searchlight to examine the cellar. They noticed a hole through one of the cold-air pipes from the furnace and another through a large wooden box on the floor. The hole in the box went through the front, about eighteen inches from the floor. Following its downward trajectory, they found a second hole.

"This box showed a bullet had entered the top edge of the box, went out at a forty-five-degree angle, and right through the bottom of the box," Freeborn said later. Moving the box from the corner, they discovered a spent .32-caliber bullet on the floor.

Freeborn said the bullet through the pipe had gone on to hit the cement floor, ricocheting to the north side of the cellar, where it struck the head of a nail in a wooden doghouse. That bullet was never found.

Ten days after John Dick's torso was discovered on Hamilton Mountain, his attractive widow, escorted by Clarence Preston, was once again brought from her jail cell to the Central Police Station. In the presence of Preston and court reporter Douglas Ewing, Charlie Wood formally charged her with her husband's murder.

"Now do you wish to say anything in relation to that charge?" asked Wood.

"Well, I know that I did not," said Evelyn emphatically. She was given the usual police warning and said she understood it.

"Now, you have given us three statements. Do you remember the contents of them?"

"Well, yes," said Evelyn.

"Are they true or false?"

"Just one."

"Or do you want to change any part of them?"

"The last one, I mean."

"Or add anything to them?"

"I'm sorry, I cannot hear you."

"I say do you wish to change any part of them, or add anything to them?"

"Change the first two," said Evelyn.

"You want to change the first two, and the last statement, I take it then, is true so far as you know?"

"It is."

"But we were interrupted, I believe, before the statement was finished," said Wood.

"Right."

"Do you want to go on from there?"

"I can't."

"Why not?"

"Because I am told to keep my mouth shut.'

"Who told you that?"

"My lawyer, Mr. W.J. Tuchtie."

"Then as I understand you now, the contents of the first two statements are false, is that right?"

"That is right."

"And you do not care to complete the third statement?"

"Well, I am told to keep my mouth shut, and bloody well shut, if I know what shut means."

"In view of this charge of murder now being laid against you, you still want to remain silent, do you?"

"I am told to."

"Very good," said Wood.

But Evelyn wasn't quite through. "Will that be laid against Bill too?" she asked.

With the word having got out that John Dick's beautiful young widow had been charged with murdering him, the crowds began gathering an hour before the opening of the small magistrate's courtroom housed in the central police building. When the doors finally opened, the room quickly filled and police had to order the overflow out of the building. Two policemen were posted outside the door to keep the curious out. But the crowd didn't disperse. Most of them stayed around hoping to see Evelyn Dick.

The realization that she was in deep trouble had subdued her somewhat, and when twenty-five-year-old Evelyn slipped into the courtroom through a side door, she was pale and decidedly nervous. Throughout the short proceeding before Magistrate H.A. Burbidge, she stood staring at the floor, her elbows resting on the oak rail of the prisoners' box. Twice she glanced up at Burbidge but not once did she turn towards the courtroom spectators.

Burbidge remanded her in custody until April 10 at the request of Crown Attorney Harvey McCulloch, who said the vagrancy charge against her would be dropped. Defense counsel Walter Tuchtie didn't argue against the remand, but asked that Evelyn be allowed to see her family "having in mind she has been in close custody, unable to see anyone, with the exception of the faces of police officers . . . I am wondering if your worship would see to arrange this."

"The matter is beyond my jurisdiction," said Burbidge. "The question of how people are kept in custody is not something I have anything to say about." He said the intention should be "to take a merciful view of it, without getting sentimental about it."

THURSDAY, MARCH 28

Unlike Evelyn Dick, a confident Bill Bohozuk bounced into the same courtroom, twenty-four hours after her appearance. The husky Leander Club oarsman and steelworker was wearing a dark suit with a military tie and a white handkerchief in the breast pocket as he faced charges of vagrancy and possession of an unregistered revolver—the .32-caliber Ivor Johnson he purchased from Robert Fonger. He showed no nervousness and smiled at his sister, Lillian, seated among the spectators.

Bohozuk was at ease huddling with his counsel, William Schreiber, while waiting for Magistrate James MacKay to commence his hearing. He ordered Bohozuk's case adjourned for one week. "It's likely this accused will appear in court again before this week has elapsed," said MacKay.

"I am not consenting to this adjournment," said Schreiber. "If you grant the adjournment, it is only fair to state, if the case is not disposed of within a week, I will move for a writ of habeas corpus."

"I feel sure the accused will be brought to trial before this week is up," said MacKay. "I don't know what progress they are making with the investigation."

Schreiber said he was not asking for bail for Bohozuk since it had been denied the week before. "I will object next week," he warned.

While much of the focus in the John Dick murder case had shifted to the courts, investigators were still slogging away behind the scenes. While Bill Bohozuk was being remanded in Magistrate's Court, Charlie Wood and Clarence Preston were delivering bone fragments in three small cardboard boxes—one black, one yellow and one blue—to Dr. Charles B. Grant in the Anatomy Building at the University of Toronto. Over the next several weeks he would keep the boxes and their contents under lock and key while he examined them in his labs.

"A few of the pieces of bone were nearly three inches long," Grant would testify later, "but most are in small fragments, and some are merely crumbs. All of them are either warped or burst apart or crushed or badly broken. Some pieces are completely burnt, and therefore white . . . and some have ashes adhering to them, and some are fused with clinkers."

Grant said that, even at first glance, it was quite obvious some of the fragments were human and except for several smaller pieces and crumbs, all "can be assigned to their proper places in the human body," including the skull, face, jaw, neck, arms, fingers, legs and feet.

"No identified piece of bone is duplicated," said Grant. "Therefore it need not be supposed that more than one human body is represented."

Dr. Roy G. Ellis, a professor of dentistry at the University of Toronto, examined the teeth found in the ashes and determined "to the best of my knowledge they compare with human teeth."

Back in Hamilton, investigators were learning more about what went on at 32 Carrick after the murder of John Dick. A local carpenter, James Waterston, had been hired by Donald MacLean to do some work at the Carrick house two days before the torso was discovered. MacLean had told him "to go down there and make some screen sash." He showed up prepared to use his carpentry skills, but when he arrived "there was no wood." Instead, MacLean had him paint a stairway window and the banister leading to the second-floor landing. Then he asked Waterston to apply stove cement around the stove casing of the furnace in the basement, and to paint the front of the furnace, including the door "and the portion which the ashes are taken out of."

MacLean paid Waterston for the work. He did the bulk of the job on Friday, March 15, and "on the Saturday I went back to finish the job, and on the Monday [when the story broke] I see the photograph of the house on Carrick Avenue. I said, 'That's enough for me. I won't go back any more.'"

Inspector Charlie Wood and Detective Sergeant Clarence Preston had other business in Toronto besides dropping off bone fragments to Dr. Grant. They attended a Queen's Park conference with Deputy Attorney General Cecil L. Snyder and Hamilton Crown attorney Harvey McCulloch. Evelyn Dick had already been charged with killing John Dick, and it was the consensus of the meeting that there was enough evidence to charge Bill Bohozuk as well, and to jointly charge Evelyn and Bohozuk with the murder of the baby found encased in cement.

FRIDAY, MARCH 29

Bill Bohozuk's lawyer, William Schreiber, need not have worried about waiting a week for vagrancy charges against his client to be heard. They were dropped twenty-four hours after his appearance before Magistrate MacKay and replaced with the charges of murder.

Shortly before court opened with Magistrate Burbidge on the bench, reporters at the press table were called to the office of John Thompson, inspector of detectives with the Hamilton Police Department, who announced the new murder charges against Evelyn and Bohozuk. Some of the reporters ran to telephone their city desks. It was supposed to be a light docket in court that day, including Donald MacLean's appearance on charges of stealing from the HSR, so there were only a few spectators.

Evelyn and Bohozuk were transported in separate police cruisers from the Barton Street jail to the courtroom in the downtown police building. MacLean, out on bail, had arrived early in the courtroom and fidgeted in his seat, glancing from door to door, watching for the arrival of his daughter.

Bohozuk entered the courtroom and chatted amiably with Schreiber across the railing of the prisoners' dock. He appeared calm and was wearing a dark suit with a light shirt and military tie. He was in whispered conversation with his lawyer and nodding and smiling to acquaintances in the body of the court, when Evelyn was led into the dock behind him. She averted her eyes from the spectators and walked with her head down.

Newspaper reporters recorded the defendant's every move. "There was a pause of a few minutes during which Mrs. Dick, wearing her gray kid coat and pancake hat, again, seated herself on the bench in the dock and dropped her head in her hands," said the *Hamilton Spectator*. The *Globe and Mail* described Evelyn as "neatly dressed in a broken check black and gray suit, a black tam and a gray fur coat thrown over her shoulders. Her face was white and drawn, although she did not seem as much upset as on her earlier appearance."

The *Toronto Daily Star* reported:

> *Throughout the hearing of Mrs. Dick and Bohozuk, the two stood some ten feet apart without once looking at each other. When Mrs. Dick sat down halfway through the hearing, she turned her back on the man with whom she is charged.*
> *While his gaze wandered around the courtroom, Bohozuk did not look at Mrs. Dick with whom he was reported to be friendly before her marriage.*

Bohozuk was standing in the dock during the hearing when a police officer motioned him to sit down. "Do I have to sit down?" asked the defendant.

"No," said the constable standing near him beside the dock.

"Thank you," said Bohozuk defiantly. He remained standing, arms folded, throughout the short court session.

He and Evelyn were charged jointly with killing her newborn child, and his name was added to hers as the purported killers of John Dick. Both were remanded in custody until April 24 for a preliminary hearing. They were led out of the court and returned to jail in separate police cruisers.

As the courtroom door closed behind them, the court clerk sharply called out the name "Donald MacLean." He stepped forward and Burbidge read the official arraignment.

MacLean didn't respond when asked if he preferred to be tried by magistrate or by a judge and jury in a higher court. "A higher court," said his lawyer, Walter Tuchtie.

"You must answer yourself as to whether you wish to be tried by a judge and jury or by me," said Burbidge, obviously annoyed.

MacLean conferred briefly with Tuchtie, then said: "By judge and jury." Once again he was released on bail until the next Wentworth County sitting of the Ontario Supreme Court.

Reporters questioning Inspector Thompson after the court hearing were told that, although two people had been charged in the death of John Dick, the case was ongoing, and other suspects were being investigated. He said police would continue working "until we clear up every angle."

FRIDAY, APRIL 12

When the police were looking for new leads or angles, all they had to do was talk to Evelyn Dick. And if they didn't go to her, she often came to them. Such was the case this day, when Clarence Preston received a message that Evelyn wanted to see him. The detective sergeant went up to the jail and met with her in a private room on the west side.

"What's on your mind?" asked Preston.

"When are you going to bring the old man in?" she asked.

"Who do you mean?"

"My father."

"Why?" asked Preston.

"Well, he is in it."

"What do you mean?"

"Well, he loaned Bohozuk his gun."

"How do you know?"

"I saw it," said Evelyn. "You have got to help me. I am not going to be left holding the bag."

"I am not able to help you," said Preston. "It's up to your lawyer. What is he doing?"

"All he says is, 'Don't tell the police anything about your father.' He is only interested in feathering his own nest and keeping my father out of jail."

"Is Bohozuk in this thing?" asked Preston.

"Absolutely."

"Well, it is my duty to prove him innocent or guilty."

"What can I do? Will it make it worse for me if I tell everything?"

"I cannot answer that question. You are putting me on the spot, but if you want to talk, I will sit and listen."

Evelyn thought a moment.

"Why did you marry John Dick?" asked Preston.

"Well, when I first met Dick, he was a lovely fellow, very kind, and he used to bring soap chips, and other things that were hard to get, up to the apartment. He used to help with the dishes. I married him before my father knew anything about it, and when my father did find out, he raised hell. He took the car away from me and he said he would disown me. My father hated John Dick's guts. Then John found out about my father stealing, and things went from bad to worse. My father paid Bohozuk three or four hundred dollars to do the job, and he was sitting in the Balmoral Hotel getting drunk while it was being done." She said her father had tested the gun in his basement before giving it to Bohozuk.

Evelyn told Preston that on March 6 she met John Dick near the Astor Hotel around 2 p.m., and they went to the King George Hotel but couldn't get a drink because it was afternoon closing time. She said she went off to buy some paint at a hardware store while her husband looked around in Kent Shoe Store. Then she said they met Bill Bohozuk and the three of them drove up to the Mountain in the borrowed Packard.

"So you were there?" asked Preston.

"If I say yes, will it be worse for me?"

"I'm not answering that. I can't say." Then he asked her how many shots were fired.

"Three," said Evelyn, counting silently on her fingers. "How many bullets in my father's gun? How many will it hold? Five, I think. There was one chamber empty."

"I don't know," said Preston. "Were you in a barn?"

"No, on a side road."

"Do you mean to tell me this thing happened on a side road in broad daylight?"

"Sure, and you will find some pop bottles and a ginger ale bottle which was left."

"That would be good—to find these," said Preston. "We might get some fingerprints."

"Would it help if you found Bohozuk's fingerprints on those bottles?"

"Well, it would certainly back up your story. What would you say if you were asked to go out and show us the spot?"

"With you alone?"

"No, not alone."

"Yes, I will go. Do you want me to go this morning?"

Preston said he would let her know. As he was preparing to leave, he asked Evelyn what was in the car when she tried to park it in the garage behind the Carrick house on Ash Wednesday.

"John Dick's body," she replied calmly. "It was left in the garage, and my father and Bohozuk looked after the disposition of it."

"Where did it go?"

"Rosslyn Avenue, I think."

"How the heck would they get a body out of the car in daylight without the neighbors seeing everything?"

"Well, we have a nice cement drive to the back, and it's near the house."

As Preston readied to leave, Evelyn asked him to come back for her later that morning. "I will see," said Preston, handing her two chocolate bars.

He returned to the jail with Inspector Wood at 1:30 p.m. Evelyn was eager to get out of the jail, and they drove off with her directing the route. As they headed along Highway 53, she had them turn south on a gravel road but then seemed confused about which direction to go. Eventually, traveling north along a road in Glanford Township, she pointed to a farmhouse on the east side of the road.

"This is the place where the drinking started," she said. "There is a gate in the fence and you will see it's locked. The house is vacant." Evelyn had them drive south for some distance, then said, "Here is where the bottles were thrown out. Stop the car."

The three of them got out of the car and made a fruitless search for bottles along the roadside.

"What are your intentions?" asked Wood [believing there were no bottles].

"Well, maybe some schoolchildren picked the bottles up and turned them in for a few pennies."

Back in the car, she told them to drive on to an intersection further south. "This is where we got stuck," she said, and a short distance further, "Here is where John started to get drunk." On another concession road, heading towards Caledonia Highway, she identified the place where Dick began worrying about being late for work.

"He had to be in to work somewhere around four o'clock."

"Who was driving?" asked Preston.

"I was." She said John was sitting in the front passenger seat and Bohozuk was in the back, and when John told her to turn north, back to Hamilton, Bohozuk signaled her in the mirror to keep going straight. When she eventually turned north on a muddy county road in the township of Ancaster, "John Dick got very mad. 'I know what you are up to now,' he says. 'Tomorrow I will start divorce proceedings and instead of you being a big shot down at the steel plant, you will be the laughingstock.'"

Evelyn told the policemen that Dick was becoming very drunk, and as they drove she had the windshield wipers going "because mud was flying all over everything." (That would explain the mud covering the Packard when she returned it to Landeg's garage.)

Wood was driving the route slowly, and as they neared the top of a rise, Evelyn said that this was where Bohozuk "shot Dick in the neck." She placed her finger on the back of Wood's neck just below the hairline, to indicate the entry point. "The bullet came out the right eye, and the blood splashed all over. He shot him again. The car was filled with gunpowder smoke. I was covered with blood, and I stopped the car. I got out the left front door and Bohozuk got out the right rear door, came around and opened the right front door and pulled the blanket that was on the back of the front seat—pulled it over and wrapped it around John's head, and John groaned, and Bohozuk shot him again through the chest or stomach."

Wood by now had stopped the car. "Is that true?" he asked.

"Yes," replied Evelyn.

"Well, that doesn't add up," said Wood, getting out of the car and walking away in disgust. He knew from the torso's chest wound that the shot had been fired from the left side, not the right.

"What does he mean?" asked Evelyn, turning to Preston.

"Well, he thinks you are lying."

"I am not lying. I'm telling the truth. Why should I take the rap for someone else?"

"Well, tell me what happened," said Preston.

Evelyn told him that after Dick was shot twice in the neck, he slumped forward. She stopped the car and got out. Bohozuk came around to her side of the car and, pulling the blanket from where she had been sitting, "covered John with it. Bohozuk then got behind the wheel." She said that when John Dick groaned beneath the blanket, Bohozuk pulled the gun from his hip pocket. "He said 'I had better finish him off' and shot him."

Wood returned to the car.

"Inspector," said Preston, "I think you misunderstood what she said."

"Well, I would be glad to hear it again," said Wood.

"Yes, you misunderstood me," said Evelyn. "You are too hasty."

"Well, you explain it."

Evelyn went through her story again, this time placing Bohozuk behind the wheel when he fired the shot into Dick's chest.

"Well, that is more reasonable," said Wood.

They headed back to Hamilton. As they approached the city, Evelyn told them Bohozuk had driven the Packard after the shooting.

"All right," said Wood, "so we have Bohozuk driving the car and John Dick's body slumped beside him."

"Yes," agreed Evelyn, "and I'm in the back seat." She said they drove to the back lane behind the Carrick house, where she got the keys to the garage and opened it. "And Bohozuk pulled the body out of the car and laid it in the garage. I locked up the garage and gave Bohozuk a set of keys . . . on the understanding that he was to come back that night and dispose of the body. Bohozuk said he was going to get good and tight that night." She said he eventually carved up the body in the garage and the parts were burned at his home at 21 Picton Street West and at her father's house on Rosslyn.

"Did you burn anything at Carrick Avenue?" asked Wood.

"Just the odd piece of skin and flesh that was left lying around the garage," said Evelyn.

"What did you do after the garage was locked up?"

"We drove downtown and I let Bohozuk off at the Royal Connaught, where his car was parked. Then I bought some 'It' cleaning fluid and went home, cleaned up my clothes, got the blood off my stockings and my shoes, and then took the car back to Landeg's garage."

"When did you next see the body?" asked Wood. "Or did you see it?"

"Yes, Thursday night. In the garage."

"What was the condition?"

"Well, the legs were missing and the arms were missing."

"And what about the head?"

Evelyn hesitated.

"Was the head off?" asked Wood.

"Well, nearly."

"Well, was it on or off?"

"It was partly off, you know, partly cut through."

"Well, that doesn't add up," said Wood. "You know, Mrs. Dick, it is only fair to inform you that we have in our possession a blue striped shirt which we believe was worn by John Dick on the day he disappeared, March 6. And this shirt was found early in the morning of March 7, with the arms cut off, saturated with blood and completely buttoned up and including the collar. Now, what is your answer to that?"

Evelyn was silent.

As they came into the city, Wood asked Evelyn if she wanted to put her latest statement into writing.

"Yes, I certainly will," said Evelyn.

They drove to the Provincial Police building, where Wood took her to Sergeant Farrow's office. Preston sat with her in the office and she was provided with writing materials.

"Now remember," said Wood, "you are charged with murder, and you don't have to make any statement unless you wish to do so, but whatever you do will be taken down in writing and may be used as evidence. You understand that, irrespective of what has happened today?"

Evelyn said she understood, and Wood and Preston left her alone, preparing to write. When Wood looked in on her a few minutes later, she was in the same position but hadn't written anything. "What's the matter?" he asked.

"Well, I am not going to make a statement. My lawyers told me not to say anything."

"All right," said Wood, "you have already said it. I just thought—so nobody would make a mistake—you would put it in writing, but it is quite all right. We'll go."

With that, Evelyn was returned to the Barton Street jail where Preston made arrangements for her to receive a pen and writing pad—just in case she changed her mind.

SATURDAY, APRIL 13

Since their conference with the deputy attorney general in Toronto on March 28, the police had been contemplating arresting Donald and Alexandra MacLean. After listening to Evelyn's latest story, Wood and Preston decided the time was now. The two were picked up for questioning and both were charged with vagrancy and held over the weekend until their arraignment Monday morning. Both were represented by Walter Tuchtie, and both denied any knowledge of the murder.

The couple had reconciled and were in the process of moving furniture from the Rosslyn house to Carrick when they were arrested. Wood wouldn't tell the press what prompted the arrests; he would only say that the two were wanted for questioning.

With both her mother and grandmother in jail, four-year-old Heather was placed in temporary foster care under the supervision of the Children's Aid Society. Officer Muriel Oliver, with the Hamilton Police morality department, told the *Toronto Daily Star* that Heather "did not seem to realize anything strange had happened, and was quite content to go for an automobile ride and finally to her new home."

MONDAY, APRIL 15

The vagrancy charges against Donald and Alexandra MacLean were to be heard by Magistrate Burbidge, but once again both the press and the spectators packed into the small courtroom were in for a surprise. The vagrancy charges were dropped, and just a month after the discovery of John Dick's torso, the murder charge against Evelyn and Bill Bohozuk was amended to include the MacLeans.

Burbidge dealt with several other cases before the MacLeans were brought into court. The stocky MacLean, looking glum and disheveled, was wearing a gray checked suit, blue shirt and maroon tie. He was holding a gray tweed cap in his hands as he entered the prisoners' dock. Weighing over two hundred pounds, he dwarfed his wife, who wore a gray fur coat and gray felt beret. They looked around the courtroom impassively, neither seeming particularly distraught.

The MacLeans were ordered held in custody until the April 24 preliminary hearing, when all four accused would appear.

fourteen

Preliminary

By 6:30 on the morning of April 24, more than a hundred spectators, some carrying brown bag lunches, had gathered in front of the Central Police Station hoping for a seat at the preliminary hearing into the torso murder and baby-in-cement cases. Police didn't expect such a public outpouring, and when they checked the tiny second-floor courtroom at 7 a.m., more than a dozen people were already inside. Protesting, they were ejected and joined the growing queue outside.

The odds of finding a seat in the twenty-foot-by-fifty-foot courtroom were zero for all but a tiny fraction of the crowd. Most of the fifty or so seats available to the public had been taken over by witnesses called to testify at the preliminary. But many in the crowd were aware they weren't likely to get into the courtroom. They were there for an event and would be satisfied with a glimpse of the defendants—in particular the now notorious Evelyn Dick.

By 8:30 a.m., a smaller but still substantial crowd had gathered at the Barton Street jail, when Donald MacLean and William Bohozuk were led with other prisoners to a waiting police van. Evelyn Dick and her mother came out later and were driven to the court in a police cruiser. "First time out of the jail in a week, the two were dressed in smart spring clothing, seemed in high spirits and walked quickly to the cruiser," reported the *Spectator*.

Inside the courtroom, Magistrate H.A. Burbidge warned members of the press that no photographs were to be taken. He said the local media was aware of the restriction but the three or four visiting American newsmen might not be. Any infraction of this rule, he said, would constitute contempt of court.

Proceeding first on the charges against Bohozuk and Evelyn Dick for the murder of the infant, Crown attorney Harvey McCulloch called Detective Freeborn, who described finding the baby encased in cement in a suitcase in the Carrick house attic. Next, doctors from Mountain General Hospital verified that Evelyn had delivered a healthy baby boy in September 1944. Pathologist Dr. William Deadman testified that the baby probably died soon after leaving hospital.

Following Deadman's testimony, Burbidge adjourned the hearing to the first-floor juvenile courtroom, banning the public and the press. The magistrate had ruled earlier that any evidence involving confessions or testimony by one accused against the other would be held in camera. The admissibility of the statements introduced in secret at the preliminary would be determined at trial in Supreme Court if one or both of the accused were remanded.

Evelyn Dick's scattergun rhetoric, which—their guilt or innocence notwithstanding—had already ensnared her father and mother and Bill Bohozuk, was about to be demonstrated in a very personal way to Magistrate Burbidge. She at first refused to testify against Bohozuk at the in camera session, but when Burbidge warned she would be held in contempt of court, she said that Bohozuk was the father of the dead baby and that he had killed it. There was no other evidence against Bohozuk—only Evelyn's words—and his lawyer, William Schreiber, set out to expose her as a liar with loose morals.

"Haven't there been many men in your life?" he asked.

"A few," said Evelyn, as if she were discussing nothing more consequential than the weather.

"Quite a few. How many?"

"I don't know."

"Nearly every man you have ever gone out with has had intercourse with you, is that right?"

"No, sir."

"How many men have there been in your life that ever had intercourse with you?"

"Just a few."

"Give me the names of all the men you ever went out with," demanded Schreiber.

Magistrate Burbidge interjected: "I have called attention very often to the fact that is a meaningless expression."

"That you have had intercourse with, and kept company with," continued Schreiber.

"The magistrate's son," said Evelyn, calmly.

There was stunned silence for a moment.

"Magistrate Burbidge's son for one," said Schreiber, "go ahead, give us some more names."

"Bill Bohozuk."

"Who else?" persisted Schreiber. "Let me help you along." He listed the names of four prominent Hamilton men, including Jack Campbell and stockbroker Albert Adams. Evelyn agreed she had had intercourse with Campbell and Adams, but not the other two.

"Any more that you haven't mentioned?"

Evelyn added the name of lawyer Reg Sloan and admitted giving silver cigarette cases to two other men, but denied having intercourse with them. She identified Campbell as the father of her stillborn second child.

"Why did you give the name of Norman White as the father of your second child?" asked Schreiber.

"Because he [Campbell] had a good position in the army and didn't want to have the military authorities get after him. He was stationed at Kingston . . . He told me to keep it quiet."

Evelyn emphatically denied Schreiber's suggestion that Donald MacLean might be the father of Peter David White, the murdered infant. And she said that although her father was opposed to another child in the house, he was fond of Heather and of children generally. That fits with Ross Hough's memories of MacLean being kindly and generous to him and other neighborhood children.

"You would of course lie to protect your father, wouldn't you?" asked Schreiber.

"No, sir," said Evelyn.

Peter Preston says that his father, Clarence, knew all about Evelyn Dick's list of lovers. "The little black book," he says. "My dad was very, very upset about the little black book, because he was told at one time, 'Put it away, don't pursue it.' They told him he would never go any farther in the department if he didn't let go. And he didn't go any farther in the department. There were names of judges, lawyers, politicians . . . judges' sons. That's not from my father; that's from everybody else that's had anything to do with the case. There were very important people. That's why they told Dad to soft-pedal it."

Retired National Parole Board member Mary Louise Lynch, who knew Evelyn in later years, said she was once in Hamilton to address the Canadian Club and was staying at the home of a wealthy friend. "He owned a dairy," she says. "He said that he knew another tycoon in Hamilton and, vaguely, something came up about all these promiscuous wealthy men. I don't think we discussed Evelyn Dick. But I never realized she had so many."

Although all of Evelyn's statements to police would later surface in open court, the list of names she spewed out before Burbidge was never publicly recorded. Marjorie Freeman Campbell, in her 1974 book *Torso*, said the list of names was suppressed "in the interest of male chauvinism."[19]

Detective John "Jack" Freeborn testified he saw Bohozuk at the police station after he was brought in. Freeborn asked him if he knew Mrs. Dick. The young rower had a reputation as a ladies' man but his locker-room response to Freeborn, indicated he wasn't much of a gentleman.

"Yes, I've had her out, Jack," said Bohozuk. "I laid her, she was easy, but I certainly had nothing to do with the murder of John Dick."

After two hours of secrecy Burbidge moved the hearings back to open court, where he ruled that Bohozuk must stand trial with Evelyn on the charge of murdering her infant son. The husky oarsman kept his composure, but Schreiber protested the decision. "It is an admitted fact that the body of the baby was found in the home of what might be called the Crown's star witness against Bohozuk," he said. "But there's not a tittle of evidence to incriminate him, other than her testimony," he said. "Her story was so improbable—so impossible."

Burbidge insisted there was "direct evidence that a jury is entitled to consider."

"We have frequently differed on some points," said Schreiber, "and we certainly differ on that one."

Twenty-seven-year-old Bohozuk, who seemed so carefree entering the court, came out of the in camera hearing looking pale and shaken. He mouthed the word "railroaded" to reporters sitting at the press table, and he said later: "I haven't one thing to do with this. Like my lawyer said, it's only the word of one person that keeps me here. I am innocent. Get them to give me a lie detector or truth serum test—they do it in the States. That'll prove I'm innocent."

With Burbidge's decision, McCulloch moved immediately to proceed on the murder charges in the John Dick case. Donald and Alexandra MacLean joined Evelyn and Bohozuk in the prisoners' box.

Before the court adjourned in the late afternoon, more than twenty witnesses had testified for the Crown, framing its case from John Dick's last hours to the discovery of his torso on Hamilton Mountain: Evelyn's Dick's actions; her relationships with her husband, family and Bill Bohozuk; the difficulties between John Dick and Donald MacLean, and John Dick and Bohozuk; the muddy Packard with blood on the seat; the victim's bloody shirt, sweater and tie; all of the evidence found at 32 Carrick Avenue and 214 Rosslyn Avenue South; the charred teeth and bones; and MacLean's theft of cash and tickets from the HSR.

The court took a day off and the case resumed on the morning of Friday, April 26. The second witness to be called by the Crown was Anna Wolski, the widow who had asked John Dick to marry her. She said that Dick came to her house two weeks after his marriage to Evelyn in October 1945, "and he seemed worried and upset." She admitted helping him spy on his wife to determine if she was seeing Bohozuk.

Police witness Constable Leonard Mattick told the court that in a search of the Carrick house on April 18 he had seized ten HSR "motorman" buttons, six of them with blood spots, from the bottom of a dresser drawer in Evelyn's bedroom. There were also bloodstains on fourteen larger brass and silver buttons found in Evelyn's sewing basket. While Mattick was testifying about the buttons, Evelyn leaned over and whispered something to her mother and then to her lawyer, Walter Tuchtie.

Since Evelyn had admitted to Clarence Preston that she put John Dick's uniform into her trunk—later broken into by Donald MacLean—there was little doubt she was the one who removed the buttons. Observers found it odd that someone could be so frugal as to save evidence that could link them to such a dastardly crime.

Following Mattick's testimony, Burbidge for the second time ordered an in camera session in the juvenile courtroom, with no spectators and no press. Again Evelyn refused to testify against Bohozuk and again she relented when Burbidge threatened to find her in contempt of court. Sticking to the last story she gave police, she said Bohozuk had killed her husband. Her multiple, sometimes contradictory statements were introduced into the record, their validity to be left to another court.

After nearly three hours in secret session, all four accused left the courtroom and the press were invited in to hear Burbidge order William Bohozuk, Donald MacLean and Evelyn Dick to stand trial for the murder of John Dick. In a surprise move the magistrate announced that there wasn't sufficient evidence to proceed against Alexandra MacLean on the murder charge, but she was held as a material witness to appear at the next Supreme Court assizes. She was freed after posting a $4,000 bond. Under police escort Evelyn had followed her mother to the table, where she was handed papers to fill out for her bond. As she looked up at her daughter, Alexandra began sobbing uncontrollably, whether in relief that she was free or distress over Evelyn's predicament was not clear. It was the first time since her arrest that she had lost her steely composure.

fifteen

Stars and Strikes

By the time the preliminary hearings were concluded, Evelyn Dick's dark eyes had danced across the front pages of newspapers across the country. Toronto writer Jack Batten described the torso murder as "the first big news story, juicy and scandalous, of the postwar years. Newspapers from the American northeast covered the story, and *Time* and *Newsweek*, in a rare tip of the hat to Canada, ran features on the case."[20]

In Hamilton, all the participants in the case had become media stars in their own right, including policemen and lawyers. The case was talked about everywhere, and the brightest star of all was Evelyn Dick. From Dr. Deadman's testimony the whole world knew that the one appendage left untouched in the mutilation of John Dick's body was his penis. Already, schoolchildren were skipping rope to a new ditty: *"You cut off his arms, you cut off his legs, you cut off his head, how could you Mrs. Dick?"*

"The war was over, people were relaxing," says Peter Preston. "They didn't have the kind of responsibilities they'd had during the war years. And I think they were ready to make a party out of almost anything. And I hate to refer to something as horrendous as this as a party, but for the people that gathered to watch it, it was a show—they watched a show, and that's what it was.

"I think to the people of Hamilton, and the people of Canada eventually, Evelyn Dick was the femme fatale. She was the Mata Hari—the person they most loved to hate, or hated to love. She was attractive—a beautiful girl—but in most people's eyes a horrendous murderess."

Television was still six years away in southern Ontario. There was radio, but people turned mostly to their newspapers for information. The public couldn't get enough of the story and of Evelyn Dick. "She had high cheekbones," remembers Jocko Thomas, "so she photographed very well and was quite demure, and people would look at her and say, 'Well, how could anyone who looks like that do such a dastardly deed as kill her husband and saw off his head and his arms and his legs?'

"People were eating it up. The *Star* loved crime. The war had just ended and people were sick and tired of war news, and this was a way to sell newspapers, and it sure sold a lot of newspapers."

Lyman Potts arrived from Regina in 1940 to become program director at CKOC in Hamilton. "And it was quite a challenge," he recalls, "because the station was not doing very well. It was having difficulty competing with Buffalo and Toronto. Both cities had access to the four American networks, whereas we were deprived of any." He remembers how the torso murder gripped the city, how it was so high-profile that the station's news director, Bill Leckie, covered the story himself. "We had two people as editors and reporters, which was pretty good for 1946 radio. And Bill covered it personally. He was a former policeman, and of course was well familiar with the routine."

Potts remembers the talk around Hamilton about who was in Evelyn Dick's infamous "black book"—talk that persists to this day. "I don't know whose names are in the book. I have no idea. You could say any person in Hamilton was in the book; somebody could just suggest it as a gag, and immediately rumor would put that person in the book. I heard there was a book and names were read to the judge. That's all I know about it."

Potts says the John Dick murder "is certainly one of the biggest stories that ever hit Hamilton. There's no question of that—and we still don't know the complete answer to it. But it was a great radio story, a wonderful radio story. If murder is wonderful, it was a wonderful radio story. And this would have been one great television story, had television been alive in those days."

Retired policeman George Lawson says that, besides the gruesome murders, it was Evelyn Dick and her mysterious dark eyes that drew people to the story. He's eighty-seven and still smitten. "She was an extremely beautiful girl," he says. "She had very deep brown eyes that, if your sight caught each other in line, you'd feel cold chills run over you. There was just something exceptionally beautiful about her. Even if you saw her walking down the street, you'd say, 'My God, that's a striking-looking girl.' But I guess she was as evil as she was beautiful."

Four days before John Dick's torso was found, Lawson was coming into work as Evelyn Dick was leaving the police station—after reporting that her husband had run out on a fistful of debts. "I think she was there voluntarily that day," says Lawson. "And I pulled the door open and she almost fell into my arms. She was a nice chunk, you know. Oh God, she had those piercing dark brown eyes. Christ, she'd look right through you. There's no question about it, if I saw her on the street today, I'd know her."

As Evelyn Dick and the other defendants sat in their cells in the bleak old Barton Street jail through the summer of 1946, the stories and rumors of her sexual exploits were a hot topic from the best of restaurants and clubs to the lowliest of beer parlors.

There wasn't much for reporters to do except listen to gossip and rumors. The court case was in hibernation until the Supreme Court fall assizes in October, and the police were as close-mouthed as ever. Jocko Thomas heard a lot of the stories about Evelyn Dick and says it was difficult to separate fact from fiction. "They said she was a nymphomaniac. As old Sid Hibbs the court reporter put it: 'She only fucked her friends, and had no enemies.' Her reputation before she married John Dick was that she was a party girl, frequenting hotels, joining in the fun, and of course a lot of one-night stands. I don't know how true all the stories were, but those things do spread, and they are exaggerated at times, but she didn't have a very good reputation."

From the end of the preliminary on April 26 until the trial in October, the only legal activity involving the principals in the case occurred on May 13, when Donald MacLean appeared on the theft charges. He elected to be tried by a judge alone, and the case was put over until after the murder charge was disposed of. The next day the HSR won an injunction against both MacLeans, freezing their bank accounts. But five thousand dollars had already been withdrawn and was sitting in Donald's lawyer's trust account to cover legal fees. To help ease the financial pressure, the Rosslyn Avenue house was sold for $5,700.

Residents of Hamilton experienced a bizarre bit of déjà vu eight days after the preliminary hearing when two young boys discovered the body of a newborn baby girl stuffed into a paper bag on Hamilton Mountain about two miles from the site where John Dick's torso was found. Murray Messenger and Malcolm Hawkins, age ten and eleven, were on their way to play baseball at Hamilton Mountain Park around 6 p.m. on Thursday May 2 when they looked over the parapet and saw the bag at the foot of a tree.

"The head was in a paper bag and the legs were sticking out just like a chicken," said young Murray. "We climbed down the ledge and found it was a baby. It looked like somebody tossed it over the edge." The boys ran home and told their parents who called police. The infant, no more than two weeks old, was found about fifteen feet below the brow of the mountain. There were no marks of violence on the body but Coroner Dr. C.J. McCabe, who estimated the baby had been dead for two or three days, said it was possible it had been smothered. Police were awaiting a final report from the pathologist, Dr. Deadman, before deciding whether to treat it as a murder investigation.

If Evelyn Dick, the MacLeans and, in particular, Bill Bohozuk were tired of the glare of publicity that had been on them since mid-March, they must have welcomed an event that consumed Hamilton and the country's labor movement for eighty-one days, from July 15 to October 4. It was the now famous strike against the Steel Company of Canada (Stelco), which resulted in a historic shift of power between industry and labor. It took an event of that magnitude to push the torso murder case off the front pages.

War had brought full employment and with it some concessions from management, which in peacetime they were seeking to reverse. But returning servicemen and women, and many who had stayed in the factories during the war, were determined to resist a regression to the exploitive conditions of the twenties and thirties. The workers wanted their week reduced from forty-eight hours to forty; a wage increase of twenty cents an hour; and improved paid vacations. Most important, they wanted full recognition and the right to unionize all plant workers.

Anticipating a strike, the governor general appointed a government controller to oversee Canada's three major steel companies, including Stelco and Dofasco in Hamilton. Any employee who refused to work was then considered to be disobeying the government and was liable to a fine or jail term. Workers who stayed, however, would be given a wage increase.

Most workers ignored the threat, and they took to the streets in the thousands, with the support of workers from Westinghouse and Firestone. Frustration turned to violence, bricks were thrown, men were beaten. On August 25 the OPP and RCMP were called in to maintain order. Folk singer Pete Seeger and wrestler Whipper Billy Watson showed up to support the strikers.

Finally the company gave in, and by October 4 the pickets had been disbanded. Besides a substantial wage increase, Local 1005 gained two thousand more dues-paying members. The era of authoritarianism was over. From now on, workers would have increased recognition, seniority protection and a proper grievance procedure.

For almost three months the twelve thousand strikers had grabbed the headlines, except for two days in late September when a Grand Jury confirmed the charges against Evelyn Dick, Donald MacLean and William Bohozuk and ordered them to stand trial October 7. The strikers went back to work three days before the trial started.

⬛ sixteen

Hanged by the Neck . . .

Whipped along by aggressive blanket newspaper coverage, the public frenzy accompanying Evelyn Dick's appearance before the grand jury in late September 1946 was a precursor of what was to follow. The unlikelihood of a young, attractive woman with mesmeric dark eyes being implicated in two horrendous murders was the catalyst. Throw in the scent of scandal over her trysts with some of Hamilton's rich and powerful, and her infamy quickly mushroomed to full-blown celebrity.

On Monday, September 23, the first day of the hearing, so many flashbulbs popped in the crowded corridors outside the courtroom that large hand-drawn signs banning all cameras went up the next day on pillars inside the courthouse. Outside the grand graystone building,[21] with its imposing Italian Renaissance columns and sweeping wide staircase facing Prince's Square, crowds swelled to the hundreds then thousands for the trial itself.

Retired Hamilton policeman George Lawson remembers "lineups more than a city block long. I can't remember any court case like it. I guess it's because she was so beautiful and magnetic—an extraordinary young woman. If they [had] sold tickets at ten dollars apiece, they would have made a hell of a lot of money."

Jocko Thomas, who didn't cover the preliminary for the *Star* but was sent to Hamilton to cover the trial, says the experience was unforgettable. "I covered a lot of murder trials in my time, but none that drew as much attention as the Dick case. It certainly was the most dramatic. I can't think of any other trial that was more sensational. And of course Hamilton was close by and all the Toronto papers were interested in it.

It had lots of intrigue, rumor, sex, and a lot of other things. It was a good murder story."

Convinced that lawyer Walter Tuchtie was more interested in protecting her father's interests than hers, Evelyn hired a new lawyer for the grand jury hearing and her subsequent trial. Tuchtie stayed on as Donald MacLean's lawyer, while Bill Bohozuk was represented by Toronto lawyer Goldwin Arthur Martin, who would go on to become Canada's finest criminal lawyer and later a Justice with the Ontario Court of Appeal.

Evelyn's new lawyer was John Sullivan, gray-haired, handsome and in his early forties. He had come to Evelyn's attention over the summer, when he gained prominence defending strikers charged in picket-line confrontations between Stelco and the union. Sullivan's son, also named John, says his father considered the chance to represent Evelyn Dick as "a hell of an opportunity, and he got involved and he loved it. I shouldn't really talk about somebody who is deceased, but he was a bit of a character and he loved being in the spotlight. He was a good-looking guy, about five foot ten, with a little bit of a hook nose. He had a silver tongue, very glib, and was good on his feet. He could have been whatever he wanted to be, but he loved the booze—which is kind of an Irish Catholic thing. And he loved the ponies—horse racing. If I had the money that he spent on horses, I'd be a millionaire. He loved all those things." Sullivan died in his early sixties, in 1966. "He drank himself to death, is what he did," says his son, an only child.

When word got out on Monday that Evelyn had been brought to the courthouse from the Barton Street jail, crowds materialized instantly at all four entrances to the building. Many lingered long after the jurors had adjourned for the day, hoping for a glimpse of Evelyn. But she and John Sullivan were inside, dining with Sheriff A.C. Caldwell in his office. "It was a treat for Mrs. Dick," Sullivan told the press later. "She has been eating jail food for a long time [five and a half months] and she enjoyed her dinner in the sheriff's office immensely."

When Evelyn finally emerged from the building, accompanied by Sullivan and two police officers, she was surprised to hear applause and cheers from the crowd. "She smiled and waved, looking cheerful and happy," reported the *Star*. "She looked very smart in a blue dress, black coat and black hat."

Evelyn remained at the jail on Tuesday. In the courtroom, the grand jury, after hearing from more than two dozen witnesses and deliberating for an hour, brought in "true bills" against the three defendants. For the second time since their arrests, Evelyn Dick and William Bohozuk were told there was enough evidence to send them to trial for the murders of John Dick and Evelyn's infant son. Donald MacLean would be tried with them for Dick's murder. Mr. Justice William Schroeder ordered them to appear for trial on October 7.

Alexandra MacLean—under bond and compelled to testify against her daughter as a material witness—for two days sat forlornly among the Crown witnesses. Late Tuesday, after the jury's decision, she and the others were told they were free to leave. Wearing dark glasses in a futile attempt to disguise herself, she left the courthouse and faced the crowd and a clutch of news photographers waiting in Prince's Square. Seething with anger as she ran the gauntlet, she suddenly stopped, wheeled around and walked back towards them. "Take a good one," she said curtly, removing the glasses.

Two weeks later, on October 7, MacLean and forty-seven other witnesses were back in the walnut-paneled courtroom for the start of the murder trials before Mr. Justice F.H. Barlow. The provincial Crown Attorney's Office brought in Timothy J. Rigney of Kingston as special prosecutor. Hamilton Crown attorney Harvey McCulloch, prosecutor at the March preliminary trials, would assist him.

Tall, with an imperial manner, Rigney's usual job was Crown attorney of Frontenac County, but he was often called in as special prosecutor for high-profile or controversial cases. Impeccably dressed, he usually wore spats—even when they went out of fashion—and pinstriped suits. *Toronto Daily Star* reporter Jocko Thomas knew Rigney well. "He was regarded as the best prosecutor in Ontario at that time. They gave him the tough cases. He was sharp, stately and very dapper. I covered cases he was on in Kingston and he'd invite me over to his house, pour me a glass of very good Scotch, and we'd sit and talk. He was a very literate man."

One of the cases that cemented Rigney's reputation was that of Bill Newell. "He was an air force guy who murdered his wife over on Toronto Island," says Thomas. "And the guy had three trials before they convicted him and hanged him. The first two ended in hung juries. Rigney prosecuted the third case, but it wasn't too difficult because by that time Newell's girlfriend had gone against him—she'd found another boyfriend. He was hanged at dawn in the Toronto jail and Tim Rigney got a lot of credit for it."

Rigney enjoyed his renown and his gunslinger image—coming to town to clean out the bad guys—and was confident of his abilities. His boss was Ontario's strong-willed deputy attorney general, Cecil Snyder, who had an equally positive view of himself. Thomas knew Snyder too, and says he loved publicity. "He was a little bit of a showman. He loved to see his name in print, and when I reported on a murder case I'd always make sure Cecil's name was in the paper, so he always trusted me with everything. When he gave me a tip, I wouldn't tell anybody where I got it, not even the office.

"Before he became deputy attorney general, and occasionally even after, he prosecuted murder trials. I think he had twenty-eight hangings in his time. I think he only lost one murder trial and that was Mickey McDonald, a Toronto gangster charged with murdering Jimmy Windsor in what was called Toronto's first gangland killing. That was in 1939. McDonald was convicted and sentenced to hang, but a retrial was ordered. Snyder took the retrial, but he lost it." (McDonald went on to become number one on Canada's list of most-wanted criminals. Sentenced to fourteen years in Kingston Penitentiary for the armed hijacking of a truck full of liquor, he escaped on August 17, 1947, and was never heard from again.)[22]

The knock against Snyder was that he only prosecuted cut-and-dried cases he was sure to win. "If there was anything a little bit tough about a case, he'd hand it over to Rigney or somebody else," says Thomas. "Everybody used to say he wouldn't take them unless they were a cinch. He didn't take the Newell case because he thought he might not win it. He didn't know the girlfriend was going to become a witness for the Crown."

It was on one of the cases prosecuted by Snyder that Jocko Thomas also got to know Mr. Justice Barlow, the judge assigned to the Evelyn Dick case. "A couple of years before, he was the presiding judge at the Hot Stove murder case in Fort Francis, where four men were found guilty of murdering a woman. They put her on a hot stove to force her to tell where she had some money hidden in the Atikokan area in northwest Ontario. And Snyder prosecuted that case." Thomas reported on the case for the *Star*. "There was nothing much to do up there after court, and Barlow invited me for a drink in his room at the hotel. I guess he didn't want to drink alone."

The way events unfolded in the Evelyn Dick trial, the sharing of a bottle with Barlow in a small northern town proved fortuitous for Thomas, probably saving him from a stint in jail and from losing his job.

"Accused, stand up please," said the court clerk in a strong voice as the trial of Evelyn Dick, Donald MacLean and Bill Bohozuk officially got underway at 11:45 a.m. on October 7, 1946. After the clerk read the formal charge of killing John Dick, he addressed each of the accused individually, starting with Evelyn.

"Evelyn Dick, how do you plead, guilty or not guilty?"

In a dramatic retelling, the Toronto *Globe and Mail*'s Eva-Lis Wuorio, assigned to write "color stories" for the newspaper, captured the moment brilliantly:

> *The court chamber was suddenly still, the panel of jurors straining forward, the counsels and clerks of the court in their black gowns and white starched ruffles frozen as in a painting against the background of the ornate dark wood paneled wall.*[23]

*Evelyn Dick lifted her head and her dark eyes snapped
and then she said, a little angrily, a little arrogantly, "Not
guilty." She had not so much as glanced at the other two
prisoners who preceded her into the court. She appeared not
even to hear her father's gruff "Not guilty" plea and
William Bohozuk's too-quick answer while the clerk was still
speaking. She was not to look at them again. It was as
though they did not exist.*

Wuorio noticed that Evelyn had gained considerable weight
during her six months in the Barton Street jail. She had gone
from one hundred and ten pounds to one hundred and thirty-
six—quite noticeable on her five-foot-four frame. Consequently,
wrote Wuorio, her mother had purchased for her a new black
dress, "short-sleeved, with a wide bow at the throat and gathered at the hips. Her skullcap was sequin-studded; her dark hair
fluffed above her ears so that her brilliant earrings sparkled; her
nail polish was the exact shade of her lipstick . . . Her relaxed,
though somewhat sullen, calm created an aura about her."

Wuorio wrote that after the three accused had entered
their "not guilty" pleas, "it was suddenly no longer merely a
business of one woman and two men standing by the polished
mahogany bar. It was assurance anew that against a grievous
wrong, the law of the land stands quiet, level and just." The
Ontario Court of Appeal would ultimately decide how "quiet,
level and just" the law stood in this particular case.

Even before the process of choosing a jury was underway,
Crown attorney Rigney announced he was planning to proceed against Evelyn Dick "alone and first, and following that,
if it is agreeable to the court, to try the other two accused
jointly." The defense lawyers didn't object, although John
Sullivan pointed out that the three accused had been indicted
together and said that Rigney's move came as a surprise to
him. Mr. Justice Barlow went along with Rigney's request in
what was to become a troubling pattern of acquiescence to
the Crown and deriding of the defense.

Sullivan's son, John, attributes his father's treatment by
the judge to social attitudes prevalent at the time. "Don't for-

get, he was Irish Catholic and came from the wrong side of the tracks. He was bright and he rubbed people the wrong way. There was animosity there. He wasn't part of the club." He says in those days his father felt that Ontario society—the establishment, including the legal system—was largely in the hands of the Anglo-Saxon Protestant elite and he didn't fit in. "I mean, growing up, he hated the Brits and anybody involved with [them]. I mean absolute hatred."

John Sullivan Jr., who was born and raised in Hamilton, says he loves the city in all its quirkiness. Where else, he says, would an exaggerated hillside become a mountain? "If you're from Hamilton it's called the Mountain, all two hundred and sixty-five feet of it," he laughs. But in the 1940s, "Hamilton was very divided. If you were in a certain religious group, a certain name group or geographic group—that's who you were and you knew it. It was an insular little town in its own way. I was raised a Roman Catholic in the west end of Hamilton, and there was a point in time when you literally had to fight your way to school. We had to go together, in groups. We were the dirty Catholics. Kids are mean to each other at a very young age."

Sullivan was only about eleven at the time of Evelyn Dick's trial, but after hearing his father talk about her in later years, his impression was that she "was a bit of a flirt. She floated around. She was very pretty and she was a party girl and therefore she touched all elements of society from high to low—and remember, Hamilton had its Mafia. Layer all that with this murder thing and it was kind of wild."

The senior John Sullivan may have been somewhat paranoid about the legal system and his treatment by Justice Barlow, but as author Jack Batten noted, the judge's attitude may have had a decisive influence on the trial's outcome.[24] "Mr. Justice Barlow was generous with the Crown and snappish with the defense." And Barlow, "who seemed consistently indisposed to defense submissions, brushed away Sullivan's arguments."

After John Sullivan's death, his son came into all his papers and records related to the Evelyn Dick trial. "I had everything, and Marjorie Campbell got a hold of me and I gave her a whole lot of material." Campbell incorporated some of that material into her 1974 book *Torso*. Sullivan, meanwhile, had married, started a family and moved to Montreal to take an advertising job with *Time* magazine. He was living there when the book came out. "I gave her all this material I'd had for years, and when we eventually moved back to the Hamilton area, I thought I'd better look her up and get it back. But I found out she was dead, and I never got any of the material back—none of it, zero."

The only bit of Sullivan's memorabilia not sent to Campbell was Evelyn Dick's wartime ration book. "It is ration book number five issued by the government of Canada in the name of Evelyn White at 214 Rosslyn Avenue South in Hamilton," says Sullivan. "Everybody had them. You couldn't buy butter, meat or many other things without them. In the back of it is an application to change her name and address to 'Dick, Evelyn, 32 Carrick Avenue, Hamilton.' There's no date on it, but there's a serial number and her signature."

Part of the material used by Campbell in her book were the notes John Sullivan made as he prepared for the jury selection process:

> *Everything pertaining to the prospective juror needs to be questioned and weighed: his nationality, business, religion, politics, social standing, family ties, friends, habits of life and thoughts, and books and newspapers he reads. All these qualities and experiences have left their effect on ideas, beliefs and fancies that inhabit his mind.*
>
> *Involved in it all is the juror's method of speech, the kind of clothes he wears, style of haircut. And above all, his business associates, residence, and origin.*
>
> *An emotional kindly and sympathetic man, if chosen as a juror, will place himself by his imagination in the dock; really, he is trying himself.*
>
> *Retain Irish, English and Germans, agnostics, Jews. No Prohibitionists, Calvinists, Lutherans, Baptists, or wealthy men.*

SHAKESPEARE: Yond Cassius has a lean and hungry look;
He thinks too much: such men are dangerous.
You may defy all the rest of the rules if you can get a man
who laughs. Few things in this world are of enough impor-
tance to warrant considering them seriously. A juror who
laughs hates to find anyone guilty. You want imaginative
individuals. If a man is instinctively kind and sympathetic,
take him.[25]

Whatever Barlow and others may have thought of John Sullivan, Evelyn Dick was pleased with him. "She would beam when Sullivan came over for whispered conversations in the prisoners' dock," recalls Jocko Thomas, whose chair at the long mahogany press table was "just an arm's length away from Evelyn Dick. I was the closest to the prisoners' box. I was the first one in that seat and I hung on to it for the whole trial. Nobody ever challenged me. I got the same seat every day.

"One thing that always impressed me, and I still remember it, was her obvious disinterest in what was going on as people were giving evidence. She seemed to be out of this world, not listening to what was going on, not too interested in it. Only once in a while, when her counsel would come back to the prisoners' box and talk to her, would she show any interest at all."

When it came to accepting or rejecting potential jurors, however, Eva-Lis Wuorio reported that Evelyn would lean forward to whisper to Sullivan

> *with quick insistence. It appeared to be in many cases her*
> *prompting which excluded the citizens, here to serve in the*
> *cause of justice, from the jury. She would stand, her chin in*
> *hand—she wore no rings but the wedding ring—her eyes*
> *sharp. There is a strange stillness about Evelyn Dick. Only*
> *her eyes move, flashing from man to man, throughout the*
> *courtroom.*

Wuorio, then in her late twenties, was just a couple of years older than Evelyn Dick and was trying to imagine what she must be feeling. Evelyn's twenty-sixth birthday was just six days away. She had spent her twenty-fifth birthday trying to figure a way out of her nine-day-old marriage to John Dick; a year later, she would spend her birthday fighting to prove she didn't murder him.

"Perhaps she thought then that here are the men who will hang me or set me free," wrote Wuorio. "These are the men from the streets I have walked, from farms I have glimpsed from a car, from garages where I have stopped to have my car serviced, and they will judge me. Perhaps she thought so, as, again and again, her counsel turned down a prospective juryman."

For better or for worse, those whom Evelyn and her lawyer would have to convince were all men. It wasn't until the mid-1950s that most Canadian provinces finally considered women emotionally and intellectually capable enough to judge the guilt or innocence of an accused.

Of the first twenty jurors considered, Evelyn, through her counsel, rejected thirteen. Finally, the two rows of seats in the jury box were filled with Wentworth County male citizenry from a variety of occupations, including: Earl B. Wright and William R. Taylor, salesmen; George Arnott, blacksmith; J. Stewart Thompson, accountant; Stewart A. Wanns, glass cutter; Ernest J. Tucker, machinist; Allan Wise, crane operator; Charles Paupst and Gordon Stutt, farmers; Alex Turner, electrical engineer; Fred Webster, roofer; and Sam Wiseburst, insurance agent.

With Evelyn Dick going to trial alone, Barlow ordered Donald MacLean and Bill Bohozuk returned to their cells. He also instructed the press not to report any evidence that would prejudice their trials. Jocko Thomas remembers MacLean as "a big dour-looking sourpuss guy. When they took his picture, he always looked like he was going to charge the photographers at any minute. He was powerfully built, with a constant frown on his face."

During an afternoon break on the first day of Evelyn Dick's trial, Eva-Lis Wuorio approached John Dick's sisters Lena (Helen) and Anna in the corridor outside the courtroom. They were with their husbands, John and Jacob Wall. The *Globe* reporter described them as *the little parade of four stolid people, two women with wide, high cheekbones, blonde faces and almost yellow hair, attended by two short, dark men . . . In the corridor, one of them stopped to say softly that they had ridden over from Vineland, and would probably have to come again. And then, her voice still low-toned, but cold now, she almost whispered: "Yes, we know the way of it—we know." And then the other one looked at her sharply.*

Wuorio described another encounter in the corridor with "a small slight woman in a gray suit, whose swift irritability seemed more a matter for great pity than annoyance. This was Mrs. Donald MacLean, Evelyn Dick's mother."

"It's no one's business what I do," MacLean told her coldly, "no one's."

In her colorful narrative style, Wuorio described the scene outside the courthouse on the first day of the trial. The moods and actions of the crowds would be repeated, with slight variations, throughout the nine days that followed:

Already at nine this morning the curious had begun to collect on the tree-shaded courthouse lawns and in the warm sunlight. Through the trees, the Mountain glinted in autumn glory, but here below, the morbid excitement was hourly more evident in the gathering crowds, the sudden shrill bursts of laughter, the loudly voiced conjectures both as to the time and place of the prisoners' arrival and as to whether Evelyn Dick would today "tell who she did business with."

Photographers had been barred from the court by the order of the sheriff and they made the spearhead of each new rush to the various doors of the building at each rumored appearance of the prisoners.

When the court day ended at 6 p.m., Wuorio reported:

[T]he strategic withdrawal of Evelyn Dick could not be manipulated for the hundreds of people who had gathered on the lawns. Suddenly again the sense of judicious, wise justice that permeated the slightly stuffy, quiet court

chamber was broken, and Evelyn Dick's story in its most glaring phases was merely entertainment for her fellow citizens. It was disturbing and tragic.

Somehow, all the worst of it seemed to be expressed in the shouting of two small girls who ran after the black car. The one with the long, light hair cried: "I saw her! I saw her! Isn't she pretty?"

With the jury in place, Rigney called his string of Crown witnesses to the stand: policemen to describe the discovery of the torso and the evidence gathered at the Carrick and Rosslyn houses; forensic experts to connect Donald MacLean's revolver to the bullet fired into John Dick's chest, and to identify as human the bones and teeth found among the ashes; and Dr. Deadman to describe the butchery inflicted on the victim's body.

During cross-examination, Sullivan asked Deadman how long it would take to dismember John Dick's body.

DEADMAN: *Assuming a proper saw, a good sharp saw, and a muscular individual, I would think those legs and arms and the neck could be sawed off within half an hour . . . by continuous effort.*

SULLIVAN: *Continuous effort. That would demand some strength on the part of the individual?*

DEADMAN: *I think that the sawing through of bones of this character would take some strength, yes—the less the strength, the more time consumed, of course.*

Ann Kammerer, the wife of John Dick's cousin, testified that while living with them he usually left the house at 10 a.m., although his HSR shift didn't start until 4 p.m.

SULLIVAN: *Did he ever tell you what he did?*

KAMMERER: *He used to watch his house on Carrick Avenue.*

SULLIVAN: *Do you mean the house of his wife?*

KAMMERER: *Yes.*

SULLIVAN: *And he would spend from ten o'clock in the morning till four o'clock in the afternoon walking around the streets in the vicinity of Carrick Avenue?*

KAMMERER: *That is what he told us.*

The witness who caught the attention of the media and the crowd more than any other was Evelyn Dick's mother, Alexandra MacLean. Rigney asked for her reaction to Evelyn's plans to marry John Dick.

MACLEAN: *I was very annoyed that she would take the license out without me knowing the man.*

RIGNEY: *Did anything take place on the third of October?*

MACLEAN: *Yes, we had a great row.*

RIGNEY: *Over what?*

MACLEAN: *Over her getting married to John Dick.*

He also asked her about returning home with Heather after walking up to wave to Dick on the streetcar.

MACLEAN: *I said to Evelyn, "John was not on his car." So she said, "Well, it's not likely he will trouble me again, and you will never see him on a car." I said, "What do you mean? He is not finished?" and her face flushed. And the way she said it gave me the impression that something serious had happened. So she told me to shut my mouth and keep my nose out of her affairs.*

RIGNEY: *She said, "It is not likely he will trouble me again"?*

MACLEAN: *Yes.*

RIGNEY: *Then what did you say to her again?*

MACLEAN: *I said, "Why, there is nothing happened to him? He has not been killed?" And she said, "Yes, John Dick is dead, and you keep your mouth shut."*

Under cross-examination MacLean told Sullivan about all the bickering between her daughter and John Dick, and how he began to stay away from the house.

SULLIVAN: *And how often would that happen?*

MACLEAN: *Oh, the first ten days he stayed in and helped us a lot with the work, and then he got this phone call on a Monday morning. Well, after that he was not home very much, and because his wife wouldn't turn the Carrick Avenue house over to him, he wouldn't do anything around the place and he wouldn't stay home.*

SULLIVAN: *Now, you said something about his wife would not turn Carrick Avenue over to him. What did you mean by that?*

MACLEAN: *Well, he didn't put a dollar in the Carrick Avenue house, because he hadn't got it to put in, but he was giving the people the impression up at the Street Railway that he had put in twelve hundred, but I know he hadn't put up a dollar.*

SULLIVAN: *And were there demands made to transfer the property to him?*

MACLEAN: *Yes. He remarked that he would give his wife a hell of a life until she turned the house over to him.*

Sullivan also asked MacLean about the arguments she had with her daughter when Evelyn attempted to drive the Packard into the garage behind the Carrick house.

SULLIVAN: *You said something about your daughter giving you sharp answers. Was she often sharp?*

MACLEAN: *Yes, very sharp.*

SULLIVAN: *And were you sharp toward her?*

MACLEAN: *Oh yes, I am bad-tempered.*

SULLIVAN: *Similarly quick tempers, mother and daughter?*

MACLEAN: *Yes, I am very quick-tempered.*

SULLIVAN: *A similar temper to hers?*

MACLEAN: *Yes.*

SULLIVAN: *And you often had disputes, did you?*

MACLEAN: *She seemed to have more temper after she married John Dick.*

When word got out that Evelyn's mother would be testifying on October 9, the crowd that turned up was the largest yet. Wuorio wrote her impressions of the end of that momentous day:

And finally a little past six, the long day was over, the still court, admonished into submission by Judge Barlow, rose to go into the night that now was nearly dark. The nightly witch hunt of Hamiltonians was about to start outside. It is impossible to adjudge the numbers which surrounded the courthouse but it must have been into the thousands. It was the biggest mob yet. There were shouts as the mob swayed from door to door and the red pinpoints of cigarette tips seemed to underline the macabre scene.

They brought Evelyn Dick out by the west door, and the mob surged, and she said breathlessly, "Oh, my feet!" Children kept pushing through the adults, hoarse with excitement. For a moment she stood spotlighted for them in the lighted Provincial Police office, and they saw how her hand shook as she took a cigarette to her mouth. But on her face that day, there was a smile.

To say Alexandra MacLean's testimony was a body blow to the defense would be an understatement, but it didn't turn her daughter against her. Evelyn even wrote her mother a note saying she looked nice on the witness stand and praising her for not breaking down during her long day of testimony. But as devastating as MacLean's testimony was, John Sullivan knew that admission of the statements Evelyn made to police would be fatal. He believed they were taken unfairly, without proper warning, and gained through improper inducements. He also believed he had a strong case against admitting them—but he had Barlow sitting on the bench.

The *Toronto Daily Star*'s answer to Eva-Lis Wuorio was Marjorie Earl, who was assigned to the Evelyn Dick case with

Alf Tate and Jocko Thomas. In those days it wasn't uncommon for reporters to become part of the story, and Earl quickly befriended Evelyn and at times defended her in print. On the third day of the trial she wrote that Evelyn,

> *whose apparent calm has puzzled and astonished everyone attending her trial . . . may not be so unfeeling as she seems. Daily she asks anxiously after her four-year-old daughter, Heather. The beautiful young mother daily pesters Mrs. Alice Hickmott, jail matron, for news of the little girl.*
>
> *Mrs. Dick's calm self-possession in court has been described by someone who knows her well as "just a front she puts up when she is very serious." She behaves in court not like a woman fighting for her life but like a spectator enjoying the proceedings.*
>
> *When the court adjourned for the day one of the first things Mrs. Dick did was to ask for the papers. "What are they saying about me?" she asks. "Who else did they mention? Are there any good pictures of me?"*

Two days later, Earl and Evelyn met in a courthouse corridor, and the reporter wrote that she couldn't believe she was facing a woman "aware that her life is at stake." She described the accused as "buoyant and cheerful as a schoolgirl with nothing on her mind but love stories."

"Everything's just fine." Evelyn smiled.

"How are they treating you, and do you get enough to eat?" asked Earl. "Shall I bring you a steak tomorrow?"

"Oh, everything's wonderful," Evelyn replied. "I get salmon salads, chicken salads, sandwiches, everything I like. I don't need any food, but I do need something to read." Earl reported that Evelyn then fumbled in her handbag and pulled out a dollar bill. "Get me some magazines, will you?" she asked. "You know, love stories, movie magazines and true confessions. Lots of them."

Earl said that in private conversation Evelyn exhibited a

> *kittenish quality. Her voice was low, but distinct, with a childish upward inflection at the end of each sentence.*

Though she tries to avoid the crowds, she acts as though she likes their interest, and some of them must like her, for she has received many gifts from admirers during the last few days. These include the pearls she was wearing, nylon hose, cosmetics, nail polish, and perfume. She also gets fan mail.

Jocko Thomas says that male colleagues back in Toronto nicknamed Earl and Wuorio the "sob sisters" for their colorful and emotional reporting, but in fact it was their stories that fleshed out the characters and personalities of the principals. Without their work there would have been a substantial gap in the historical record.

Earl's talents went beyond ingratiating herself with the star of the show. She was a shrewd reporter, and on the first or second day of the trial she learned from John Sullivan that Evelyn's statements to police were included in the transcripts of the preliminary trial. She also learned that copies of the transcripts were left out on a table in a second-floor room that doubled as a law library and barristers' room. When Earl told Jocko Thomas about the transcripts, his newshound competitive juices started to boil.

Thomas thought Timothy Rigney might let him see an advance copy of the statements if he promised not to use them until they were introduced to the jury. Rigney acknowledged the existence of the transcripts but refused to provide an advance copy. "We'll be introducing them in a few days," said Rigney. "Of special interest will be Mrs. Dick's statements about bloodstains in a car she borrowed at the time of her husband's murder."

Thomas had politely asked permission to see the statements; now he would simply steal them. He left the courthouse with Earl and the other reporters when the trial was recessed sometime around six that evening. An hour or so later, he was back.

"The doors were open," he recalls. "And there were no security guards around like there would be today—just the janitors and cleaning staff." Thomas had befriended one of the senior janitors. "I told him I had to look up something in the law library and I gave him a crock of whisky. I went up and the door was open and the transcripts were sitting out on a table. I took them and left."

Marjorie Earl was waiting at the Royal Connaught, where the *Star* had put its reporters up for the duration of the trial. They were stunned when they saw that Evelyn's statements ran to thousands of words—and what words they were. "We were shocked because some of the statements were so far-fetched," says Thomas. "And I remember in one part they said that she was giving a statement to police and there was some argument that she would stop talking until one of the detectives had gone out and brought back her favorite chocolate bar. And when she ate a couple of chocolate bars, she started talking again. I think defense counsel tried to indicate that this was not a voluntary statement; it was induced by the fact that she had a taste for chocolate and she needed some chocolate.

"Now, those statements didn't admit any guilt, they were just a bunch of lies, and any sensible jury listening to her would know she was lying. The guy coming to the house and calling her up and saying, 'We got his body in a sack here,' and rolling it down the Mountain and all that—I mean, that's how far-fetched the statements were. Of course that was to cover evidence the police had of bloodstains in the car she borrowed. And any jury couldn't help but believe that she was implicated in it. 'Your husband has been running around with the wife of one of our gang and they're going to get him': now that's the type of statement that convicted her."

From the Connaught Hotel, Thomas and Earl went to the railway terminal building. "There was a telegraph office there. They were out for business and they had a lot of typewriters." Thomas was fortunate that Earl had another talent: she was a touch typist. "I read the statements while she typed," says Thomas. "She was very fast, but it still took us until about four or five in the morning to transcribe everything. I wanted to get them done so I could get them back to the library before morning."

It was just before 8 a.m. when Thomas slipped back into the courthouse and replaced the transcripts. "So nobody knew they were gone, not even the janitor." The copies of the statements were sent to the *Star* by bus express that morning. They were set in type but would not be released until the editor heard from Thomas that they had been admitted as evidence. Thomas had no idea when, or even if, the statements would be introduced; that would be up to Barlow after he heard arguments from Rigney and Sullivan.

Meanwhile, Thomas, Earl and Alf Tate went back to the daily grind of trying to stay ahead of the competition. "We had our own telex machine—Teletype machine, as they called it," says Thomas. "It was hooked up by Canadian National Telegraph and they had an operator there to run it. The *Star* had eight main editions a day. The first edition was at eleven o'clock in the morning, then about every hour after that, right up until 5:05 at night. And we filed copy on the Teletype in a little office in the courthouse, and the headlines were different in every edition during the Dick case. It was the latest equipment. We wrote out our copy in longhand, and the operator would send it out. We called it running copy. And as the evidence was introduced, our running copy was sent right back to the newspaper and published that day.

"Running copy is an art that's gone out of newspaper work now, because the papers only have one edition a day, and all the stuff they print is news of the day before. In the days of the Dick case, people got their news from the newspapers. There was a limited amount of radio newscasts, and no television, of course. And on every case I covered, even on the police beat, you'd phone in stories and they'd be in the paper. When I covered the courts in the city hall in Toronto, stuff that I wrote at 12:30 would be sent down a tube directly to the *Star* office and would be in the 1:30 paper. So you did running copy. It's a part of newspaper work that's lost now because it's not necessary."

The new telex machine gave the *Star* a leg up on its Toronto competition, and its afternoon editions were consistently beating the *Globe and Mail* and the *Telegram*. "They were just sending their copy down to the CN or CP telegraph office," says Thomas, "which would be a guy in a telegram office typing it out . . . and sending it."

In Hamilton, the Toronto papers were facing stiff competition from the local *Spectator*. "The *Star* used to sell a lot of papers in Hamilton," says Thomas. "We had a Hamilton correspondent—an editorial office to compete with the *Spectator*."

Saturday, October 12, would prove to be a momentous day in the trial and in the newspaper career of Jocko Thomas. In the courtroom, Mr. Justice Barlow was rebuffing John Sullivan's attempts to keep out Evelyn's statements. Each statement was considered separately, with Charlie Wood and Clarence Preston explaining the circumstances under which they were obtained. Sullivan argued that some of Evelyn's statements were made while she was facing a vagrancy charge, not a murder charge, and therefore should not be admissible. Rigney argued the statements were voluntary and therefore admissible, and Barlow agreed with him.

When Sullivan argued that one statement—which Evelyn gave to Wood and Preston while driving out to the location where Bohozuk allegedly shot John Dick—should not be allowed, Barlow said it all resolved "down to whether or not it was voluntary, and whether or not there were any threats, promises, inducements, or anything of that kind held out to her." He totally ignored Sullivan's position that his client had not been properly warned.

"Well, my lord, it seems to be quite apparent that there was no warning given to this woman before she was taken on this trip, a trip of slightly over thirty miles, consuming most of the afternoon," said Sullivan. "She evidently was on friendly terms with at least one officer, and it seems to me that it was more or less in the nature of an outing, and unless a warning was given to her before they departed on the trip and not afterwards, as both officers have sworn, I hardly see how they can really insist on this as a statement."

With Barlow refusing to accept his no-warning argument, Sullivan said that while there were no promises made by the police officers, "there may have been an inducement . . . an indirect inducement, by reason of the chocolate bars provided by Sergeant Preston, and talking about getting movie magazines, a decent meal other than jail fare provided for her, and little matters like that. Of course this woman was very young and very impressionable."

Sullivan closely scrutinized the friendship between Detective Sergeant Clarence Preston and Evelyn Dick. The policeman said he had known her father for many years and knew her casually from seeing her on buses and streetcars when she was younger. He had not asked to be assigned to the case but happened to be on duty when OPP inspector Wood came to the station looking for assistance in the investigation. Preston denied using his friendship with Evelyn to obtain a statement from her.

"Do you not think it might have been better if an entire stranger had dealt with her?" asked Sullivan.

"I don't think a stranger could have been any fairer than I have been to this woman," replied Preston.

When Sullivan pressed him about providing chocolate bars, a chicken dinner and movie magazines as inducements, Preston said Evelyn paid for the chocolate bars and chicken, and although she had requested he stop to purchase movie magazines, he refused. Preston admitted posing for a photograph with Evelyn.

Preston's son Peter says that his father "used to take her in cigarettes and chocolate bars to get her to talk, and she used to talk and that didn't go down well at home, you know. Oh God, there were pictures that would come out in the *Spectator* with her just looking up with her big brown eyes at my father, and it didn't go over well."

In her book Marjorie Campbell describes one *Spectator* photograph introduced as an exhibit by Sullivan: "It showed Detective Sergeant Preston and Evelyn at the entrance to the courthouse—a spectacled middle-aged man in a dark, pin-striped, well-tailored suit and light fedora, obviously conscious that he was having his picture taken, and an extremely pretty young girl smiling up at him."[26]

Peter Preston says the Evelyn Dick case cost his father a promotion. And after his retirement in 1962, "he never really talked about not getting promoted, but it was indicated in the way he talked about it. Evelyn Dick was not a good subject around the house."

Retired Hamilton policeman George Lawson says Preston was "influenced a great deal by Evelyn Dick . . . and here she was lying through her teeth all the time. And most of the guys up in the CIB [Criminal Investigation Branch] office knew this. As a matter of fact, someone said, 'Clarence, you want to ease up and take it easy,' but no way, you know. He was really a bombastic sort of man. And he really, beyond the shadow of a doubt, thought that she was innocent. That was his problem. He was a good uniform officer, I'll put it that way; but as far as taking statements from people, you could tell him the moon was green cheese and [he'd say], 'That's it, my friend is right, the moon is green cheese.' He was over-influenced by the magnetic beauty of this here woman that was supplying him with information. It was all lies. And the result was, his mind was set that Bohozuk is guilty and Evelyn Dick was an innocent passerby."

Peter Preston agrees that his father initially believed Bohozuk had something to do with John Dick's murder. "There's no question, at one time he was a very heavy suspect. But it was proven in court that he didn't do it—another one of her stories. Was it true? I don't know. And nobody at the time knew." But contrary to Lawson's analysis, Preston says of his father: "Unfortunately, he found the guilty party, but the law would not convict her, in my opinion."

Lawson says he felt sorry for Clarence Preston. "If somebody came up on the street and asked me [about Preston], I'd say, 'I don't know what you're talking about, I'm a dumb-dumb,' because he was one of us."

Whatever role chocolate bars, movie magazines and chicken dinners may have played in gaining statements from Evelyn Dick, Barlow ruled it was not sufficient to ban the statements. "I'm of the opinion, Mr. Sullivan, that I must rule that this is voluntary. I cannot see where it does not come right within the rules. This statement was made and this trip was made and she talked all at her own suggestion, without any threat or promise or inducement of any kind. I must rule that it is voluntary and admissible."

That was that. The first of Evelyn's statements was to be introduced the same day.

"I asked Tim Rigney about the statements, and he said they were going to read them into the record when the jury came back from their afternoon recess," says Thomas. The timing put him in a quandary. "If I waited until after the recess to signal the *Star*, there would be no time to insert the statements into the last two editions of the day. Also, it was a Saturday; there were no papers on Sunday, and Monday was Thanksgiving, when we didn't publish either. Therefore, if we did not run the statements that day, the *Globe and Mail*, which did publish on Thanksgiving Day, would scoop us on Monday morning. But I figured, since the statements were now as good as read to the jury and we already had them in type, there would be no harm in getting a jump on the court."[27]

Thomas decided to make that jump as his deadline approached with the jury still out. "The night edition deadline was 5:05, so I had to release them before 4:30. And I figured, well, they're going to read these statements, I'll send the release." He went to the Teletype in the room around the corner from the courtroom. "I sent the message 'Release statements' and God, they took up pages in the *Star*. Stan Davies, the afternoon news editor, even pulled ads out to make room for all this stuff. It ran a full eight columns. And it was an absolute big scoop, because the *Star* sent a truckload of papers to Hamilton and the *Hamilton Spectator* didn't have it."

Trouble was, Barlow and the jury didn't have it either. In the late afternoon, as Thomas squirmed in his seat with one eye on the clock, the jury foreman came out and spoke to Barlow, and a few minutes later a sheriff's officer informed the press table that one of the jurymen was ill and a doctor had been called. "He might still be able to sit for the reading of the statements," said the officer.

In a panic, Thomas ran for the nearest telephone. "It was clear to me the jury might be adjourned back to their hotel until Monday. [The *Star*] said it was too late, the presses were running by then. The last edition went at 5:05 p.m., and I think by the time I phoned it was about 5:15. It was too late." All he could do was sit and hope the juror recovered enough to listen to the first statement. "I have always said I was sicker than he was, because there was no way I could kill the story then. It was gone. He had dyspepsia or something. I think it was something he had eaten for lunch."

Whatever the juryman's illness, word finally came: the doctor said that although the juryman was feeling better, he was not well enough to continue. He would have Saturday night and Sunday to recover at the hotel where the jury was sequestered.

Thomas was devastated. "I was very upset about it, because I wasn't a novice in police reporting or court reporting. I knew that no confession should be published in the paper or disseminated in any way until it's read to the jury. I was thirty-three years of age, I'm now eighty-eight, and I don't think I was ever so nervous—I was nervous the whole weekend. I knew there was going to be trouble."

It didn't help that the *Star* sent a transport truck full of papers to Hamilton. "And of course the radio stations in Hamilton picked it up, you see," says Thomas, "and said that this was in the *Toronto Star*, and the people went out and they bought the paper. And they told me they sold all the papers down there. It was a big scoop, but I wasn't so proud of it. I was afraid, you know. I knew that this was going to get me into trouble."

His worry was justified. After six straight days presiding at Evelyn Dick's trial, Justice Barlow was looking forward to a day off, and when he returned to Toronto early Saturday evening, he headed straight to one of his favorite watering holes—the Ontario Club, on Wellington Street. Sinking into a plush leather chair with his drink, he was interrupted by a voice from a couch just behind him.

"Hey Judge! That's quite a case you're sitting on there in Hamilton. I'm just reading about it."

Barlow turned in his chair to see the man holding up the *Star* with the screaming headline: **MOBSTERS SLEW HIM—MRS. DICK**, and a smaller subhead: JOHN KILLED FOR BREAKING HOME HIS WIFE SAYS.

Barlow was flabbergasted. "I'm sorry, I don't know anything about that," he muttered.

The *Star* had printed the complete text of Evelyn Dick's statement to police about Romanelli, the borrowed and bloody Packard, and the dumping of John Dick's torso on Hamilton Mountain. Barlow had ruled the statement admissible, but at this point he had no knowledge of its content.

When Jocko Thomas returned to Toronto on Saturday, his first stop was the office of the *Star*'s lawyer, Alexander Stark, who would later become a Supreme Court justice. At the time, Stark was also a director of the *Star*. "I'm in trouble," began Thomas, explaining what had happened. "But I know the judge. I met him in a previous murder case—had a drink with him—and he's always been a nice man. Should I go and talk to him? I can explain to him, you know, it was a mistake."

"Absolutely not," said Stark. "You stay away from him, Jocko. Don't go near him. You'll get in more trouble than you're in."

Reluctantly, Thomas heeded Stark's advice and, with great trepidation, headed back to Hamilton for the Thanksgiving Day sitting of the court, the day after Evelyn Dick's twenty-sixth birthday.

His scoop had been accidental, but even if the statements had been read to the jury, the *Star* would still have beaten the other papers. "We'd still have had reams of copy in," says Thomas, "and on a late Saturday afternoon the other papers would only have had a bit of it. It was a clean scoop, and the statements were absolutely the gist of the whole murder trial—the best part—the part that the people wanted to read."

Realistically, other than the bruise to Barlow's pride, the early release of Evelyn's first statement had no effect on the trial because the sequestered jurors didn't get to see or hear about the *Star* story. "The only other harm done," says Thomas, "was to the *Hamilton Spectator*, in that the *Star* outsold them on their own ground that night. But it was still contempt of court."

At the opening of court on Monday, the smarting *Spectator* was seeking the *Star*'s comeuppance. "Their lawyer stood up flashing a copy of the *Star* and saying, 'My Lord, I want to speak to a contempt motion here,'" says Thomas.

Barlow didn't need the *Spectator* to prod him. "I'm aware of it," he said, jowls shaking. ". . . where they got the copy of this statement I know not, but I know that it did not come from the court. It had not been put in evidence; I had not read it; the jury has not had it before them. It was entirely an improper proceeding for any newspaper. The other newspapers, fortunately, so far as I know, did not do anything of this kind, I am very glad to say." He said he would deal with the matter at the conclusion of the trial.

The other newspapers gleefully reported Barlow's criticism of the *Star*, and the *Spectator* threw an additional dart when it derided the *Star* for reporting that, as the statement was read in court on Saturday, "a hushed courtroom listened as if to grasp every syllable . . ." As the *Spectator* acidly pointed out: "Court was adjourned Saturday before the 'hushed courtroom' could hear any syllable of the statement. The statement, read in dialogue form by Crown Attorney Harvey McCulloch, K.C., and T.J. Rigney, K.C., was given to the jury on Monday, and the courtroom did not seem to be particularly 'hushed.'"

A day or so later Thomas went to lunch with Dick Dickson, the official court stenographer assigned to travel with Justice Barlow from trial to trial, taking down evidence in shorthand. Thomas quickly lost his appetite. "You know, Jocko, the judge is really mad," said Dickson. "He's made up his mind. He's going to fine the *Star* ten thousand dollars and the guy that's responsible for putting that in the paper is going to go to jail for sixty days."

"It was me," said Jocko, the color draining from his face.

"Oh no," said Dickson, "the judge was certain it wasn't you. He said you would never do anything like that."

"Well, I did it."

"Well, you're going to get sixty days in Barton Street jail. You better go and see the judge."

Thomas was in shock. "Holy Joe Atkinson was a penny-pincher, and I knew if he had to pay ten thousand dollars, I'd be fired in no time. And sixty days in the Barton Street jail—it was a hellhole, always had been. So I said the hell with what Stark told me, I'll go and see him."

He entered the judge's chambers timidly. "Well, sir," he began, "I'm in great trouble. I'll lose my job and I'll be fired for sure and I'll never get a job anywhere else. It was just a mistake."

Barlow was convinced that the leak had come from Queen's Park, that a *Star* reporter obtained the statements from a source within the Attorney General's Office. It may have been wishful thinking. Barlow was a long-time Liberal and probably envisioned embarrassing the Conservative government of George Drew, in power since 1943, the first premier of a dynasty that would last forty-two years.

"Barlow was a man with a very jowly face," says Thomas. "And he shook his head and he said, 'Are you sure you did this? Are you sure it didn't come from your man at Queen's Park?'"

"No, sir, it had nothing to do with Queen's Park at all, sir."

"Then who told you where to get those statements?"

"I'm sorry, I can't tell you that, sir."

"Well, I would like to know that, because whoever told you that had no right to tell you."

"I'm sorry, sir, even if I have to go to jail, I can't tell you anything about that."

Barlow seemed more upset that the leak hadn't come out of Queen's Park than he was over the leak itself. He told Thomas that he had planned to force the *Star* to produce the reporter responsible, and that a fine and jail term were on the cards.

"I told him I'd be fired for sure if there was a fine like that against the paper," says Thomas. He explained to Barlow that Rigney had told him the statements were going to be read after the break, and that if the *Star* hadn't got them in, the *Globe* would have had two cracks at it—on Thanksgiving Day and Tuesday morning—before the *Star* had a chance to publish them.

"Well," said Barlow, "technically, I don't think you've done anything too bad here. The jury was sequestered and didn't get to read the statement. But I was embarrassed by it." He went on to describe what had happened at the Ontario Club. "So it was embarrassing to me. There he was, holding up a copy of the *Star*, and I had to tell him I didn't know anything about it. He looked at me as though I'd lost my mind. Here it was all in the *Star* and I didn't know anything about it."

Thomas apologized profusely and was breathing easier when he left Barlow's chambers.

At the end of the trial Barlow would be asked if he had decided on any action against the *Star*. "No, I haven't," he said. "I'll have to give this further consideration in my chambers in Toronto."

"Boy, was I relieved then," says Thomas. "And of course I'd see him on Bay Street a long time afterwards and he'd wink at me as he walked by on his way to the Ontario Club." A *Globe and Mail* reporter covering Osgoode Hall told Thomas that whenever he asked Barlow about the matter, "he was always considering it. And somebody told me he could rule on that any time—it didn't matter if it was a year old or more, he could rule on it. So when he died a few years later, I must admit I was kind of glad—relieved."

Things weren't going well for Evelyn Dick inside the courtroom. Outside, the last three days of the trial were almost surreal, with thousands of onlookers continuing to circle the elegant seventy-year-old courthouse, rushing from door to door with every rumor that Evelyn was arriving or leaving. Always composed and impeccably dressed, she was treated like a visiting dignitary or movie star. A fellow female prisoner—a hairdresser by trade—kept her perfectly coiffed for the daily court appearance. And Tom Rouse, the sheriff's officer assigned to escort the prisoner to and from the Barton Street jail—sometimes in a taxi and sometimes in a police cruiser— each day made a ritual of presenting a slice of his wife's special cake to Evelyn. Taxi drivers fawned over her and there was fierce competition to see who would get the fare. Evelyn promised the drivers an autographed photo of herself. And the *Spectator* quoted her thanking all of her lawyers, past and present, and saying to her fans and custodians: "I would like to pay tribute to everyone—to the senders of letters, the senders of gifts, and to matrons and officers for kindness shown during my custody."

The court didn't sit on Sunday—her birthday—but on Saturday, John Sullivan arrived with a huge bouquet of red and white carnations, left for her at his office by an admirer. Birthday cards, letters and gifts poured into the courthouse.

The next day, Thanksgiving, the crowd of more than two thousand was in a festive, holiday mood. Marjorie Earl wrote:

> *A lucky few got into court—one group for the morning session, another for the afternoon. Hundreds went home to their Thanksgiving dinners, foot-weary and disappointed, leaving the grounds littered with paper. Special police who had their dignity and their good natures severely scorched by mob determination, nevertheless managed to prevent any storming of the quiet courthouse interior. They picked up two purses which women had dropped in the crush of the sardine-packed queues. These handbags symbolized the collective anxiety to see Evelyn Dick on trial.*

The crowd began forming in four lines outside the main courthouse at 6:30 a.m., four hours before the doors opened. Extra police were brought in to keep order. When a hundred or so of the crowd were allowed in to fill the courtroom, the lines moved up—those in front hoping to get seats for the afternoon session. Earl described the scene:

> *In the morning and in the afternoon, when Evelyn Dick arrived and departed, the crowds rushed around the building to get a close look at the young prisoner. They swarmed around the taxi, in a wild pushing, tugging, elbowing effort to see her. When she came out of the court in the afternoon, she looked at the crowds with a puzzled expression and without any suggestion of interest.*
>
> *It is possible that Evelyn Dick is beginning to regard the people outside not so much as admirers, but as just people who rush and crowd and squeeze and argue for a chance to see what she looks like.*

At the same time, the newspapers were receiving nasty telephone calls and letters to the editor condemning the star treatment afforded a woman accused of two horrible murders. In response, the *Hamilton Spectator* interviewed Thomas Gourlay, Ontario's inspector of prisons, who said, "as a remanded prisoner, there is no objection to another woman in the corridor helping Mrs. Dick to look presentable. Naturally a woman prisoner does not want to appear in court looking like a tramp."

Mr. Justice Barlow was anxious to complete the trial of Evelyn Dick, and to that end he held an unusual night session on Tuesday, October 15. By the time Crown attorney Timothy Rigney announced, "That, my lord, ends the evidence on behalf of the prosecution," it was 9:15 p.m.

Throughout the trial there had been a lot of conjecture—in the courthouse, in the newspapers, and in every bar, restaurant and office in Hamilton—over whether or not Evelyn Dick would be called to testify in her own defense. Now the courtroom was deathly quiet, with all eyes on John Sullivan as he rose from his chair. "My lord, the defense is not offering any evidence," he said.

Sullivan had strongly recommended that Evelyn not testify, but ultimately it was her decision. She had made one brief appearance on the witness stand when Sullivan was challenging the admissibility of one of her statements to police, but that was in the absence of the jury. Attempting to defend or explain her multiple, contradictory statements would have been disastrous. And after watching the accomplished Rigney in action for nine days, and realizing that all her talking to police had put her in serious jeopardy, she wisely heeded Sullivan's advice.

With no evidence to offer, Sullivan would have to convince the jury of Evelyn Dick's innocence in his final address. He knew Rigney would be a formidable foe and, once again, lurking in the background, there was the unpredictable Barlow.

As the import of Sullivan's announcement took hold, a murmur went through the crowded courtroom.

"That closes the case then, gentlemen," said Barlow. "We will adjourn until ten o'clock tomorrow morning, when we will proceed with the addresses."

Evelyn Dick didn't appear the least bit drained by the long day in court. Smiling as she went down the stairs from the courtroom to the first floor, she said to the matron escorting her, "Well, I guess my public is waiting to see me." She was right about that. The crowd facing her as she stepped out the courthouse door was larger than ever.

The next morning, for the first time since her trial began, Evelyn was impatient and appeared tense. Perhaps it was a delayed reaction to the night session. Or was it the realization that this was her day of reckoning? That the evidence against her, piled up over eight days, and coupled with intimate details of John Dick's death revealed in her statements, led in only one direction—to the steps of the gallows?

Leaving for court from the Barton Street jail, her walk to the taxi with sheriff's officer Tom Rouse was slow and plodding, not her usual sprightly step. And when waiting photographers asked her to pose, she smiled wanly and told them to "please hurry up, the governor doesn't like this." On any other day she would have said with a broad smile: "Make this a good one, boys."

Before the jury was called in to hear final arguments from the Crown and defense, John Sullivan's young associate counsel, Frank Weatherston, attempted to introduce a motion to have Barlow throw out the murder charge on the grounds of insufficient evidence. "You should have made that motion before you announced that you had no evidence to submit," said the judge. "Having announced that—the case was closed."

Sullivan jumped to his feet. "That, my lord, if I may submit respectfully, was an announcement with respect to the production of evidence."

"No, no, don't misunderstand me, Mr. Sullivan. That closed the case. I asked if you had any evidence. The proper time for a motion of this kind is at the conclusion of the Crown's case . . ."

"Then, my lord, I probably should not have made a statement at all last evening, and let the court adjourn, because it was adjournment time," said Sullivan.

"No, it was not adjournment time necessarily," countered Barlow. "I called for the defense, and would have gone on with it if there had been any defense to offer."

Weatherston got back into it. "I respectfully submit, my lord, that the motion can be heard at this time. If in fact there is not sufficient evidence on which the jury can find a verdict of guilty, then your lordship has the power and you should take it from the jury at this stage."

Barlow relented and agreed to hear the motion; he could slap them down later.

Weatherston's first ploy was to suggest there wasn't sufficient evidence to prove that the torso found on Hamilton Mountain was actually that of John Dick.

Barlow was having none of that. "Well, you need not spend much time on that," he said, "because I am against you on that. I am of the opinion that, so far as that is concerned, there is sufficient evidence on which a jury may find that it was the body of John Dick, and that it has been properly identified."

Weatherston got the message and moved to the main thrust of his motion: that there might be evidence for the jury to consider the possibility that Evelyn Dick was an accessory after the fact, but no evidence to warrant a charge of murder. "There is not one iota of evidence which points to the accused being guilty of murder. There is quite sufficient evidence, perhaps, that she is guilty of assisting in disposing of the body, but that is not sufficient evidence on which the jury can infer that she is guilty of the crime of murder."

He said that in all of Evelyn Dick's statements, except the final one, "she denied having any hand at all in the murder. The last statement as to the trip, up over the Mountain, is the only one where she claims to have been present, and in that case . . . there were no less than nine lies . . . But even taking it as true, the evidence was that the murder was committed by Bohozuk, after both Bohozuk and Dick had been drinking and arguing, and Dick was drunk. There is no admission by the accused that they had gone up on the Mountain for the purpose of disposing of Dick.

"There is nothing . . . to suggest that she had any hand in it, or knew anything about it beforehand. Her statement at that time would show only that she was driving along and suddenly Bohozuk shot the deceased through the right eyeball."

Barlow quickly dismissed the motion, saying it would be "quite improper if at this stage I were to say to the jury there is no evidence, because in my opinion there is evidence which should go before the jury. Furthermore, I think the motion was too late in any event, but I did hear it. Now bring in the jury, please."

Evelyn Dick slouched in the prisoners' dock and doodled and sketched on a notepad, as she had done through much of the trial, while John Sullivan, imposing in his flowing black robes, began his address to the jury. He said the case was "unusual in criminal trials in this country" because of the massive publicity and an atmosphere rife with rumor and innuendo. "It has many unusual angles and possibilities. It has attracted attention all over the country. The white light of publicity has beaten down on it. There have been a great many tales circulated of this event which have not come out in evidence. I wish you to wipe this gossip from your minds."

Sullivan said it was also unusual and "unknown in the annals of criminal history for a mother to take the witness stand against her daughter—her only child—on a capital charge and give evidence of that sort. Perhaps Mrs. MacLean has her own theories of what happened. Perhaps she had her own motives." He reminded the jury that she too had originally been charged with the murder of John Dick but was released under bond requiring her to testify, and that she was a self-admitted "woman of considerable temper."

Sullivan said it was suspicious that there was so much evidence lying around to connect Evelyn Dick with the murder of John Dick. "There were unlimited possibilities at the Carrick Avenue house. There was a conductor's punch, skirt, car tickets, rubber boots and bone fragments. There was so much left that it seems impossible that a guilty person would leave so many exhibits that would enable the investigating authorities to place the finger of suspicion. It seems incredible."[28]

Referring to Dr. Deadman's testimony about the dismembering of John Dick's body and the splintered bone of one arm, Sullivan said the pathologist had "made a gesture with his large, capable hands of a person sawing partway through, and then snapping off the bone." Pointing to the prisoners' dock, Sullivan said, "Such cutting up was a task unequal to this little girl." It was one of the few moments during his two-and-a-half-hour address that "this little girl" paid much attention to the proceedings. She yawned a couple of times but mostly had her head down, doodling on her notepad.

"There is nothing presented here to show that this little woman could do it all by herself, although she may have known something about it afterwards," said Sullivan of the murder. "She could neither carry the body, nor cut it up . . . There is a great deal of evidence connecting her with the case, but not of the charge of murder."

Even if jurors felt no sympathy for Evelyn, Sullivan said "it should not make you any the less ready to accept the evidence. I mention this because of the gossip, the stories, the general feeling of nausea on the part of the public when this crime was first discovered. Evelyn Dick has been in jail for seven months. She is twenty-six years old, pretty, photogenic. She can't help that. I am not saying this to arouse sympathy, but it must be considered . . . in the light of the statements: She is not one of very high mentality, perhaps, but a lot of people are not of particularly high mentality when put under the spotlight."

Sullivan described Evelyn Dick as a girl who "never wanted in her life and never did a day's work. She is a pretty young woman, an only child, who by her mother's testimony led a rather unhappy life. Maybe it's not her fault that today she stands before you accused of the most serious crime in the code books. Parents have a serious responsibility these days."

As to a motive for John Dick's murder, Sullivan contended there was none. The usual motives were money, love or passion, and "it is not shown in the evidence that money was involved." He said there had been "no great exhibition" of passion. "Rather there seems to be indifference—if anything. And there wasn't much love."

Concluding his address, Sullivan said the Crown had failed to prove that Evelyn had either a weapon or a motive. "On the evidence it is shown that she was connected with it after death, but that is not murder. There are two verdicts you can give, first, guilty of murder, and second, not guilty.

"But there is a third view—that although there is a considerable element of doubt . . . the verdict is *not proven*, and in this country that is *not guilty*. Unless the Crown has brought home to you, without the shadow of a doubt, that Evelyn Dick is guilty of the murder of her husband, I am convinced you will find her not guilty—which only means she has not been proved to be guilty."[29]

Special Crown prosecutor Timothy Rigney exuded confidence as he took his turn before the jury and the packed courtroom. He said it wasn't up to the Crown to ascribe motive for the crime. "Perhaps you will bear in mind that the function of the Crown is to stand neutral in matters of this kind."

Rigney said that from the time Evelyn Dick provided a $200 loan in late January or early February as part of a down payment for "a job that was expected to be done . . . there existed in the minds of at least two people the idea of doing away with John Dick." He said that, according to the accused herself, "the job" was "John to be fixed . . . put out of business . . . murdered, I guess," by a gang from Windsor. That, said Rigney, was the cornerstone of the Crown's case.

As expected, he reiterated Alexandra MacLean's testimony about her daughter telling her, before the torso had been discovered, that John Dick was dead and to "keep your damn mouth shut." Rigney reviewed Evelyn's penchant for deception, beginning with the creation of her non-existent husband, naval commander Norman White; lying about the blood in the Packard; and asking at the police station if there was a warrant out for her husband when she knew he was dead. And in one of her statements she told police, "I am not going to take the rap alone." Were those the words of an innocent person, wondered Rigney. "No," he said. "It implies that she was in it, but so were others," and the only conclusion is that "she was in this thing—an active participant."

As must have been obvious to the police, Rigney said, a thread of truth ran through all of Evelyn's wild stories. As an example, he said she told police that she had passed Dr. Frank Boone, the child care specialist who gave a clean bill of health to her baby—later found encased in cement—on her way down the Mountain after John Dick was shot. That statement was indeed true, said Rigney.

Regarding the police finds in the ashes at the Carrick house, the prosecutor asked the jurors if there could be "any doubt in your minds about these bones being human bones; that the teeth are human teeth; and that those bones fit only the members of this body that were missing? She did it. Her mother says she did it. There cannot be any doubt.

"She admits out of her own mouth that there was no such person as Romanelli. Then why did she talk about him? To lead police on a false scent? What purpose would she have in leading them on a false scent if she was not involved?"

Rigney asked the jurymen if they had given any thought to how the revolver used in the killing "found its way back into a man's [Donald MacLean's] home where it was found? If you and your wife go for a drive, do you find it necessary to arm yourselves with a revolver on a pleasant afternoon's motoring?"

Closing his address, Rigney urged the jury to consider the evidence impartially and in its entirety.

Now it was Mr. Justice Barlow's turn. At the start of his fifty-minute address he told the jurymen that they would be the sole judges of the facts in the case but that he was the boss when it came to the law, "and it is my duty to interpret it to you as I find it, and it is your duty to follow my interpretation of it. If I have made any mistaken rulings in this case or if I misinterpret the law to you in any way, it will be taken care of elsewhere, but not here. You take the law as I give it to you, and you decide the law as I give it to you."

Barlow said the case had been subjected to "considerable newspaper notoriety" and instructed jurors to "put that out of your minds. Do not allow yourselves to be prejudiced by anything of that kind in this case."

It didn't take him long to go after John Sullivan. "In the address of the accused's counsel this morning he said that you must be satisfied beyond a *shadow* of a doubt. That is not the law. You must be satisfied beyond a *reasonable* doubt, which is a very different thing; so put that out of your minds . . . It is not a fanciful doubt, gentlemen; it is not a doubt conjured up perhaps by a weak juryman to escape responsibility in the case . . . So I tell you, gentlemen, that a reasonable doubt is a doubt that remains in the mind of a juryman after he has honestly considered the evidence and endeavored to come to an honest conclusion upon the same. You may not, gentlemen, create materials of doubt by resorting to trivial suppositions and remote conjecture as to a possible state of facts different from that established by the evidence." In other words: don't be chicken, a little doubt is normal but not in itself enough to warrant a *not guilty* verdict.

And, he told them, don't worry about convicting on circumstantial evidence. "True, it requires to be scrutinized carefully, but to say that a person should not be convicted upon circumstantial evidence is entirely wrong . . . Perhaps fifty, perhaps seventy percent of important criminal cases that come before the courts are decided upon circumstantial evidence . . . You might describe it as a network of facts cast around an accused. It may be a mere gossamer thread, as light as air, that vanishes. On the other hand, it may be very, very strong. It may be close and so coherent that there is no escape from it."

Before an accused can be found guilty based on circumstantial evidence, he said, "you must be satisfied not only that the circumstances are consistent with the accused having committed or having been a party to the act, but you must also be satisfied that the facts are such as to be inconsistent with any other rational conclusion than that the accused is guilty."

Barlow said the jury could pick and choose what they wanted to believe of Evelyn's statements, but "I would think you would not believe all of it . . . You are the sole judges of the weight to be given to the facts in these statements. You may determine that the statements or parts of them are untrue and not entitled to any weight, on the ground that they were not voluntarily made." That remark must have been confusing to the jury since Barlow had already ruled that the statements were voluntary and he had just told them he was the sole arbiter of the law. And he went on to say that if the jury thought that some or all of the statements were not voluntary but they believed some or all of their contents were true, "you should act on that."

After reading from the Criminal Code and defining *murder* to the jury, Barlow said: "If you conclude that the accused Evelyn Dick killed her husband intentionally, then she is guilty of murder. And . . . if you conclude beyond a reasonable doubt that she did not actually shoot John Dick, but that someone else shot him—that Bohozuk shot him—but conclude that she aided or abetted Bohozuk in the murder, then she is a principal and she is just as guilty as the person who fired the shot; she is equally guilty." And, he said, she would be equally guilty if she did "counsel or procure it to be done."

"Evelyn Dick is not being tried here for what she did after the killing. That evidence is merely helpful to you in aiding you . . . to come to a conclusion as to her guilt or innocence of the actual killing." In case they missed the point, Barlow stressed again that "a person who before the offense is committed or at the time of its commission does something for the purpose of aiding any person to commit a criminal act is a principal and is equally guilty with the person who committed the crime."

He said the jurors might think there was no motive for John Dick's killing, but he could certainly see one. "I would think there was plenty of motive. She was married on October 4 and shortly after that apparently there was trouble." He referred the jurors to one of Evelyn's statements which defined the trouble: Evelyn not allowing her husband to live with her, having sex with Bill Bohozuk five days after the wedding, etc.

"Then there was the trouble with Bohozuk down at the plant where he worked," said Barlow; "and how she went down and used his car; and then how Dick went down there and saw Bohozuk. Then there is the evidence of the quarreling that went on, and finally they separated on the second of February, and Dick went off to live with his relatives.

"Then to show whether or not she was connected with this, what about the two hundred dollars that she gave to Bohozuk? . . . There is probably a thread of truth running through this, and you will have to try to pick that thread out and follow it through, from the circumstantial evidence and from the evidence which appears from her statements. You remember how she talked to Bohozuk about getting rid of Dick."

Building his own drama, Barlow declared, "Then, gentlemen, isn't it a most extraordinary situation?—we have not heard it all." He suggested the jury should accept Ann Kammerer's evidence—obvious hearsay—that John Dick had told her he was going to meet his wife on the day he disappeared, and relying heavily on her last statement to police, Barlow went on to build a case against Evelyn almost as strong as Rigney's. He related her story about the drive up the Mountain, with Bohozuk and Dick drinking and arguing, "and then she tells the story of the shooting. Then she says that the revolver was her father's. She says that he gave it to Bohozuk. She is very familiar with that revolver; she apparently knows all about it.

"So I say, did she aid in this killing? Sometimes, gentlemen, circumstantial evidence is likened to a jigsaw puzzle; you have all the pieces and you fit these pieces in, and when you get them all fitted in, they may not be all there, but if you get enough there—there you have it."

You can almost envision Barlow twisting his forelock and bowing to the jury as he repeats over and over that's it's all up to them but, as in the case of the story of the Windsor gang, "you might wipe out of your minds entirely—although it is entirely for you—this fantastic story of gangsters from Windsor, and Romanelli. The accused herself says there is no such man as Romanelli. But that is something you will have to go through in your own mind.

"Then you remember she says herself that the limbs were burned up in a furnace, in the north end I think she says, but

I wonder. Perhaps you gentlemen may be satisfied that they were burned up in the furnace at 32 Carrick. Her mother says she carried out the ashes, although they had a man for carrying them out."

Although the evidence might not indicate exactly where John Dick's body was dismembered, Barlow said "it would seem to be pretty certain that the body was dumped over the Mountain on the night of March 6, because the bloody shirt was found on the morning of the seventh. There may be slight discrepancies in the evidence; in fact, oftentimes discrepancies show the truth of the evidence rather than otherwise." He said it was significant that much of Dick's conductor's equipment was found at 32 Carrick.

However, before the jurors could find Evelyn Dick guilty, he said, they must be satisfied beyond a reasonable doubt that "the circumstances and all the evidence" pointed to her guilt, and also that there was no other rational conclusion. "Then I say to you, gentlemen, are they consistent with any other rational conclusion? Personally, I would not think so, but that is entirely within your province. You do not need to accept what I say . . . if you do not agree with it. If you come to the conclusion that, beyond a reasonable doubt, she assisted in the killing, then your duty is clear."

Barlow said the jury had two choices in their verdict— guilty of murder or not guilty—and the decision must be unanimous. The jury left the courtroom at 4:05 p.m. to begin their deliberations.

Barlow asked if the defense had any objections to his charge to the jury. Frank Weatherston said that, although Barlow had told the jury that some of Evelyn's statements to police "were fantastic—the story of Romanelli, the story of the gang from Windsor—" he had failed to point out that the story about the trip to the Mountain with Bohozuk and John Dick "is also fantastic, and I thought perhaps your lordship should have pointed out to the jury that there were a great many obvious lies on the face of the statement. I think Mr. Sullivan pointed out nine in his cross-examination which were quite inconsistent with the sworn testimony of other witnesses, and I think that perhaps should have been pointed out to the jury . . . Of course they are entitled to believe part of the story if they wish."

"Oh, yes," said Barlow.

"But I submit that it should have been pointed out that there were lies in the story," said Weatherston.

Barlow asked Rigney if he had any objections.

"No, my lord," he replied. "I thought that the matter was completely set out—correctly, if I may be permitted to express a humble opinion." Rigney said he was surprised that Weatherston would expect Barlow to instruct the jury "as to what lies have been told."

"That is entirely for the jury," said Barlow, sweeping aside the defense's objection and adjourning to his chambers to await the decision.

In the courtroom, the spectators weren't about to give up their seats, but after listening quietly and intently to the long defense and prosecution's final arguments and the judge's charge to the jury, they were able to stand and stretch and were soon engaged in lively, if hushed, debates over Evelyn's guilt or innocence, and over the performance of the lawyers and the fearsome, heavy-jowled judge.

Down the hall from the courtroom, Evelyn Dick waited in the small, dingy room she had seen so much of over the past ten days. With her were her usual companions: sheriff's constable Tom Rouse and jail matron Alice Hickmott. If anything, Evelyn's mood had improved as the day went on. She was puffing one cigarette after another, and reporters waiting in a nearby room could hear her occasional laughter through the door.

Spectators were expecting a long wait, and when they noticed sudden activity, they anticipated an adjournment to 8 p.m. for the jury's evening meal. But reporters overheard Sheriff Caldwell tell John Sullivan, "The jury is ready to report," and there was a rush back to the courtroom. It was just before 6 p.m. The jury had been out less than two hours. Spectators' heads turned in unison as Evelyn entered the courtroom between Rouse and Hickmott. She was wearing her familiar black dress with a beige coat over her shoulders. Once she was seated in the prisoners' dock, Sullivan approached and leaned against the rail, and the two chatted and smiled.

Conversation ceased and spectators rose as Barlow was escorted to the bench from his chambers. Evelyn scanned the unsmiling faces of the jurymen as they were led into the jury box. Court clerk George Inch called the names of each juror in turn, and each answered "Here."

"May I say to the audience that I do not wish any demonstration in this courtroom," warned Barlow. "I have instructed the constable to take into custody anybody who causes any demonstration of any kind."

"Gentlemen of the jury, have you reached a verdict?" asked Inch.

"We have, sir," replied jury foreman Charles Paupst.

"Do you find Evelyn Dick on the charge in this indictment guilty or not guilty?"

"We have found the accused guilty, with a recommendation of mercy, sir," said Paupst.

"Gentlemen of the jury," said Inch, "harken to your verdict as the court hath recorded it: The jury finds Evelyn Dick guilty, with a recommendation of mercy. So say you all?"

The jurors nodded affirmatively. John Sullivan stood and turned to say something to Evelyn.

"Evelyn Dick, stand up," ordered Barlow. "Sit down, Mr. Sullivan, please." The lawyer quickly sat and the judge turned again to Evelyn. "Have you anything to say, why sentence should not be passed upon you according to law?"

"I would like my case appealed," said Evelyn in a firm, soft voice. It's probable that Sullivan, feeling the cards were stacked against him, had told Evelyn to expect a guilty verdict, with plenty of grounds for appeal.

"Evelyn Dick," said Barlow, "the sentence of this court upon you is that you be taken from here to the place whence you came, and there be kept in close confinement until the seventh day of January in the year 1947, and upon that date that you be taken to the place of execution and that you be there hanged by the neck until you are dead. And may the Lord have mercy on your soul."

Where to Find It

The Globe and Mail

Rain, Cooler

103rd Year. No. 30,215.   Metropolitan Edition ★   TORONTO, THURSDAY, OCTOBER 17, 1946.   5 Cents Per Copy   30 PAGES

MRS. DICK HANGS JAN. 7

Turning to the jurors, Barlow said their recommendation for mercy would be "forwarded to the proper authorities. Gentlemen, I want to thank you for your service in this case. It has been a long, difficult, trying case, and I do not see how you could on the evidence have brought in any other verdict than the verdict you brought in. You are now discharged."

Jocko Thomas described the scene in the *Star*: "Mr. Justice Barlow pronounced the death sentence in somber tones as Mrs. Dick stood at attention, her dark eyes flashing. There was no wavering or holding of the dock rail which so often is seen when men hear those dreaded words 'hanged by the neck.'"

"My recollection today was that there was a gasp in the courtroom when the jury returned the verdict of guilty, and certainly a gasp when the judge read the death sentence," Thomas says. "The uniformed officer and the jail matron walked her out of the courtroom. Everybody had to remain there until she was taken out, and then everybody left."

The *Hamilton Spectator* said: "Even in this terrible moment, the young woman did not flinch. It was an unreal moment for those in court. A woman had been sentenced to death." The reporter said Evelyn, with her escorts, walked from the court "steadily, a strained smile on her face. Officials feared she might collapse when she was away from the eyes of the crowd. But no, her composure was unbroken."

Thomas says he heard the death sentence read many times in murder cases he covered, and "years and years ago, when I was a copy boy at the *Star*, I remember going to the city hall courtroom where a judge read the death sentence to a man and he put on a black hat. That's what they used to do, but they hadn't

175

done it for a long time by the time Evelyn Dick was sentenced."
He says Barlow had plenty of experience reading death sentences, including the three in the Hot Stove murder case. "It was all written out in front of them and they just read it," he said.

Before leaving the small waiting room in the courthouse, the condemned woman warmly thanked her lawyers as they smiled and shook hands. Then, as she walked with her escorts along a corridor on their way out of the building, she saw Timothy Rigney leaving his office. She smiled at him. "Keep your chin up," he said.

The word *guilty* rolled out of the courthouse on a verbal wave that washed over the growing crowd outside. There was a surge towards the entrance, where they hoped to get a glimpse of the condemned woman. Evelyn and her escorts struggled to a waiting police cruiser. Flashbulbs popped like gunfire and there were taunts and cheers from the noisy mob. Finally, the car moved slowly through the crowd, into the dark night.

Alexandra MacLean wasn't in the courtroom to hear her daughter sentenced to death. Thomas says she had early on "given up on the chance of getting her daughter off. She didn't think Evelyn could be saved from the gallows. She wouldn't say anything during the trial, but afterwards Marjorie Earl went to her house and got a very graphic interview."

MacLean told Earl that Evelyn

> *"had her faults. She may have been wicked, but she is my daughter, my only child, and I idolized her. I don't know what I will do without her. I miss her every day in hundreds of different ways, and now—oh, how can I stand it."*

Earl said MacLean began weeping as she sat in the

> *tastefully and expensively furnished living room at 32 Carrick Avenue, the house that has become known in every quarter of the Dominion. Tears coursed down her cheeks continuously. Every few seconds she covered her face with her hands and sobbed.*
>
> *"I loved her so much and she loved me. We were very, very close, until she married John Dick," said MacLean.*

Earl reported:

[A]s she spoke the dead man's name, some of the bitterness she displayed in the courtroom showed in her voice and in an involuntary compression of her lips. Her grief and terror were so real and so terrible, so pitifully responsive to sympathy that I wept with her. From a corner of the room, the condemned woman's little daughter gravely watched the adult drama without comprehension but with childish fear as the noise of her grandmother's sobs filled the silent, darkened room.

The *Star* reporter described MacLean as a tiny woman with graying dark hair

done up in a bun on the nape of her neck. She was wearing a printed cotton house dress, flat-heeled shoes and cotton stockings.

At one point in the interview MacLean leaned forward,

her face contorted and, tears streaming down her tired, aged cheeks, she clutched my arm, put her head down on my coat front and wept. She was just an ordinary heartbroken mother.

"How can I bear it?" sobbed MacLean. "Tell me quickly, what is going to become of her? We had a terrible row the day before her wedding. It lasted from morning until night. I was very bitter about that."

MacLean was eager to know what her daughter was wearing in the courtroom that day.

"She wanted a change of clothes, and I sent her a pretty plaid skirt and a sweater. Was she wearing them? No? Ah well, I guess she didn't like them. She really wanted a new dress, but I couldn't afford to buy her one."

(In fact Evelyn did like the clothes her mother sent but wasn't allowed to wear them.)

MacLean apologized to Earl for the uncontrollable tears.

"I've been crying all day," she said. "I left my glasses off. I'd just get them wiped dry when I'd start to cry again. This is the first day I've really cried. For weeks I've been trying so hard not to cry I thought sometimes my head would crack. Today I did a washing and cleaned the whole house, not because it needed doing, but just for something to keep me busy. I couldn't just sit and wait."

MacLean said she had been trying to see her daughter,

"but they won't let me. She wants to see me, too. Her lawyer told me she has asked. I can't bear to go to the courtroom and just watch her. Besides, I have to look after little Heather. She's all I have now. I have to live for her."

By then Heather was sitting at her grandmother's knee in a tiny stuffed chair, said Earl.

She was combing her doll's hair. When she heard her name, she reached up to caress her grandmother's wet cheek. The childish gesture of affection brought a new rush of weeping.
"You should have seen Evelyn," said MacLean when she regained her composure. "She had everything. Everything a girl could want—a good home, friends, money. We loved one another and she was a good daughter to me. My only child and I love her." She said she had visited her daughter every week since she was committed for trial six months earlier. "They only let me stay ten minutes, once a week, and then only behind an iron grille. I don't always take Heather, because she cries to be in her mother's arms."

With her husband and daughter in jail, Heather was MacLean's only company.

"Nobody ever comes to see me now. I had friends, but they're afraid to be seen coming here after all this. I'm so lonely, so terribly lonely, and I'm too old for such sorrow and trouble. My husband, my girl . . ."

MacLean suddenly went to the kitchen cupboard and pulled out a letter from Evelyn.

"I got it yesterday," she said. "She writes me every week. I write her every week too. She tells me the jail matron laughs at my letters and calls them books. I just sit and scribble as though I were talking to her."

She handed the letter to Earl. The handwriting was round and neat, and the letter was dated October 14, the day after Evelyn's twenty-sixth birthday. "Barton Street jail" was written above the date in the upper right-hand corner.

Dearest Mother

I guess my case will be over this week. I will never forget my 26th birthday as long as I live. I wish I had listened to you and never got married. Thanks for bringing the things up to me. If you happen to be uptown again do you think you could buy me a pair of shoes? Size five-and-a-half "C". These black ones I have are so tight I have to remove the right one in court every day.

How is Heather? I sure miss her and wish every day that I was home with her. If I could just put my arms around her once.

I noticed that when you were on the witness stand that you had a pretty new brown hat. I liked it. I saw Dad the first day but didn't have a chance to speak to him.

Please write and tell me all the news and how you are feeling. I have tried and tried to see you but they won't let me.

Your loving daughter,
Evelyn

MacLean took the letter from Earl and sat back in her chair.

"You know," she said, "even now that she has been convicted, she doesn't realize the seriousness of her situation. She never did. She was never serious about anything. She doesn't understand."

seventeen

Another Day and J.J.

When word of Evelyn Dick's conviction and death sentence reached the tight-knit, religious Mennonite communities in Vineland and Beamsville, it was reported that John Dick's elderly mother wept, and his brother-in-law John Wall, who had identified the torso at the city morgue seven months earlier, said: "We hate the sin that has been committed, but we do not hate the sinner. We believe in the Christian way of life. Each night we pray for the souls of John's wife and the others charged with his murder." While not an advocate of capital punishment, Wall said there was nothing in his religion against it, and "it is the law."

Evelyn's death sentence was picked up by *Time* magazine and *Newsweek* in the United States and was given prominent play in British newspapers. A torso on a mountainside, a baby in cement, and a beautiful doomed young woman was an irresistible combination.

Meanwhile, a small, windowless cell at the end of the third-floor corridor at the Barton Street jail was Evelyn Dick's new home. As required by law, this was her isolated "death cell" with round-the-clock guards outside the new steel door.

At the same time, Alexandra MacLean's social isolation took a sinister turn when she was inundated with threatening and abusive telephone calls for testifying against her daughter. How could a mother do that, they wanted to know. "Several persons phoned," she told reporters outside the witness room, "some hanging up without saying anything. Since the verdict there have been many calls. On Thursday I received eighteen. I'll have to put something in the paper. People have the wrong idea over what I said in the witness box . . . I didn't let my daughter down, I only told the truth. I want people to know that." She said that after Evelyn's arrest in March, police questioned her for three hours and she told them everything she knew, and then she simply repeated it on the witness stand. Even her husband, she said, had told her in a letter that she shouldn't have said the things she did in court.

What some people couldn't understand was how MacLean—who admitted she despised John Dick—could help send her only child to the gallows when she could simply have said nothing. They wanted to know if her moral or religious principles were more important than Evelyn's life.

The judge and jury were gone; Evelyn Dick and her lawyers were gone; Mr. Justice Barlow was gone; but there was no respite for the cleaning staff at Hamilton's courthouse. The morning after Evelyn's conviction a new cast of characters showed up as William Bohozuk and Donald MacLean replaced her in the prisoners' docket, facing the same charge.

Some of the spectators were the same and they were relieved that on the bench, in place of the glowering, irritable Barlow, was Mr. Justice George Urquhart, a younger judge with a pleasant personality. Walter Tuchtie represented MacLean and G. Arthur Martin represented Bohozuk. Once again special prosecutor Timothy Rigney would represent the Crown. The accused, guarded by two Hamilton police officers, were handcuffed together until they reached the prisoners' dock.

Bohozuk was wearing a stylish blue pinstripe suit. The husky steelworker smiled slightly as he looked out at his sister Lillian, sitting among the spectators. MacLean, described by the *Star* as "red-faced and tight-lipped," wore a brown suit and seemed less rumpled than in his previous appearance.

Once the jury was chosen, Urquhart told them not to form any opinions before the trial was completed and to rid themselves of any preconceived ideas formed as a result of the wide publicity the case had received.

Urquhart denied a request from Martin to have Bohozuk tried separately. Martin then asked that the indictment against his client be quashed. "The case of Evelyn Dick has been disposed of and she has made four or five statements, one of which refers to Bohozuk," he said. "There is no evidence—and I say that without fear of contradiction and take full responsibility for it—to place Bohozuk on trial except the evidence of Mrs. Dick in her depositions in the police court."

Tuchtie used the same argument to have the case against MacLean dropped.

Urquhart denied both motions.

John Sullivan showed up as a spectator on the first day of the trial, and during a break MacLean motioned him towards the prisoners' dock. Sullivan obliged and MacLean asked him how his wife was holding up after Evelyn's conviction. "This is a terrible blow to her," he said. "I don't know how she will stand the strain." He also wanted to know how soon Sullivan could file an appeal on Evelyn's behalf. Sullivan did his best to reassure him.

Evelyn was brought to the courthouse at 2 p.m. on Thursday but was not called to testify. The large crowds had all but disappeared and she entered unseen through a rear door. She was kept near the sheriff's office in a small room, its single low window covered with heavy wrapping paper so she could not be seen from the street. There were reports that she was to meet with prosecutor Rigney, but the meeting didn't happen and she left the courthouse about 8 p.m.

Spectators who had sat through the preliminary and Evelyn's trial were subjected for the third time to a long parade of Crown witnesses repeating the same evidence about the crime.

When word got out that Evelyn Dick had been at the courthouse on Thursday and would likely return on Friday to testify, more than one hundred spectators lined up outside in drenching rain hoping for seats. Those who found a place in the courtroom weren't disappointed. Evelyn arrived by taxi just before noon, accompanied by Sheriff A.C. Caldwell, a jail matron and a police guard. They slipped in through a side door, but as they rounded a corner to the stairway, a flashbulb fired. Evelyn continued up the stairs, but Caldwell said loudly, "I want that man." A police officer escorted the photographer to the sheriff's office. He was released a short time later, without his camera and film.

Outside his office moments later, Caldwell said: "If that picture is published, it will scandalize the entire administration of justice. The taking of the picture was a terrible act. This woman is legally dead. She is in my custody to be hanged. It is only by force of circumstance that she had to be here. I am going to confer with the judge and if possible I am going to ask for a penalty of at least six days."

Evelyn's mother too arrived at the courthouse on Friday, carrying a new pair of shoes she had purchased for her daughter. She left them with a sheriff's officer who promised to pass them on to Evelyn.

At 3 p.m. Evelyn entered the courtroom with her police escort and walked directly to the witness stand. She glanced quickly at Bohozuk but did not look at her father, whose eyes filled with tears and chin quivered when he saw her.

When court clerk George Inch held the Bible out to Evelyn, she refused to take it. Urquhart waited a few moments, but Evelyn was adamant. "Do I understand that you refuse to give evidence and refuse to be sworn?" he asked.

"That's right," said Evelyn. "I have not had a chance to talk to my counsel."

Urquhart told her she could appear the next morning after meeting with her lawyer. "You may want to think it over until tomorrow morning," he suggested. She nodded and was allowed to leave the witness stand.

She was back in court the next afternoon, still refusing to be sworn or to testify. "You refuse to give evidence?" asked Urquhart.

"Yes."

Urquhart then read the subpoena that had been served on Evelyn, requiring her to appear in court. "I think you received such a subpoena when you were here yesterday?" he asked.

"Yes," said Evelyn.

"Have you had the benefit of counsel?"

"Yes."

"You saw Mr. Sullivan?"

"Yes."

"We can't induce you to change your mind?"

"No."

"That's your last word?"

"Yes."

Bohozuk's lawyer, G. Arthur Martin, said he was still waiting to see any evidence "that would tend to connect [Bohozuk] with the crime charged. There is none so far." Both he and Donald MacLean's lawyer once again petitioned Urquhart to throw out the charges against their clients.

"Quite so, Mr. Martin," said the judge, "your position is clear. But it would not be politic for me to rule her out at this time as a possible witness." He dismissed the motion, citing the possibility that Evelyn might change her mind over the weekend and agree to testify on Monday.

While the argument went back and forth, Evelyn had been standing quietly in the witness box. "All right, you may stand down," said Urquhart.

She was escorted to a seat in the front row of the courtroom, but a few minutes later she was back on the stand as contempt of court charges were considered. She held the Bible but again refused to answer when asked if she would swear to tell the truth.

Timothy Rigney approached the witness box. "Have you taken an oath?" he asked. Evelyn was silent. "You refuse to do so, after being requested to do so?"

"Yes."

Urquhart asked Rigney if he wanted him to hold Evelyn in contempt of court.

"Oh no, your lordship," said Rigney. "I feel Mrs. Dick might be given another opportunity. She might change her mind."

"She says her decision is final and she has refused," said Urquhart.

Martin was again on his feet. "She has again refused to be sworn. She has stated her refusal is final. My lord, I protest any further delay in the presentation of her evidence. This seems to be a cat-and-mouse game."

184

"Not at all, Mr. Martin," said Urquhart. "I trust that no pressure is put upon her and, knowing Mr. Rigney as I do, I'm sure there won't be. Her counsel may think it over, and she may think it over, and she may think it advisable to give evidence. A woman can always change her mind. If she does change her mind, her evidence should be heard."

"This is a capital charge and it seems to me there should be some finality," said Martin. But the judge could not be swayed.

After Evelyn left the courtroom, her mother took the witness stand, dressed in a black and white checked suit, a red sweater, pearls and earrings—a considerable improvement over the subdued, dark clothing she had sworn in earlier appearances. Martin objected to her being called as a witness because he wasn't prepared to cross-examine her until after Evelyn had testified. Urquhart assured him he had the right to reserve cross-examination for a later date. Rigney took her through much of the same evidence covered in Evelyn's trial, and Martin and Tuchtie reserved the right to cross-examine at a future date.

After hearing from four more witnesses, including John Dick's brother-in-law, John Wall, who testified about identifying the torso, court was adjourned for the weekend. When court resumed on the morning of Monday, October 21, Crown attorney Rigney was absent, attending a Queen's Park conference in Toronto with Ontario's attorney general, Leslie Blackwell, and deputy attorney general, Cecil Snyder. It was obvious they didn't know what to do about Evelyn and her refusal to testify. Without her evidence there was certainly no case against Bill Bohozuk. And the jury had already heard Dr. Deadman—under cross-examination by Martin— testify that he had found no trace of blood on Bohozuk's clothing or in his car.

Rigney was back in Hamilton for the afternoon session. He, Blackwell and Snyder had come up with a plan, but it didn't go over well with Martin or Tuchtie. Because Evelyn's evidence was "not available at the present time," the Crown was asking Urquhart to discharge the jury and put the case over until the next assizes, in January 1947.

Martin protested that Bohozuk was a working man who had already spent seven months behind bars and couldn't afford another long delay. He said the Crown's application amounted to the jury "being discharged for want of evidence." And Tuchtie wanted to know what assurances there were that the evidence would be available at a second trial. Rigney argued that he was asking for the jury to be discharged because "evidence is not available and justice is not being done."

Urquhart said he regarded this "as a very exceptional case. We have here Mrs. Dick, who is a material witness, and one might almost say a vital witness, to the prosecution. She has been subpoenaed to give evidence. She has refused to give evidence. I could therefore have sentenced her for contempt of court. In view of her situation, to sentence her would have been a futile gesture. She cannot be compelled to give evidence by any means of which I know. The Crown has done all in its power to have her give evidence.

"At the moment the Crown can do nothing more. But the situation may change, and change in a very short time. The trial of Mrs. Dick has just concluded. She has thirty days in which to appeal. This time has not expired. At present she may feel that if she gave evidence now, her evidence might incriminate her and this would prejudice her appeal. For all I know she may be on solid ground. Whether she failed or succeeded in her appeal, she might in either case change her mind and decide to testify."

Agreeing that discharging the jury and putting the case over to the next assizes might be somewhat unfair to Bohozuk and MacLean, Urquhart said he must consider the interests of justice and the public. The gruesome manner in which John Dick's body was dismembered was unequaled in any case he could recall, and it was highly probable "that one or more strong men" participated in the crime. Urquhart said it was not in the public interest that the case remain unsolved, and for that reason he was allowing Rigney's motion to discharge the jury and put the trials of MacLean and Bohozuk over to the spring assizes. He also put over the charges of murder against Bohozuk and Evelyn Dick in the death of her infant.

That decision to move the cases to the spring prompted John Sullivan to ask the judge to stay Evelyn Dick's execution, set for January 7. "There is some possibility that the next sitting of the assizes may not be held before January 7, the date set for the hanging of my client," said Sullivan.

"I would rather not deal with it at the present time," said Urquhart.

"You have that power," said Sullivan.

"I would rather not do it."

Sullivan gave up, but before sitting down he said he wanted the record to show that Evelyn Dick was not refusing to testify on his advice; he said it was her decision.

Urquhart recalled the jury, informed them of what had occurred, and discharged them.

Martin and Tuchtie complained to the press afterwards that the Crown was subjecting their clients to double jeopardy by forcing them to undergo two trials for the same offense. "No person, under criminal law, should be placed in jeopardy twice," said Tuchtie. He declared it was contrary to the guarantees of the Magna Carta.

Martin said Bohozuk was quite ready for his defense, but "by the time of the January trial his witnesses might not be available. They might have left the country, or even be dead. The unusual action taken by the Crown is without precedent in my experience." He said his client had asked early on for a lie detector test or truth serum to prove his innocence, and now, after seven months in jail, he was being deprived of the opportunity to present a defense.

The spotlight in the torso murder case moved from Hamilton to Toronto on November 14, 1946, when John Sullivan filed to appeal Evelyn Dick's conviction with the Ontario Court of Appeal. The court granted leave to appeal and January 9, 1947, was set as the date to hear the case before the Chief Justice of Ontario, Robert S. Robertson, and four other judges at Osgoode Hall. Since the date fell two days after Evelyn's appointment with the hangman, she was given a one-month reprieve.

In her isolation cell Evelyn was undergoing a transformation of sorts. With hours to fill every day, the prisoner continued to read some of her usual trashy magazines, but she also graduated to weekly newsmagazines, *The New Yorker*, and books such as Somerset Maugham's *The Razor's Edge*. Because she was a condemned prisoner, the law required that someone be with her twenty-four hours a day. To that end the sheriff's office hired "matrons" to sit with her. These women, who sat outside Evelyn's cell door, provided welcome company. If she felt like talking, there was always someone nearby.

Hamilton lawyer William Warrender, who would go on to become a judge in the city, was called by Frank Lalonde, the long-time governor of the Barton Street jail, and asked if he could recommend a woman to sit with Evelyn Dick. "I had a charlady [cleaning lady] called Mrs. Helen Wharrie, so I phoned and asked her if she'd be interested," Warrender told the *Hamilton Spectator* years later.[30] "She said she would be. She could use the extra few dollars."

Wharrie took the job and began sitting with Evelyn at night. Often they played cards, placing them on a newspaper or magazine and sliding them under the steel door. One would make a play and shove it back to the other.

Evelyn had the insight to realize she needed the best lawyer she could find to argue her case in the Court of Appeal. Sullivan had done the best he could at her trial, but she had seen him steamrolled by Timothy Rigney and Mr. Justice Barlow. She wanted somebody tougher, and Wharrie had mentioned she knew a lawyer.

"I need a lawyer for my appeal," said Evelyn one night, "and you mentioned you knew one. Could you get him to recommend somebody?"

Wharrie called Warrender, and as he later recalled: "I told Mrs. Wharrie, 'Yeah, I'd recommend J.J. Robinette, and I happen to have a lawyer's calendar here and I'll give you his phone number.' I was a young fellow, on city council, engaged in provincial politics and practicing law, and in those days J.J. Robinette was not well known to the public, but he was well known to the profession. I'd used him quite a few times myself."

Evelyn contacted Robinette and sometime before Christmas he drove down from Toronto to see her in jail. He brought along his fourteen-year-old daughter, Joan—now Joan Sadler. "At that time he had an old black Pontiac which he'd had to keep all during the war because you couldn't buy new cars," Sadler recalls. "I still remember that car, and finally, after the war, I think he just decided he'd had enough of the black Pontiac. He decided he was going to spread out, but then he bought one of those godawful turquoise and white Buick convertibles, which he had for about two years—and then he went back to being sensible."

It was the old black Pontiac that took Robinette and his daughter to the Barton Street jail. "I can remember sitting outside the jail, which was not a particularly lovely place. It looked awful. And as a young person I just thought, my God, I don't want to be in there. It sort of reminded me of the old Don Jail—just bleak. I was there for about half an hour while Dad went in and interviewed Mrs. Dick. And I think that was when he decided to take the case."

When the appeal got under way at Toronto's Osgoode Hall on January 9, Robinette was Evelyn Dick's lawyer. She had traded in John J. Sullivan for John J. Robinette—a move that would have a dramatic impact on both their lives. "He went on from there and became a nationwide public figure," Warrender told the *Spectator*.

The switch from one lawyer to another was not smooth. Evelyn had already paid Sullivan almost $7,000 in legal fees, but in a December 23 letter to Wentworth County sheriff A.C. Caldwell she complained that Sullivan wanted $600 more and had refused to turn over evidence and records or "have anything to do with Mr. Robinette" unless he was paid the additional fee.[31] Believing her life was at stake, Evelyn sold more of her jewelry and paid Sullivan off.

Sullivan's son, John, says there was "a tremendous jealousy in the legal profession, and Robinette was kind of the other side—he was the elite. I think underneath it, if my father had ever talked about it, I think there was an admiration for ability, but I don't think he would ever admit it up front. That was my feeling."

With Sullivan now co-operating, Robinette began poring over the transcripts. His daughter, who became a lawyer herself, recalls: "The first thing he thought when he read the evidence was that definitely all the statements that she had made should not have been admissible in the first trial. She just went off the wall, told seven or eight different stories. She was prodded by the police, and she was taken by them to different places, and he felt that was very unfair. He felt there were strong grounds for an appeal, so he took the case. And afterwards, when he got to know her and talk to her, he really felt she was innocent of that crime. I think he felt, in his heart of hearts, that her father was the guilty person in the whole thing. Not that she was perhaps unaware of what was happening, but maybe she wasn't directly involved."

Robinette told his biographer, Jack Batten, that the police work in the Evelyn Dick case was terrible. "They should have sealed off Mrs. Dick's house and Donald MacLean's house right away because it seemed to me that someone must have been moving objects—evidence—between the two places," said Robinette.

John Josiah Robinette, then forty-one, wasn't well known to the public, but at Osgoode Hall, where he had taught for a time, everybody was aware of his skill at explaining complex legal issues in simple terms. It was his reputation and the notoriety of the case that drew more than sixty law students to the small, fully packed courtroom to hear the appeal. When he officially retired at the age of eighty-four, Robinette said the Evelyn Dick case "was a cause célèbre, the most publicized case at that time in Canadian legal history. The appeal trial lasted for a week and reporters came from all over, even from the New York area."

The case was so high-profile that Ontario's deputy attorney general, Cecil Snyder, appeared at the court with special prosecutor Timothy Rigney to oppose the motion for a new trial for Evelyn Dick.

Robinette told the five-judge appeal panel that his argument would have two pillars: that Mr. Justice Barlow had made "vital errors as to non-direction and misdirection" in his charge to the jury; and that he was wrong in admitting into evidence Evelyn Dick's statements to police. He said Barlow should have told the jury that if they had reasonable doubt whether Evelyn was an accessory before or after the fact, "she must be acquitted of the charge of murder." Not only did Barlow fail to put that defense theory to the jury, "he actually removed it from the consideration of the jury . . ."

Robinette said Barlow also failed to tell the jury that if Donald MacLean had done the killing, "there was no evidence that the accused was an accessory before the fact"; and that if Donald MacLean did indeed kill John Dick, "then at the worst, Evelyn Dick was an accessory after the fact only, and not guilty of murder."

And on he went, thoroughly and dispassionately tearing apart the Crown's case and the actions of Barlow and the police. He concluded that Evelyn's statements to police "were not voluntary and that the learned trial judge erred in permitting them to be read to the jury."

Barlow, said Robinette, had improperly charged the jury; allowed evidence related to Donald MacLean but not to the accused; and wrongly accepted as evidence Evelyn's statements to police. On those grounds, he said, Evelyn Dick should be granted a new trial.

It was evident early on that Robinette was scoring points with the Court of Appeal justices. "I did not know that a British subject is liable to be taken away to a police station for questioning and held, in effect, in custody . . . and charged with vagrancy," said Mr. Justice Henderson. "If that can be done in Canada, it's time we found it out." He said that if police had the right to arrest on suspicion, that would give them the power to put citizens "in cells on fake charges like vagrancy—that is a dangerous situation."

Chief Justice Robert Robertson said vagrancy "is a pure formality . . . as empty a formality as one could imagine, and was done for the purpose of taking her [Evelyn Dick] into custody. She was warned with respect to vagrancy, but police asked her questions not concerned with vagrancy at all."

"She was not under arrest," countered deputy attorney general Snyder; "she was being detained."

"What's the difference?" asked Henderson. "Her freedom was taken from her. It means if the police have a suspicion, they have the right to arrest on suspicion. I deny that right. This thing seems to be fundamental and I think it's time we did something about it."

"Shouldn't that move come from the courts?" asked Snyder. "Sometimes police officers have to take unusual means to solve unusual crimes."

"Do you mean unlawful means?" asked another of the justices.

"Oh, no," said Snyder, who insisted that the statements made to police by Evelyn Dick had been properly admitted into evidence by Barlow.

Mr. Justice R.E. Laidlaw said that Barlow erred when he told the jury that "slight discrepancies" in Evelyn Dick's auto-ride statement to police on April 12 "tend to strengthen the case for the Crown. It was the only statement directed to the jury and yet it can't be believed, and I think that should have been told to the jury."

Henderson said that at no time was Evelyn Dick charged with murder when she made a statement to police.

"Would you go so far as to say no statement obtained from her while she was illegally detained is voluntary?" asked Laidlaw.

"I would," said Henderson.

These and several other positive comments from the five justices prompted Robinette to up the stakes. Now he was asking for an outright acquittal, with a new trial as his backup demand. "It is true I started off seeking a new trial," he told the court, but "encouraged by favorable comments from the bench, I have elevated my appeal now to seek acquittal. I only reply that as the appeal unfolded, I saw the true picture better."

The self-centered Snyder, sensing his case slipping away, became testy. "If no statements had been taken, and I had

Evelyn Dick leaving
Magistrate's court in Hamilton.
(Lloyd Bloom/*Hamilton
Spectator*)

John Sullivan, the dashing
Hamilton lawyer who represented Evelyn Dick in her first
trial. (Courtesy John Sullivan)

The furnace at the Carrick
house where John Dick's head
and limbs were likely incinerated.
(Courtesy Ontario Provincial
Police)

Evelyn Dick leaving the Barton Street jail with her usual escort. (*Toronto Star*)

Crowds outside the Hamilton courthouse hoping for a seat inside or for a glimpse of Evelyn Dick. (*Hamilton Spectator*)

Bill Bohozuk and Donald
MacLean after pleading not
guilty to murder charges in
court. (*Toronto Star*)

Four-year-old Heather prays for
her mother's release from
prison in front of a framed
photo of Evelyn. (*Toronto Star*)

Evelyn Dick posing with
Detective Clarence Preston. The
photo raised some controversy
during her trials. (*Hamilton
Spectator*)

Evelyn returning to jail with a new supply of romance and fashion magazines. (*Toronto Star*)

Alexandra MacLean on her way to court to testify as a Crown witness against her daughter. (*Toronto Star*)

Some of the large crowd jostling for position outside the court-house. (*Toronto Star*)

Evelyn and her mother pose in front of the suitcase in which police discovered the remains of an infant encased in cement. (*Hamilton Spectator*)

The 1946 Stelco strike, which competed for headlines with the Evelyn Dick trials. (*Hamilton Spectator*)

J. J. Robinette entering court to represent Evelyn Dick. It was the case that made him famous. (*Hamilton Spectator*)

Evelyn's daughter, Heather, and mother, Alexandra MacLean, after learning she had been found not guilty of killing John Dick. (*Toronto Star*)

Jurymen who would decide Evelyn Dick's fate in her second trial. (Toronto Star)

Expectant crowd learns Evelyn has been found not guilty. (*Toronto Star*)

Evelyn goes to court for trial of Bill Bohozuk. She gained considerable weight after more than a year in custody. (*Toronto Star*)

Alexandra MacLean is joyous after learning of her daughter's acquittal. (*Toronto Star*)

Donald MacLean with his lawyer Walter Tuchtie. (*Toronto Star*)

Alex Edmison, the prison reformer who arranged for Evelyn Dick's secret life when she left prison in 1958. He was appointed to the new National Parole Board the following year. (National Archives of Canada).

Lawyer Mary Louise Lynch, the first woman appointed to the National Parole Board. She became friends with Evelyn Dick after her release from prison. (National Archives of Canada).

Kathleen Robertson, who plays Evelyn Dick in the made-for-TV movie, *Torso: The Evelyn Dick Story*. (Shaftsbury Films)

been the judge or Crown counsel at the trial, I would have thrown in the sponge and said there was insufficient circumstantial evidence to warrant a conviction of murder against Evelyn Dick," he said.

"Are you saying that, disregarding the statements, we should acquit?" asked Mr. Justice Laidlaw.

"As a matter of fact, if I [had been] the Crown counsel and these statements had not been admitted, I would have thrown up my hands," said Snyder.

"But I have my doubts that there is no circumstantial evidence on which a jury could reach a verdict of guilty," said Laidlaw.

"I have always tried to play fair with this court," said Snyder. "I have given this matter a great deal of thought and this is my considered opinion."

"But I have some doubt on that score," said Laidlaw.

"I agree with my fellow judge," said Mr. Justice Aylesworth.

"Was it a mere coincidence that Mrs. Dick borrowed the murder car at certain critical times?" asked Laidlaw. "Are you asking us to close our eyes to the possible motive of Evelyn Dick to dispose of her husband? Do you say if there had been no statements admitted in evidence, there was insufficient circumstantial evidence to support a verdict of guilty?"

"Yes, your worship," said Snyder. "I am placed in an embarrassing position, I know, of prejudicing trials now pending in Hamilton, out of the same set of circumstances."

"Suppose you leave a certain amount of discretion to the court," said Chief Justice Robertson. "After all, we have certain arguments before us from an appellant—that there has not been a fair trial and there should be a new trial."

As Snyder began reviewing the evidence "as seen through the eyes of the average juror at the trial," Robertson interrupted him. "I don't think we're making much progress here," he said.

"This was a difficult case for the trial judge too," said Snyder, "after spending a night in a third-class hotel . . ."

". . . But what has this to do with the case?" asked Mr. Justice Henderson.

"Mr. Snyder, let me explain that the functions of a jury and Court of Appeal are quite distinct," said Robertson.

"I can only repeat, your lordship, that excluding the accused's statements, there was insufficient circumstantial evidence to support the verdict," said Snyder. It was as if he was telling the Court of Appeal to leave the statements in or the case would be lost and it would be their fault.

"But this court is not bound by your admission," said the chief justice.

"I am afraid to say more before the court because of the pending assizes in Hamilton," said Snyder.

"You have no right to say more," said Robertson.

"This is a very horrible crime," said Snyder. "There are a great number of cases which rule that a Court of Appeal should not go out of the way to interfere with the discretion of the trial judge. If this court were to interfere with this verdict, I submit such would be an unwarrantable interference with the administration of justice in this province."

Snyder's associate, special prosecutor Rigney, disagreed. He said the trial would not necessarily be lost without the statements, although he too insisted "there was nothing in the record to deprive them of their voluntary character." Rigney also said Evelyn Dick was "in no way prejudiced" by being tried separately, as Robinette had contended. "Mr. Robinette has built his two-story appeal into a skyscraper," Rigney told reporters later.

Jack Batten best sums up Robinette's presentation to the appeal court, describing it as "a bravura performance in the art of persuasion. He didn't miss a trick, or an argument. He would offer the court one ground for granting the appeal, and in the next breath he would turn the argument around, examine its reverse side and contrive a way of serving up that side as an alternative ground of equal strength . . . He picked his way through the case law on statements and cautions and admissibility, leading the court by the hand . . ."[32]

Robinette led them well, and on the morning of January 17 the appeals court unanimously set aside Evelyn Dick's conviction. "This appeal is allowed," said Chief Justice Robertson in a one-paragraph judgment. "The conviction is set aside and a new trial is directed. We hope to be able to hand down written reasons on this judgment early next week."

The newspapers immediately trumpeted the story, while Evelyn Dick fretted in her isolation cell in the Barton Street jail. The governor of the jail, Frank Lalonde, said there were formalities to be followed. "The court registrar must notify the sheriff by letter or telegram, and the sheriff in turn will advise me," he said. "When I receive official word, Mrs. Dick will be moved from the death cell to another part of the jail for prisoners awaiting trial." Lalonde said Evelyn had been a model prisoner, and with her new status she would have more privileges. She would be allowed access to newspapers and would no longer be under the constant watch of the three matrons who worked eight-hour shifts.

The *Toronto Daily Star* reported that visitors to Evelyn's death cell "agree that she is not now the chic Mrs. Dick she was at the trial. Her hair, which once received weekly care from a hairdresser, is straight and straggly, they report. Her olive skin has paled and a housedress is her wardrobe. She has put on weight—some say as much as twenty pounds. Newspapers are denied her. But she still reads her love stories and her Bible."

In Robertson's written decision four days later, he said there did not appear in evidence "anything to indicate any motive" on Evelyn's part "for desiring to bring about the death of John Dick." He said Ontario's courts were kept busy with divorce actions in which "quarrels and jealousies and marital misconduct" similar to those in the Evelyn Dick case were common, "but divorce, and not murder, is the usual outcome." He said it was difficult to see anything in the relationship between Evelyn and John Dick, "as disclosed in the evidence, to explain his murder only five months after their marriage."

He wrote that some evidence that was in no way related to Evelyn Dick had been introduced at her trial. "For example," said Robertson, "the evidence of what was found in Donald MacLean's house, and the evidence that Donald MacLean broke into a trunk at the Carrick Avenue residence after the appellant was in custody. Donald MacLean was not taken into custody for some weeks after appellant's arrest."

Robertson said it was beyond all doubt that John Dick was murdered on March 6, 1946, and that "his body was then mutilated and disposed of in a most inhuman way. This much would seem to be clearly established by the evidence . . . It is also a fair conclusion upon the same evidence, that [Evelyn] knows a good deal about these matters. The vital question is what, if any, part she had in the crime itself."

The chief justice took a swipe at Cecil Snyder for saying that if Evelyn's statements were excluded, the Crown had no case. "Mr. Rigney, who had been senior counsel at the trial and was associated with Mr. Snyder on the hearing of the appeal, said just as definitely that he did not subscribe to Mr. Snyder's view.[33] I do not think this court, in a criminal case, is entitled to take refuge behind the opinion expressed by any counsel as to the effect of evidence, but must act upon its own opinion."

The written decision contained a detailed analysis of each of the statements Evelyn made to police, and it concluded that none were admissible. It was his opinion, said Robertson, that the statements were either taken without a proper caution or taken before police charged Evelyn with murder.

Snyder didn't take kindly to Robertson's decision, and the Ontario attorney general's department quickly filed an application with the Supreme Court of Canada for leave to appeal the decision. But in a ruling on February 11, 1947, Mr. Justice F.L. Taschereau refused to hear the appeal. "Counsel for the applicant have cited many judgments and endeavored to show that the ruling of the Court of Appeal on the admissibility of confessions conflicts with views adopted by other courts of appeal," he said. "No judgment of other courts of appeal have been cited that would conflict with the Court of Appeal of Ontario on the point that there was non-direction and misdirection by the trial judge in his charge to the jury. Therefore, this appeal must be dismissed."

The legal haggling was over, and February 24, 1947, was set as the new trial date for Evelyn Dick. The appeal was an important victory for J.J. Robinette, and he accepted her request that he represent her at the second trial. To that point in his career Robinette had acted in only one capital murder case—in Barrie, Ontario, in 1943. His client was found not guilty by reason of insanity. "It wasn't much of a case," Robinette later told Jack Batten. He said he took the Evelyn Dick trial because "I thought I'd see the thing through to the end."

eighteen

Trial Two

For three and a half months Evelyn Dick's only exercise had been sliding playing cards under the steel door of her isolation cell. Mostly she slept, read and ate . . . and ate. The only privilege associated with the death cell, it seemed, was the right of the condemned to eat pretty much whatever she desired. By the time her second trial began in late February, Evelyn had been behind bars almost a full year. She was roly-poly and she didn't like it. In an off-the-cuff remark that ended up in print, John Sullivan, after visiting Evelyn at the jail, exclaimed, "She's hog fat" and "She eats like a horse." In the month between her release from her death cell into the general jail population and the start of her second trial, she went on a crash diet.

As it turned out, her second performance would be even grander than her first, drawing larger crowds and even more newspaper and radio reporters from across Canada and the United States. However, this time Jocko Thomas was not included among the army of reporters who descended on Hamilton. "They figured I got into trouble in the first one and I might get into trouble in the second one, so they didn't assign me to it," says Jocko. "I didn't worry about it. I was on the police beat and there was lots of other news going on." Despite all the new interest in the case, Thomas thought the second trial would be anticlimactic. "The zing went out of the trial, anyhow. It was a foregone conclusion that she probably would be acquitted—that she couldn't be convicted without those statements."

This time Evelyn Dick had to share the spotlight with J.J. Robinette, the man who brought her to the dance. She didn't mind sharing, because she knew that without him there probably wouldn't have been a second dance.

"He got very good press out of it, too," says Robinette's daughter, Joan Sadler. "Up until that time he'd never done much criminal work, and certainly not of that nature. He had done appeal work and he was a lecturer in law at the law school. And so it was for him the first major case that was in the papers, and I think, quite frankly, he rather liked it."

Robinette exuded confidence going into the trial. He had won the battle in the Ontario Court of Appeal; now it was time to fight the war. The war, he believed, would be less of a challenge than the battle. He was always aware, however, that if he failed, the hangman stood waiting. "One thing my father was against, all his life, was the death penalty," says Sadler. "And so I don't know how he would have ever dealt with that."

Five years later Robinette would have to deal with the death penalty when his client, Steve Suchan, of Boyd Gang fame, was hanged, along with Lennie Jackson, in Toronto's Don Jail. Suchan had been the shooter, but both were convicted of killing a police detective in downtown Toronto. The day before Suchan went to the gallows, Robinette visited him in his cell and left in tears. The judge who passed sentence in that case was Chief Justice James C. McRuer, the same man Evelyn Dick was about to face in her second trial.

When the trial opened on Monday, February 24, Evelyn Dick shared the prisoners' box with her father and Bill Bohozuk, but before the morning was out, the men were back in their cells; once again Evelyn would be tried first and tried alone. And once again, after the jury was picked, the Crown's parade of witnesses began. Robinette thought the problem of the troublesome statements was over, but he was wrong.

Although the Ontario Court of Appeal had ruled all of them inadmissible, Timothy Rigney moved to enter them. Instead of flatly denying the Crown's request, McRuer sent the jury out and put Robinette through a torturous two-day rehashing of his arguments for banning the statements.

"There was no doubt McRuer wanted to allow some of the statements to go as evidence," Robinette told Jack Batten years later. "He disagreed with the Court of Appeal judgment, and you could just see him straining in the courtroom to get those statements in. And there was something else in his motive: McRuer didn't like [Chief Justice] Robertson and Robertson didn't like him. So they took any legitimate opportunity that might come along to snipe at one another."[34]

Robertson's Court of Appeal was a higher court than McRuer's trial division, and in the end McRuer had no choice but to keep the statements out. With no statements, and with Robinette diligently keeping out some of the hearsay evidence the Crown had managed to slip into the first trial, Rigney and his co-counsels, C.R. Magone and Harvey McCulloch, didn't have a lot of wiggle room. They did, however, have a new witness with a startling story.

Frank Boehler was a nineteen-year-old farmhand who said that after six months in the Canadian army, from May to October 1945 (with postings in Orillia, Ontario, and Exhibition Barracks in Toronto), he was given a medical discharge and went home to Dundas, Ontario, where he worked for a time at Ferguson Foundries. He left there and in January 1946 was hired on at the farm of Gaines Hamilton at Glanford Station. The farm was on Ancaster Road between Glanford's fifth and sixth concessions. That job lasted about six months and then he moved on to Tillsonburg, Ontario.

"Do you have occasion to do anything else besides farm work?" asked Rigney's associate, Magone.

"Well, pulling a few cars from the mud—cars that got stuck. I would pull them out with either a team of horses or a tractor." During his six months on the farm Boehler said he had pulled out about a dozen cars—one of them on March 6, and "they didn't pay me. I was paid by all the other cars I pulled out."

He said he was sitting in the kitchen in the mid-afternoon when he saw the car stopped in the road, facing south, about half a mile from the farmhouse. "I had gone out to the barn to take a look at a cow we had that was sick," said Boehler, "and I was coming back in and I was looking down the road, and I saw the car again, and I heard two shots, possibly spaced thirty seconds apart, and then another one."

Back in the farmhouse, he said he picked up a magazine and went up to his bedroom for about three-quarters of an hour, and then went out to the barn to start his chores. It was then that he saw a man walk up to the house. He went out to see what he wanted. "He said that the car was stuck in the mud. The tractor would not start, so I hooked up a team of horses, took a rope, and I went down to the car." He said the man was standing beside the car and there was a woman in the driver's seat.

"I hooked on the team of horses and the rope broke," said Boehler. "So I had to go back for a chain. I wrapped the chain around the bumper and on the axle of the car." He said he approached the car and told the woman to "leave the car in neutral and leave the motor off." Her window was rolled halfway down and he glanced inside. "I saw a handbag with a package of cigarettes on her lap, and the lady was smoking a fresh-lit cigarette, and in the handbag there was the handle of a revolver sticking out." Boehler said the woman was wearing a "very large" diamond ring on her left hand.

"Is there anything else that you saw in the car when you were talking to the driver?" asked Magone.

"On the floor of the back seat there was part of a man's leg. I could only see part of it . . . the part below the knee—the calf of the leg and the foot. It was up against the right rear door, over against the cushion of the back seat. There was a black oxford shoe and there was a black sock, and dark blue or black pants. The shoe was about a foot and a half below the window. I couldn't see where the leg ended."

"You just saw the shoe?"

"Yes."

"And the sock and the trouser leg?"

"Yes."

Boehler said he pulled the car to the top of a hill, and before he unhitched the horses, the man, "about twenty-eight or thirty," said he had no money but offered a cigarette as payment. "I said, 'No, I got cigarettes of my own.'" He told Magone that after unhitching the horses, he walked past the car. "And the man had opened the door and had slid under the wheel, and the lady, when she slid over, had taken a Hamilton Street Railway conductor's cap and thrown it into the back seat."

Boehler said he didn't tell anyone what he'd seen until the police heard about it and OPP inspector Charlie Wood came to see him.

"Will you take a look around the courtroom and tell me if you see in the courtroom the woman who was in the car on that day," said Magone.

"Right there, the lady in the gray coat," said Boehler, pointing to Evelyn Dick.

"Mr. Boehler, will you tell me how you recall this day as being the sixth of March?"

"Well, sir, I had bought a radio two days after, and my pay-day was on the eighth of March . . . and I had drawn enough money from my employer to go and buy the radio, and I also made an entry in a book I kept of the people I pulled out, the cars I had pulled out of the mud."

If Boehler's testimony held, it would cement the Crown's case against Evelyn Dick. But it was all too suspicious to Robinette—the timing and the minute details, perfectly matching other Crown evidence. Boehler was in for a blistering cross-examination.

ROBINETTE: Did you tell the Hamiltons anything about it? The people you were working for?

BOEHLER: No, sir.

ROBINETTE: Did you read the newspapers during the first trial?

BOEHLER: Yes, sir.

ROBINETTE: Did you ever see a picture of Bill Bohozuk?

BOEHLER: Yes, sir.

ROBINETTE: And I suppose the man who was there that day was Bill Bohozuk?

BOEHLER: Yes, sir.

In answer to Robinette, Boehler said he was married but wasn't living with his wife.

ROBINETTE: Did you ever threaten to shoot your wife?

BOEHLER: No, sir.

ROBINETTE: Did you ever point a gun at her?

BOEHLER: No, sir.

ROBINETTE: Did you ever clean a gun in her presence and tell her you would shoot her with it? Come on, now, did you?

BOEHLER: I cleaned a gun in her presence . . .

ROBINETTE: Yes, when you were fighting with her.

McRUER: Now, Mr. Robinette . . .

ROBINETTE: I am cross-examining this witness, my lord.

McRUER: You must let him answer one question before you ask the next, that is all.

After asking several questions about Boehler's spotty work record—more than a dozen jobs in less than two years—Robinette went back on the attack. Boehler agreed with him that he had read all about Evelyn Dick's first trial but had not come forward.

ROBINETTE: You did not give any evidence whatsoever at the first trial?

BOEHLER: No.

ROBINETTE: And the first person you told this story to was Inspector Wood . . . about six or seven weeks ago?

BOEHLER: Yes.

ROBINETTE: Had you told it to anyone else—your friends or anyone? You didn't tell it to the Hamiltons?

BOEHLER: No.

ROBINETTE: How long were you in the army?

BOEHLER: Around five months and twenty-eight days.

ROBINETTE: How much of that time were you AWL [Absent Without Leave]? More than half, weren't you?

BOEHLER: No. Approximately twenty-eight days.

ROBINETTE: When you were discharged from the army . . . what were the medical reasons?

BOEHLER: Nervous.

ROBINETTE: Did you see a newspaper account a week or ten days ago, reporting that you had been stabbed by a Chinaman? That was published, wasn't it?

BOEHLER: Yes.

ROBINETTE: Where were you stabbed? What part of your body?

BOEHLER: I was not stabbed, sir.

ROBINETTE: Did you tell the police you were stabbed?

BOEHLER: No, I said I was attacked . . . I had come out of my apartment on King Street . . . to go up to the Selective Service . . . and I saw this fellow coming towards me, and he stopped and asked me for a match.

ROBINETTE: Who, the Chinaman?

BOEHLER: He was either a Chinaman or a Jap, yes, sir. I reached in my pocket to give him a light, and as I brought my hand up to give him a light, he brought his right hand up . . . with a knife.

ROBINETTE: You were stabbed then, were you?

BOEHLER: No, I was not stabbed.

ROBINETTE: That is a pretty dramatic episode. How did you ward that Chinaman off?

BOEHLER: I saw it and I knocked the hand aside like that. It went through my leather windbreaker, through my sweater and through my shirt.

Boehler said he reported the incident to the Ontario Provincial Police but no arrest was ever made. Robinette went back to the medical reasons for Boehler's discharge from the army and determined that he was released because he tested poorly for mental stability.

When Robinette asked Boehler if he had forged his mother-in-law's name on a couple of baby bonus checks, Boehler refused to answer until McRuer guaranteed him immunity from future prosecution. "Your answer cannot be used against you," said McRuer. Boehler admitted forging the checks but said he later repaid the money.

Robinette had done his homework, and Boehler's credibility was in shreds when he left the witness stand. For good measure Robinette later called as a witness Earl Jack, chief of police in Dundas, Ontario, Boehler's hometown. "Do you know the reputation of Frank Boehler for truth and veracity in the community?" asked Robinette.

"Yes, sir," said Jack.

"Is that reputation for truth or veracity good or bad?"

"I would say bad."

"Would you believe him on oath?"

"I would be very skeptical."

Under cross-examination by Rigney, Jack said he wasn't judging Boehler's honesty "in this particular case," but he would be skeptical "if I were dealing with him personally as to his honesty."

"I asked you what the opinion of the community was for truthfulness," said Robinette on re-examination. "My friend has emphasized honesty. What do you say about truthfulness? It may be the same thing."

"That is the interpretation I got," said Jack. "Honesty and truthfulness was the same thing."

"Honesty and truthfulness was the same thing—and bad?" asked Robinette.

"Yes."

Robinette had been informed well enough in advance to prepare for Boehler's testimony, but he was upset when he learned at the last minute that the Crown was introducing a new piece of evidence: a second spent bullet, this one recovered by police from the cinder floor of the garage at the Carrick house. OPP inspector Wood had, in November 1946, delivered the bullet to RCMP inspector James Churchman, in charge of the detection laboratory in Rockcliffe, just outside Ottawa. Under cross-examination by Robinette, Churchman said the bullet had been fired by Donald MacLean's .32-caliber revolver. And Wood said there was no evidence that the bullet had been fired in the garage. Dr. Deadman testified that he had found particles of bone on the bullet but couldn't say definitely that they were human.

The other worrisome witness for the defense was Alexandra MacLean. Evelyn did not look at her mother when she was in the witness box; she kept her eyes locked on Crown counsel Harvey McCulloch, who was doing the questioning. It remained like that until the lawyer asked MacLean about her conversation with her daughter after she noticed John Dick missing from his streetcar route. At that point Evelyn trained her stare intently on her mother. Eva-Lis Wuorio described the scene in the *Globe and Mail*:[35]

> *It seemed somehow an almost visible struggle of wills. The courtroom was so still that the hissing of the steam pipe was a thundering sound. The mother and daughter continued to look at one another, one of them just out of the death cell, the other once jailed on a murder charge and later freed.*
>
> *Here again, as if rerun on a mechanical screen, was the most dramatic moment of the first Dick trial: a mother testifying against her daughter. That heavy steady look across the still courtroom seemed on the part of the impassive Evelyn Dick to hold curiosity. Mrs. MacLean looked close to tears.*
>
> *The resemblance between the two women was suddenly obvious. They have the same sharp black line of eyebrows, the sudden snapping black eyes. They are about the same height. However, where Mrs. MacLean has thin, taut lips, Evelyn's lower lip is full and protuberant, sticking out further and further when she becomes annoyed at the testimony.*

MacLean, after her previous appearance, didn't have a lot of choice in her testimony, but there was one concession to the defense, planned or not: she did not use the words *killed* or *dead* when relating her conversation with Evelyn. When asked, at the first trial, what was said, MacLean had told Rigney: "I said, 'Why, there is nothing happened to him? He has not been killed?' And she said, 'Yes, John Dick is dead, and you keep your mouth shut.'" This time Harvey McCulloch questioned her:

MACLEAN: I said John was not on the car, and she said, "Well, it wouldn't be likely," giving me the impression that something had gone wrong.

McCULLOCH: So what did you say?

MACLEAN: I said, "He is not finished, is he, or has anything serious happened to him?" And she said, "Yes. He won't trouble me again."

McCULLOCH: Did she say anything else than "he won't trouble me again"?

MACLEAN: She told me to keep my damn mouth shut and my nose out of her affairs.

McCULLOCH: And was there anything else said then concerning this matter?

MACLEAN: No, not that I remember.

McCulloch returned to that incident later in Alexandra MacLean's testimony, but again she avoided the use of the words *killed* and *dead*.

In his cross-examination Robinette established that Donald MacLean had been a frequent visitor to the Carrick house after John Dick left in February; that MacLean had had no use for Dick; that he had smashed the lock on a trunk in the attic and kept his wife out of the room so she would not see what he was removing; that Alexandra MacLean had never seen Evelyn with a gun but knew Donald MacLean owned at least one; and that MacLean had hired a man to paint over the front of the Carrick house furnace.

The media coverage was intense throughout the trial, and it even affected Robinette's wife and three young daughters in Toronto. "When I'd go to school, people would ask about the trial, and you felt a bit, in a secondary way, like a celebrity," says Joan Sadler. "And as a fourteen-year-old I found it extremely exciting. It was at the dinner table that a lot happened, because my father would come home and tell us all these wonderful things that happened during the day. One sister [Dale] was just a year old, and of course she doesn't remember any of it and feels quite left out, because she's become a lawyer and would have loved to have been in on the whole thing. But we did discuss it a lot. My father always discussed his cases with us, which probably is why two of his daughters became lawyers."

Robinette, who died in 1996 at the age of ninety, appreciated the love and support of his family throughout his long career. His widow, Lois, is ninety-five and lives in a Toronto nursing home. "The Evelyn Dick case was so exciting," Lois says. "You know, we read every line that came out. It was a lovely case—with sex, and the baby, and bones ground up and all that. I guess it was the first really sensational one that there'd been for a long time, and it caused a lot of talk. John thought they had a chance going into the trial because some of the evidence was badly done. Sometimes, though, he purposely talked about other things when he came home—just to forget. He would have had enough during the day."

Lois Robinette had her own problems to worry about related to the Evelyn Dick case. "I got a few very nasty calls. It was [this] sort of thing: How could I marry such a man? or How much did he get for that? So I just said that was part of the way people defended people. One call troubled me more than the others, because she was really sort of nasty about it. I can't remember the exact words, but she was just saying, How could I put up with somebody that was that awful?"

Joan Sadler recalls, "My mother would be getting phone calls most of the day and into the evening saying, you know, how could your husband represent this terrible woman who had done these dreadful things? And my mother at first tried to sort of appease these people and say, well, you know, you're innocent until proven guilty. Then, by about the fourth day, she just gave up and put down the phone whenever she heard one of these calls, because some of them were quite vitriolic." Lois Robinette says her husband believed Donald MacLean was responsible for murdering John Dick. "But he was always very good about not talking about anything like that. Even some of the cases that he had that were noteworthy as far as gossip was concerned, he never mentioned who the people were or anything. So I guess they trusted him."

Joan Sadler says it was her mother who provided the home atmosphere necessary for her father's successful legal career. "She's—she's an incredible person. Without her, my father would never have been able to do the things he did. He needed that support at home to do these things, really. My father was a bit of a dreamer and—well, he was an intellectual person. So practical matters just had to be dealt with by my mom, and were.

"I think she probably didn't find the Evelyn Dick case quite as exciting because she would have been more worried about my father and what he was going through at the time, even though he loved it. She's a very private person and I don't think she really liked the publicity that much, whereas we thought it was great, you know. Her role in life was always to look after my father and the family, and that she did, and she did it incredibly well.

"I guess one would say my father was very practical when it came to the law and not so practical when it came to just life. I think that's probably it. I mean, I don't think he could, for instance, know where a pot was to boil water in our kitchen. He just never stepped foot there, except to eat."

Sadler says that even though the case was going well for her father, she believes public opinion was still against Evelyn Dick. "My husband said that at his family table, at that time, that's what they were always discussing—this awful woman— because it was a pretty horrific crime."

As in Evelyn Dick's first trial, it was an all-male jury that leaned forward in their seats as J.J. Robinette began his summation on Wednesday morning, March 5, 1947.

Robinette conceded early in his address that his client might be guilty of being an accessory after the fact, but "if she is an accessory after the fact, she is not guilty of murder, and that is the only charge you are to consider.

"The Crown must prove the guilt of an accused person beyond a reasonable doubt. The defense doesn't have to prove anything. And if I ever saw a case in which there is doubt, gentlemen, this is it. Mr. Rigney said at the beginning of this trial that we were about to investigate a mysterious case."

Robinette spent considerable time debunking Frank Boehler's evidence. "The key, the kingpin in the Crown's case against Mrs. Dick, is Frank Boehler. Remove Boehler's evidence from this case and it is like taking an important bolt from an intricate piece of machinery—it just doesn't work. I say to you with all the force at my command that Boehler is not telling the truth.

"Look at his fantastic story. Using Inspector Wood's words: 'it just doesn't add up.' He says he pulled a car out of the ditch. Mrs. Dick was in the front seat, Bohozuk was there, and he sees part of a leg sticking up in the back seat. He sees a gun. I suppose, if questioned further, he would have seen the gun smoking. He doesn't tell anyone. He goes back to his room and reads a western—the most ridiculous thing I've heard. He puts Bohozuk into this. He reads something out of the paper in the first trial, sees his picture and puts him into it."

Robinette said Boehler was incapable of holding a job, and that his story about being attacked by a Chinaman proved he was "just an imaginative teller of lies." He challenged the jury: "In business you have to believe in the word of your fellow men. In any decision in business, would you men believe the word of Frank Boehler? No. On something vitally affecting the welfare of your family and friends? Obviously, no. Would you accept the word of Boehler in this case, where a woman's life is at stake? No."

Robinette acknowledged that the blood found in the Packard borrowed by Evelyn, and her statements to her mother about John Dick being "finished," could indicate that his client was an accessory after the fact. But he questioned Alexandra MacLean's motives. "Did it strike you that she was a sympathetic mother, or a pretty hard, self-interested woman who was looking after her own interests and trying to clean her own skirts first?"

Robinette suggested that if John Dick had found out that Donald MacLean was stealing from the Hamilton Street Railway, it would be a motive for MacLean to kill him. "Evelyn had no motive for killing her husband. There was something more sinister as a motive than a separated woman."

He said the spent bullet found in the Carrick Avenue house came from Donald MacLean's gun. "That bullet may have been fired at Rosslyn Avenue and come over from MacLean's house in the body. It may have fallen out of the body. Dr. Deadman says the members were cut from John Dick with a saw. Is there a saw at Carrick Avenue? No. But at the Rosslyn Avenue basement you find a saw, a carving knife and an ax. And John Dick's shoes are found at Rosslyn Avenue.

"Far be it from me to point the finger of accusation at any man. It is a terrible responsibility, but we are after justice here. Human feelings wouldn't permit me to say that I want you to find that Donald MacLean killed him. The evidence is there—the suspicious circumstances. Perhaps Evelyn Dick helped to conceal the crime after it had been committed. Have you heard a single tittle of evidence that a fingerprint of Evelyn Dick was found on anything? No. It's just not there.

"I ask, on her behalf, no sympathy. I never do it for a client. You must give your verdict on the evidence. There is nothing on which you can convict Evelyn Dick of murder. Gentlemen, you just can't do it. You would not hang a dog on the evidence you have heard."

Speaking slowly and in a low voice, Timothy Rigney reviewed most of the evidence in chronological order, taking pains to counter Robinette's characterization of important Crown witnesses Frank Boehler and Alexandra MacLean. Of Boehler, he said: "The witness has been characterized in terms that are quite unfair. What motive did this man have for concocting such a story, if he did concoct it? You will recall that he didn't seek out the police, they sought him out. Would a man who had never seen the car fabricate such a story, providing such a wealth of details?"

What the jurymen didn't know was that during a hearing in which the jury was out of the courtroom, the Dundas police chief, Earl Jack, had outlined several examples of Boehler's dishonesty, including one incident in which he helped push a taxi that was stuck and then insisted they pay him thirty-five dollars for a watch he said he lost while helping. The watch was seen on his wrist a few days later.

Regarding Alexandra MacLean, Rigney said she "took the Holy Bible in her hand and swore to tell the truth." He suggested she was motivated to do what was right with as much sincerity as the jury had in doing its duty. "Wouldn't it have been easier for her to say nothing of certain things? Did she pull her punches when she was telling of this man, John Dick, borrowing money from her?"

Rigney completed his summation at 2:45 p.m. and McRuer announced that he would not charge the jury until the next morning. "I suggest that you keep your minds open," he said. "Do not start to try to finalize your judgment until you have heard my charge on the law. I think we might start at nine-thirty in the morning if that is agreeable to you. That will be the last day you will have to be here."

McRuer began his charge, which would take almost three hours, by thanking the jury for their attention and "great personal sacrifice" over the eleven days of the trial.

"Mr. Robinette contends there is no motive," he said. "Mr. Rigney points to the strained family relations. Bohozuk was friendly with the accused; he was calling her up; her husband was jealous; she was married to Dick—all those circumstances. Mr. Robinette points to the marriage ties [that are so] easily dissolved in the divorce courts these days. You will consider all that. It is not necessary that you find motive in order to find the accused guilty, but if there is no motive shown in the evidence, it is an important circumstance to take into consideration in arriving at your verdict."

Aware of the importance of Boehler's evidence to the Crown's case, McRuer said he was first going to present the case to the jurors "as if Boehler did not exist in it. Then we will consider Boehler's evidence."

He started by reminding them of the gruesome crime they were dealing with. "The head was removed; four upper bones of the neck were gone; both arms were cut off; both legs were cut off; and the bowels were slashed open. It appears to me that there have been in some quarters attempts to throw glamor around this loathsome and sordid crime, and to treat it as if it were fiction taken from some cheap storybook. That there has been a deliberate destruction of a human being seems not open to the slightest doubt."

Of Alexandra MacLean's evidence, McRuer said he did not see any reason "for feeling that she was coming here to commit perjury in these trying circumstances—perjury of a most dreadful sort if it were perjury."

He asked the jury if, after the evidence of bone specialist Professor John Grant, there could be any doubt that the bones found in the ashes at the Carrick house and garage were John Dick's. "Human bones are not things that accidentally get into the ashes. Bones of the human head and the human neck are not things that accidentally get into the ashes. They get in there by carefully calculated plan and design."

McRuer said that the shot fired into John Dick's chest "came out, but did not pierce the clothing on going out, and that is the only shot that was apparently fired into the torso. If the deceased was killed by a bullet, it must have been fired into his head." The bullet found on the floor of the garage on Carrick Avenue was fired by Donald MacLean's gun, but police did not recover the gun at his house until March 19, thirteen days after John Dick's disappearance. "The revolver was not cleaned," said McRuer. "You will ask yourselves whether a guilty man would have left the weapon on the dresser after all the publicity of the case."

He said the jurors had to weigh the significance of Donald MacLean forcing open the trunk in the attic at the Carrick house. "On the one hand, the defense points to that as an indication he was a participant in the crime. On the other hand, the Crown points to it and suggests that he may have been endeavoring to remove some evidence that he had learned would incriminate the accused."

McRuer said it was his duty to deal with Boehler's testimony. "I can say very frankly to you gentlemen, if this case depended on Boehler's evidence, and Boehler's evidence alone, I would hesitate a long time before I would convict, if I were a jury. I would suggest to you that he is far from the kingpin in this case. I think the circumstances I have been recounting to you . . . are very, very important."

Nearing the conclusion of his remarks, McRuer said that if Evelyn Dick "borrowed the car, or drove the car, for the purpose of taking John Dick out to the country so that his death might be brought about, she would be guilty." But if all she did was to help cover up after the murder, she would be not guilty.

The jury began deliberating just after noon.

McRuer's charge was much more even-handed than Mr. Justice Barlow's at the first trial, but Robinette had several objections. He said the judge had failed to tell the jury that Boehler had made no mention of the two outboard motors on the floor of the Packard's back seat. He said it was unlikely Boehler could have seen what he claimed with the motors there. And Robinette said McRuer was wrong when he told the jury that MacLean's revolver had been found on top of the dresser; in fact, it was found in the bottom drawer of the dresser. "It was not lying casually about," said Robinette.

The jury was recalled to the court and McRuer addressed the points made by Robinette. Deliberations resumed over lunch and it took the jury five hours to reach a decision.

In stark contrast to her first trial, Evelyn Dick appeared stressed and anxious as she listened intently to McRuer's charge, and some reporters covering the trial said she seemed terrified as she watched the jury leave the courtroom. "The whites of her eyes gleamed as she gazed in seeming horror after them," said one report. Later, in her dingy waiting room, she vomited and wept.

At the Carrick house, Alexandra MacLean prayed and kept busy with housework on a day that she described to a reporter as the longest of her life.

Evelyn, pale and nervous, was brought into the courtroom about ten minutes before the jury. She sat looking at the floor as she waited. The *Toronto Daily Star*'s Alf Tate described the scene:

> *Anyone sitting close to her could see she was breathing heavily —as if trying to still a hard-beating heart. She was also frequently licking her lips.*
>
> *The jurymen sat down, cleared their throats, shifted their positions, smoothed their hair or scratched imaginary spots and then, one by one, began to slide quick glances at Evelyn . . . They waited—the prisoner and the jury and the spectators. The only sounds to be heard were city sounds from outside.*
>
> *His Lordship took his place on the bench. Evelyn Dick watched him, controlling every evidence of emotion except the staring brightness of her eyes.*

"Gentlemen of the jury, have you agreed upon your verdict?" asked the court clerk. "Do you find the prisoner at the bar guilty or not guilty?"

Jury foreman Alex Bryce rose and faced McRuer. "Not guilty, your worship," he said.

"The foreman sat down and color began to flood back into Evelyn Dick's face," reported Tate. "Suddenly she was smiling. She looked around her. With her fear lifted she was now unable completely to control her emotions."

Robinette leaned back in his chair "in an involuntary manifestation of surprise and pleasure." Tate said McRuer recorded the verdict without the slightest change in his expression.

"The smile would not leave Evelyn Dick's face," he reported. "The moment she reached the prisoner's room, Evelyn wheeled, threw her arms around Tom Rouse, her regular guard, and kissed him."

"Well, that's that, the jury has spoken," muttered Rigney as he left the courtroom.

Lyman Potts was working with CKOC radio at the time of the trial. Through hand signals the station's man in the court signaled the jury's verdict shortly before 6 p.m. "I just ran into the studio, cut the program off and said, 'Here's a bulletin from the CKOC newsroom. Evelyn Dick has been found not guilty,'" recalls Potts, who still lives in Hamilton. "And of course we repeated that. Now, what we had going for us was the fact that the newspapers had printed their final editions, and there would be nothing on the streets until the *Globe and Mail* started publishing the paper for the next day, which would come out around 10 or 11 o'clock at night. But the radio had it."

Clarence Preston's son Peter says, "It [the reason for the verdict] wasn't the law, but Robinette—a pretty good lawyer. And she said at one time that she was going to tell so many stories that sounded true that nobody would really know the true one. And I think that's what happened. On top of that there were some very highly placed people involved."

"This was our red-letter day," said Alexandra MacLean when she heard Evelyn had been acquitted. "It's the power of prayer. I told Evelyn to keep praying and I prayed a lot myself. We're Anglicans and we believe strongly in the power of prayer." But she told a *Telegram* reporter the next day that she "really didn't think Evelyn was going to get off."

Joan Sadler says the victory was a milestone for her father. "He was very pleased because it was a spectacular win in many ways, and he had got to the jury and he realized that he had this ability to speak to juries. It just meant that his whole life really changed in that time, and we were all very happy for him, including my mother.

"All I remember is my father coming home and saying, 'Evelyn's been acquitted.' And he probably poured himself a Scotch and soda and we all sat around talking about it. It was a very euphoric time. We were probably more pleased with Dad than we were with anything, and he was so pleased with himself. We all felt very good."

Robinette described his feelings in Jack Batten's 1982 book *In Court*. "When the trial ended, the front page of the *Star* carried a double red banner, 'Evelyn Acquitted.' Nobody needed to be told what that meant. I've never seen a case for such sensation, and overnight I went from being an academic lawyer to being a criminal lawyer."

Evelyn's smile vanished when she tried to leave the court-house under police guard. Flashbulbs were firing from every direction. The crowd, estimated at six thousand, was in a raucous mood, and there were many more jeers than cheers. Once again the taxi assigned to take her to the jail was surrounded. But with horn blaring and a phalanx of a dozen policemen leading the way, the car was able to drive off.

It was exactly one year to the day since John Dick was murdered.

nineteen

A Baby in Cement

Through both of Evelyn Dick's trials, Bill Bohozuk and Donald MacLean were confined to Barton Street jail, so antiquated it was described by some as "dungeonlike," or as Jocko Thomas put it, a "hellhole." It must have been particularly distressful for the much younger Bohozuk, used to vigorous training for competition as a top-flight oarsman with the Leander Boat Club. He had already missed a full season of training and competition, and now a new spring was approaching.

For an athlete confined to pacing a dingy cell, Bohozuk remained in surprisingly good spirits, with strong support from his family and his estranged wife, who had returned from California to be a witness for the defense. MacLean, in contrast, constantly grumbled about his predicament. As a heavy drinker forced on the wagon, he probably daydreamed about quaffing a beer at his favorite haunt, the tavern at the Balmoral Hotel.

Each man had lost ten pounds during almost a full year of incarceration, but Bohozuk said it wasn't because of worrying. "The food has been pretty good the last little while," he told a reporter. "Of course you have a lot of mush and stuff like that—sort of birdseed—but two days a week lately we've been having a grand fish filet."

Twenty-eight-year-old Bohozuk had been bleating from day one that he was innocent, and all he wanted was a chance to prove it in court. However, each time he was set for trial, it was put over. He had to wait patiently through Evelyn Dick's first trial, through her appeal and through her second trial.

Now, on Monday, March 10, he was heading back to court with MacLean and Evelyn. She and Bohozuk were charged with murdering baby Peter David White, and he and MacLean with killing John Dick. But once again the Crown was asking for an adjournment, because the Ontario attorney general, Leslie Blackwell, was planning to file an appeal of Evelyn's "not guilty" verdict. Crown attorney Harvey McCulloch asked Mr. Justice A.M. Lebel to postpone the trials until the appeal was dealt with.

Attorneys for Bohozuk and MacLean—G. Arthur Martin and Walter Tuchtie—were furious. They denounced the way the Crown had proceeded from the start of the case, in March 1946—failing to keep the defense informed of their plans. "I never know what to expect until I arrive in the courtroom," said Tuchtie. MacLean had marked his sixth-ninth birthday in his cell two days before, and his lawyer said, if not released soon, "my client . . . will most likely die of old age. He is not in the best of health."

"Something must be done to put an end to this stalling," Martin told Lebel. He said that the Habeas Corpus Act "provides that the accused be indicted in one assizes and be tried in the next assizes at the latest. I contend my client must be tried at this assizes." He said the case was "fast assuming the appearance of a national disgrace."

Martin's growing reputation as a defense lawyer had been greatly enhanced four months earlier when he won freedom for eighteen-year-old George R. Sears, sitting in a death cell in Windsor, Ontario, after his conviction for stabbing a policeman to death. He had also been charged with one count of murder and two counts of attempted murder in other stabbing incidents, but those charges were stayed when he was found not guilty in the policeman's death.

Two weeks before Sears's December 3 date with the hangman, Martin convinced the Ontario Court of Appeal that confessions made by Sears to police had been improperly obtained and could not be believed. Sears had been arrested a year after the murder and charged with the series of slashings that had terrorized the Windsor area. He denied any involvement in the crimes, but police kept him in custody and he was not allowed to see his father. Then he was kept in a cell with nothing to eat, and was questioned again for several hours before making the confessions. A doctor testified at his trial that Sears was in a state of "complete physical exhaustion" when police were through with him, and he had to be assisted into court when he appeared before a magistrate two days later.

The appeal court ruled that the confessions, the only evidence against Sears, were not voluntary. "The appeal should be allowed and the conviction quashed," said Chief Justice Robert Robertson. It was only the third time in Ontario's history that an accused had been freed without having to go through a new trial.

Now Martin's frustration was evident as he and Tuchtie argued before Lebel that if the court decided to adjourn their clients' trial once again, it should at least allow them to be freed on bail. But it wasn't only the Crown asking for a delay. J.J. Robinette was also in court, representing Evelyn Dick once again, and he asked for a two-week adjournment, to March 24. He said his client had "just gone through a trying experience" and "it would hardly be humanitarian to put her through two murder charges in so short a time."

Lebel had a little for each of them. The Crown would get an adjournment but only until March 24, as suggested by Robinette. The case would go ahead then, appeal or no appeal, and he sided with Tuchtie and Martin on the matter of bail for Bohozuk and MacLean. "These men have been held altogether too long without bail," he said. He was granting the postponement on the understanding that Evelyn would be tried first, and alone, on the charge of murdering her baby, and that it would not be a lengthy trial. "All counsel must be ready to proceed on the Bohozuk and MacLean cases as soon as the trial of Evelyn Dick is completed. There will be no further delay if this court can prevent it."

Lebel allowed Bohozuk and MacLean to be freed on $5,000 bail each. Still in handcuffs, both men left the courtroom with broad smiles. The next day at 9:30 a.m., Bohozuk was a free man. His father, Frederick Bohozuk, and Reverend Dean Waterman, rector of Christ's Church Cathedral, each posted $2,500 property bonds to meet the $5,000 bail. Bondsmen for MacLean were a King Street East merchant,

Robert Inkster, and Lawrence Crooker, a superintendent of the Hamilton Street Railway—an odd source considering that MacLean was still facing charges of massive theft from the streetcar company. It was noon before MacLean was released from custody.

Bohozuk had been in jail ten days short of a year, and the first thing he wanted was his favorite meal—southern fried chicken and lemon meringue pie. Then he and his sister Lillian and his wife, Helen, were going to the movies.

Donald MacLean, carrying two parcels of clothing as he left the police station after signing release papers, told reporters he wanted "to get a lot of fresh air. After that, I want a great big steak with lots of mushrooms." Like Bohozuk he said he was also looking forward to lying down "on a real home bed" again.

It must have seemed strange to the Ontario Court of Appeal to receive a motion from the Crown to appeal Evelyn Dick's "not guilty" verdict. The request, filed by the Ontario attorney general on March 15 at Osgoode Hall, listed only one reason for the appeal: "That the learned judge [McRuer] was wrong in law in rejecting as evidence statements made by the Crown at the trial." But McRuer had rejected the statements because the Court of Appeal had already ruled against admitting them, and the province's appeal of that ruling to the Supreme Court of Canada had been rejected. It would be more than six weeks before the latest appeal was heard at Osgoode Hall.

On Monday, March 24, Evelyn Dick appeared in a Hamilton court to face a charge of murder for the fourth time in a year—including her preliminary trial. Robinette didn't think he had much chance of getting Evelyn off on the charge of murdering her baby. The most he hoped for was conviction on the lesser charge of manslaughter.

"When it came to the baby, that was a different kettle of fish," says Joan Sadler, "because I think my father definitely thought she had killed the baby—put it in cement and left it in the attic—which was not a very pleasant thing to have done. But she was scared, upset; afraid she was going to be thrown out on the street. You know, she didn't have a particularly happy life with her mother and father. I imagine she was frightened of her father. He was a very terrifying man, I think. I mean, anybody that I've heard speak of him thought he was a frightening sort of person.

"Her mother had really, really dominated her. She slept with her mother most of the time—all her adult life, even when she was acting as a call girl or whatever. Jack Batten said in his book that she wasn't a call girl, but I think it's a perfect description of her, because she accepted gifts. He preferred to think of her as a courtesan. Well, that's stretching the point a bit, I think.

"And she got herself into terrible difficulties with this, you know, saying one thing after another, particularly about Bohozuk, who really had no part in it whatsoever, but she kept trying to bring him in."

Jocko Thomas didn't think Evelyn had a chance in court. "Well, she had something to explain about the baby, because the hospital records show that she left with a baby and the baby was alive, healthy and everything, and now it's encased in a suitcase of cement. Oh, I'm sure that she killed the baby. I mean, if the baby died naturally, why would she want to encase it in cement? If she had tossed that club bag in the Hamilton Bay, it goes down to the bottom and that's it. But she kept it a long time."

Evelyn came into court wearing her familiar gray fur coat, which she kept tightly around her during the morning session. She was pale and there were dark circles under her eyes. Before proceedings began, OPP sergeant Carl Farrow carried in the suitcase in which the baby had been found encased in cement. A few moments later Bill Bohozuk and Donald MacLean for the first time entered the courtroom unshackled. They were there to have their cases officially put over, as agreed earlier, but G. Arthur Martin told Lebel, "Frankly, I would prefer a joint trial," and suggested the Crown be forced to state its reasons for trying Bohozuk and Evelyn separately. But Robinette said that if Timothy Rigney and the Crown hadn't petitioned for separate trials, he would have insisted on it. Lebel ruled that it wasn't necessary for Rigney to state the Crown's reasons, and granted the application.

After the jury was selected, Rigney outlined the Crown's case for the jurymen, telling them that Evelyn had given birth to a healthy baby boy on September 5, 1944, but the baby was not seen alive after she left the hospital by taxi ten days later. Police discovered the remains eighteen months later, encased in cement in a suitcase at Evelyn's Carrick Avenue house.

The first witness he called was Alexandra MacLean, and for the fourth time it was mother facing daughter in the courtroom. "Dr. Adamson accompanied her from the house to the hospital," said MacLean. "I went to see her there when the baby was a week old. I saw it just once. I think she was in the hospital about ten days. She came home to live at the Rosslyn Avenue home.

"Evelyn told me before she went to the hospital she had made arrangements to have the baby sent to the Children's Aid Society the day she would leave the hospital. And when she got home, she said a representative of the Children's Aid had taken the baby."

"Was your husband aware of Evelyn's pregnancy?" asked Rigney.

"Yes," said MacLean.

"Was she ever known by any other name, other than Evelyn MacLean?"

"Yes, Evelyn White. That was in connection with the birth of the first one."

"Do you know a White?" asked Rigney.

"No."

"Did you know whether Evelyn was married?"

"I understood she was."

"What is Heather's full name?"

"Heather Maria White."

"Previous to her going to the hospital, what was the family attitude towards the baby being brought home?"

"My husband didn't want a baby at home."

"Did you have any cement at Carrick Avenue?" asked Rigney.

"No."

"Was there any cement at Rosslyn Avenue?"

"Yes, there was a bag of cement at Rosslyn."

Hamilton detective John Freeborn was called into the courtroom and began removing contents from the beige suitcase Alexandra MacLean had brought to the hospital for Evelyn. He removed a burlap bag; a cardboard box; a small wicker basket; and articles of stained, ragged baby clothing. The quiet of the courtroom was broken when spectators, straining to see the items, stood up, sending court attendants rushing over to order them to sit down.

Under cross-examination MacLean told Robinette that the beige suitcase contained books when she saw it in the attic of the Carrick house in January 1946. She said Evelyn had purchased baby clothes before entering the hospital and had hired two prominent doctors to assist in the birth and after-care.

"In other words, every preparation was made for a normal birth?" asked Robinette.

"Yes," replied MacLean.

"And your husband said the baby was not to come into the house on Rosslyn Avenue?"

"Yes, he thought one baby was enough." Prompted by Robinette, MacLean again told about her husband breaking into a trunk and telling her, "in a rougher way, to get out of the attic and get on with my work."

Pathologist William Deadman told of finding a piece of coarse string around the baby's neck when he examined the body after the cement was chipped away. Considering its position, he said the baby was probably strangled by the cord. Under cross-examination, however, he admitted it was only a theory and the baby could have died from natural causes.

By noon on Tuesday, the second day of the trial, Rigney informed Lebel that the Crown had completed its evidence. As in her last trial, Evelyn Dick did not testify and Robinette said he had no witnesses to call. He would address the jury at 2:30 p.m., following the lunch break. Outside, although a snowstorm was raging, more than two hundred people were lined up to get into the afternoon session. However, most of the public seating had been taken over by a panel of potential jurymen on standby for the Bohozuk and MacLean trials. Police had to call in reinforcements when the crowd, mostly women, charged the entrance when the doors opened.

As Robinette began his address to the jury in the afternoon, he fretted over a mood he sensed in the courtroom.[36] "There was a definite feeling that Mrs. Dick had to pay some kind of penalty for the sort of life she'd led," he told Jack Batten years later. "The court was determined to punish her, so was the jury, and they were just reflecting what was going on out in the whole community. Mrs. Dick wasn't going to be allowed to get away with her freedom."

Robinette told the jury that the pathologist had been unable to determine the cause of death and therefore the Crown could not prove murder. But, he said, if the infant was murdered, "Who did it?"

He asked the jury also to consider Evelyn's Dick attitude towards children. Was she ruthless "or a loving mother? First of all she had a child by the name of Heather. Where that child's father is, no one knows. She gives birth to that child, takes it to her home, and treats it lovingly." Evelyn had invented a father for Heather, said Robinette. "Is that the act of a ruthless woman? Was it not an act of thoughtfulness to protect Heather from the stigma of illegitimacy? We are trying a woman for murder. Mrs. Dick is not a murderess, she is an affectionate mother."

He said the fact that Evelyn had not been a good woman was not evidence that she had murdered her child. "Did she seek to get rid of the child by abortion? No! We don't know anything about that father. But remember, Mrs. Dick is sitting here alone today—you don't see any of the fathers."

Staying in the hospital for ten days and getting the best doctors demonstrated that Evelyn wanted her child to live. "Who did not want it? There is evidence that Donald MacLean said he would not have the child at his house on Rosslyn Avenue." And it was at that house that the cement and the trowel were found, he said. Another possibility, according to Robinette, was that it was the father of the child and not Evelyn who didn't want the child.

"The accused is charged with murder and nothing else," said Robinette. "Murder is killing with intention, premeditation, malice aforethought. Manslaughter is killing another person with gross or wanton carelessness." The mention of manslaughter would give Lebel something to think about in his charge to the jury.

Timothy Rigney told the jury that if Robinette's suggestion that the father may not have wanted the infant was true, it was likely an embarrassment to Evelyn as she left the hospital. He also reminded the jury that, although living with her parents on Rosslyn at the time of the baby's birth, Evelyn was also renting the James Street South apartment at that time and it was possible she killed the baby there.

There was already a stigma on Evelyn because of her illegitimate child; having a second one would bring further shame, said Rigney, speaking to motive.

"We hear juries addressed on the rights of the accused," he said in closing. "We hear little about the rights of the rest of us. And now, you have a duty to perform which can be comforting to your conscience."

In his charge to the jury Mr. Justice Lebel said, "This is a case of murder, not a question of morals." After a cursory review of the evidence Lebel said that Robinette's mention of manslaughter as a possible verdict had given him some concern, but after considerable contemplation he had decided the jury could consider the possibility of manslaughter. "What's manslaughter? It is culpable homicide but without malice, aforethought or intent, as in murder. The presence or absence of intent to kill is the difference between manslaughter and murder as far as this case is concerned." He was giving an out to jurors who might be reluctant to see the death penalty imposed on Evelyn but who still wanted her punished.

"You must not allow sympathy to play any part," said Lebel. "And this is of special importance in this case because the accused is a woman. Our law makes no distinction between race or sex."

Lebel said the verdict must be "guilty of murder, guilty of manslaughter, or not guilty. You are not sitting here as members of the public who accept everything they read and hear. You represent law and order in the community and it is your duty to see the accused gets a fair trial."

The jury retired at 4:30 and Evelyn once again waited nervously in the small anteroom down the corridor from the courtroom. This time her wait was five hours and twenty minutes.

"We find the prisoner not guilty of murder—guilty of manslaughter," said jury foreman James Bell in a strong voice just before 10 p.m.

"As a child surprised and disappointed by an unexpected misfortune, plump and pretty Evelyn Dick last night frowned and bit her lip when the jury foreman announced she was . . . guilty of manslaughter in the death of her nine-pound baby boy, Peter David White," reported the *Star's* Alf Tate.

When Lebel asked if Evelyn had anything to say before he passed sentence, Robinette was on his feet before she could respond. He asked the judge to wait until after he presented "some evidence of a medical character" the next morning. Lebel agreed and told the jurymen they too would have to be present.

On Thursday morning Robinette called Dr. R.A. Finlayson, a psychiatrist with the city of Hamilton's health department. He had examined Evelyn Dick on March 17 and March 19. He said her "mental age is about thirteen years. She is what is known as a constitutional psychopathic personality. There is an inherent factor which shows up in her behavior. On top of that, this woman's life was one of insecurity.

"I also interviewed her mother and the only reason for the insecurity was the constant bickering at home, and the separations. The only time she cried, and she cried like a baby, was when I talked about her early home life. She showed just emotional distress."

"The occasion when she cried—was that unusual for her?" asked Robinette.

"Very unusual."

Robinette asked Finlayson about Evelyn's potential for rehabilitation.

"There is a real hope," said Finlayson. "These people have to be studied, have to be understood. And if they are, they can improve a great deal. My own feeling is that, with discipline and a better sense of duty towards others, something might be done. One of the faults of these people is that they do not have much concern for the feelings of others."

Evelyn stood for nearly ten minutes with her hands folded in front of her while Lebel discussed the enormity of her crime. Most of the spectators in the crowded courtroom were members of a panel of potential jurors from which twelve would be picked for the trials of Bill Bohozuk and Donald MacLean.

"You will be cared for better, apparently, in your place of confinement than you have ever been cared for before," said Lebel. "There is hope that you may even reform. But my function is not the function of a penal institution. It has been said that you have the mental age of thirteen years. I can only regard you from a layman's point of view, that with a mind of thirteen you would have a thirteen-year-old's understanding of right and wrong.

"There are no mitigating circumstances that I can see insofar as sentence is concerned. I have come to the conclusion, and it is not an easy one for me, that you must be sentenced to the maximum sentence I am allowed to impose. I sentence you to spend the rest of your natural life in prison."

There was an audible gasp in the crowded courtroom.

"Remove the prisoner," ordered Lebel.

The scene was described by the *Hamilton Spectator*:

> *In a tense and crowded courtroom, with more apparent composure than the judge who sentenced her, Mrs. Evelyn Dick was committed today to penitentiary for the rest of her natural days. She was calm, erect, unflinching. A peevish lip dropped briefly, but the uncommon composure was unshaken. She wheeled sharply, lowered her head, and marched from the courtroom under guard.*

A week later Dr. G.E. Wilson, a psychiatrist with the Ontario Hospital in Toronto, wrote an open letter to Finlayson in the

Hamilton Spectator. He said he was amazed by the doctor's psychiatric portrait of Evelyn Dick.

I am reliably informed that she attended high school. For an individual with low borderline intelligence such a thing is impossible. Dr. Finlayson gives her a mental age of thirteen years. We must understand that in intelligence tests, a mental age of fourteen is considered normal adult intelligence. Again, if Evelyn Dick's mental age was thirteen at the time of the testing, it is quite possible that normally it might be even greater, as it is a fact that persons under mental strain do not score well on such tests. In all likelihood her IQ would probably be higher if taken under normal conditions.

Therefore, said Wilson, Finlayson was wrong and Evelyn's intelligence was average. And he said that labeling her a "psychopathic personality" on the one hand and saying she could be cured on the other was contrary to all psychiatric study. "It is a recognized fact in psychiatric circles that psychopaths never learned by experience or training." Wilson concluded that Evelyn Dick was probably not a psychopath, but if she was, there was no cure for her.

No doubt Robinette called Finlayson as a witness to mitigate Evelyn's guilt—hoping to lessen her sentence. That didn't work, and it's certain even Robinette didn't believe she had the mental capacity of a thirteen-year-old.

"He thought she was much more intelligent than she was given credit for," says Joan Sadler. "He quite liked her. *Like* isn't quite the right word, I guess. I think he felt he had a job to do and he did it. But there was some empathy for her. I don't think she was brilliant, but she was not subnormal. I mean, she had a lot of friends in high places and they wouldn't put up with a real moron, would they?

"Some things she did were intelligent, but she really did some very unintelligent things too. I'm thinking more around the trial, where she could have saved herself earlier on, but she just talked her way into trouble by just talk, talk, talk. Now, that's not sensible."

Through the years there have been rumors of an incestuous relationship between Evelyn and her father, but Sadler says her father never hinted at it even in later years.

Jocko Thomas also heard those stories. "There were all kinds of rumors at the time that she and her father were engaged in an incestuous relationship. I never ever believed that. I think it was just a story. There was never any proof, but there was ill-feeling between the husband and wife. Her father and mother were not very friendly to each other."

Public sentiment in Hamilton was running against Evelyn Dick, and there was relief when she was sentenced to life for killing her baby. Many thought she deserved more. "They all thought she was guilty," says Faith Reed, one of the children who discovered the torso on the Mountain fifty-five years ago. "And then when she got acquitted of that and only got manslaughter for killing the baby—even that was not good enough. I mean, manslaughter, you kill your own baby, and you only get eleven or twelve years—whatever it was."

Faith's brother David says people were satisfied when Evelyn was found guilty of killing John Dick and sentenced to hang. "Even my parents, eh? She deserved what she got. But when J.J. Robinette came in and it all blew up again, not too many people were happy."

Joan Sadler says that people thought Evelyn "was a bad woman, but mostly because of her sexual exploits, I suspect. In those days, you know, times were different. I don't think she was ever thought of as the evil presence that Karla Homolka has developed into. She was a much nicer woman, really, I think.

"But she was acquitted of murdering her husband. And the baby, while it's horrific—I think there are a lot of women who, under certain circumstances, if they'd had a baby they didn't want—I won't say they would have done the same thing, but I think there was, not a sympathy, but an understanding. Whereas Karla Homolka—nothing she did was understandable, I think, in a sane person."

David Reed says Hamiltonians were angry "because they all figured money talks. And everybody thought that politicians and people whom she had been involved with were paying the bill. I think J.J. charged her $100,000. That was an awful lot of money in those days."

Many years later Evelyn Dick would tell National Parole Board member Mary Louise Lynch that a "prominent Hamiltonian, who was her last lover," paid Robinette $150,000. "Today, you know, that wouldn't be so much, but of course then it was a lot. And Evelyn said, 'He got the noose off my neck, so he doesn't owe me a thing.' I just don't know how it came up, but I do remember that—I can't say where the conversation was, but she did say that this man owed her nothing because he paid $150,000 for Robinette.

"He was a very prominent man. I never knew what he was. I know he was very prominent, very rich, and was married and very respectable, and had a very nice family, I think mostly in their teens. And I think he had given her a car, and jewelry, I think, as well. All the lovers she had were rich men, except that other man [Bill Bohozuk], you know."

Alexandra MacLean had testified that once Heather was born, Evelyn seemed to have much more money, some of which she gave to her. But Lynch insisted that Evelyn told her the money used to pay Robinette came from "the father of the one that she strangled. He wasn't Heather's father. He was the last one."

Sadler, like Lynch and many others, could never understand why Evelyn married John Dick in the first place. "She liked handsome, virile men. I mean, Bohozuk was one and this John Dick was anything but. He was a streetcar conductor and he didn't have any money. He didn't have any of the things that she really liked. Perhaps it might have been a case of Evelyn taking a stab at respectability. I think maybe that might have been it, you know—'I can be married.' But it was obvious that she wanted to get rid of him because he was a nuisance to her life."

Evelyn, perhaps relieved that she had cheated the hangman, was in a cheerful mood as she contemplated leaving the dreary Barton Street jail for the women's prison in Kingston. She knew that if she was on her best behavior, it wouldn't be unusual to be released after serving anywhere between seven and twelve years. But she would not be transferred to Kingston until after the appeals in her case were exhausted. In addition to the Crown's appeal over the "not guilty" verdict in the death of John Dick, Robinette filed an appeal of the life term she had received for the death of her baby. He said he was appealing the sentence but not the manslaughter conviction. It would take almost four months for both appeals to be heard and dealt with. It would be midsummer before Evelyn would see the last of her Barton Street cell—and the last of Hamilton.

t w e n t y

Vindication and Grief

Five minutes after Evelyn Dick left the courtroom, Bill Bohozuk took her place in the prisoners' dock. Dressed in a well-tailored dark blue suit, blue shirt, and red and blue striped tie, he conferred with his counsel, G. Arthur Martin, while a jury was selected to hear the case. His wife and sister were there to support him, along with his brother, a corporal with the RCAF who had flown in from Dartmouth, Nova Scotia, at his own expense.

Like a rerun of a bad movie, the Crown once again trotted out Alexandra MacLean as a witness. She said she had never met Bohozuk but had talked to him a couple of times on the phone for a few seconds and had seen the picture of him at the Henson apartment.

In cross-examination MacLean said Evelyn had told her the fictitious Norman White was the father of the infant Evelyn said she had given up to the Children's Aid Society. She said Evelyn didn't work and never told her where her money was coming from.

"It started to come in more rapidly after the birth of Heather than before?" asked Martin.

"Yes," said MacLean.

"From whom?" he asked again.

"Evelyn didn't tell me."

"But there was some connection between the money and Heather's birth?"

"Yes."

"Did you find Evelyn was untruthful?" asked Martin.

"Yes."

"Did she, after she was arrested, tell you she would tell the police so many stories they wouldn't know where they were at?"

"Yes."

While MacLean was testifying, Evelyn was nearby, in the familiar holding room, waiting to be called as a witness. The question whispered around the courthouse was, would she appear? She was called, but again refused to testify.

Over Martin's objections Mr. Justice Lebel agreed to have the statement from her preliminary hearing, incriminating Bohozuk, read into the evidence. Harvey McCulloch and Timothy Rigney read her questions and answers to the jury.

Lebel ordered a publication ban on the names of seven men Evelyn had mentioned in her testimony, including one whom she identified as the father of her stillborn second child. "I want the press to refrain from mentioning any one of these names," said Lebel. "Names must be entirely left out of print." When they came to the portion of the testimony mentioning the names, Rigney leaned in and whispered them to the jury.

The testimony included Evelyn's statement that after the dead infant was discovered, Detective Clarence Preston asked her if Bohozuk was responsible and she said he was. She also said she got pregnant when a drunk Bohozuk "took advantage of me."

Preston was called to testify, and he said Evelyn told him "the baby came to his death when Bill Bohozuk knotted a blanket around its neck . . . in his car near the Royal Connaught Hotel . . . She said she left the baby in the car with Bill Bohozuk and went across the street and bought a coat and then joined him in the hotel. She said that he had a key to the room, and that she went to the room, stayed half an hour and then went home."

The detective said Evelyn also told him that the first time she was intimate with Bohozuk was on October 6, 1945.

"Thirteen months after the infant Peter White was born?" asked Martin.

"Yes," replied Preston.

In her preliminary hearing testimony, Evelyn said a plumber doing work on the Carrick house had seen Bohozuk deliver a box purportedly containing the baby encased in cement. Martin called plumber Len Lane to the witness stand. He said he had worked at the house on three or four occasions in November 1945, and in February and March of 1946, but had never seen Bohozuk or the delivery of a cardboard box.

Unlike Evelyn Dick, Bill Bohozuk was anxious to defend himself on the witness stand. "I did not kill the baby," he said forcefully. "I am innocent. I have served a long term in prison to which I am not entitled. I took no box, no cement, no infant to 32 Carrick Avenue."

The first time he saw Evelyn Dick, he said, was when his wife pointed her out to him in the summer of 1944, before they were married. The first time he spoke to her was in the spring of 1945, and he said he was intimate with her "on only one occasion," after a movie in October 1945. The previous Sunday, while they were on a drive with Heather, they took the photographs that police subsequently found in Evelyn's bedroom.

Bohozuk said that as he arrived at work on the morning after he loaned his car to Evelyn, a man came up to him and asked if he knew she was his wife. "I said I didn't know. It was quite a shock to be accosted by this man and told she was his wife. I am not in the habit of going out with married women."

After that, said Bohozuk, he picked up the extra set of keys he had lent to Evelyn and never asked her out again. But he said he drove Evelyn home at 10:30 one morning in late November or early December 1945, after bumping into her at the liquor store. And after smashing up his car he borrowed $200 from her, in late January 1946, and paid her back two weeks later when he got a bank loan to pay off all his creditors. He called to tell her he had the money, but she couldn't pick it up because she had had a difficult tooth extraction, so he drove over with his young neighbor, Rocky Cupido, and dropped the money off at the Carrick house.

"Whom did you see?" asked Martin.

"Evelyn and Heather," said Bohozuk.

"What did you do?"

"I handed her the money, thanked her for her kindness, and left."

"Did you ever see her again after that?"

"The first time I saw her after that was . . . at the Barton Street jail."

In his summation to the jury Martin said the case had been given nationwide publicity and that there had been a lot of "poisonous gossip and rumors . . . with no foundation in fact."

He said Evelyn Dick's motive for lying was that "the infant's body was found in her home, in her suitcase, and unless she pinned it on someone else, she was going to hang. Hasn't she every motive in the world to lie? Why did she pick on Bohozuk? Maybe it was because he was one of her later friends, or maybe it was vengeance because he would not have anything more to do with her. Maybe it was suggested to her when Detective Preston asked: 'Did Bohozuk have anything to do with this?' I find it very hard to forgive Detective Preston if he planted that thought in her mind.

"Why did she not go into the witness box and tell her story when her own life was at stake? She did not dare risk going into that box. She just sat there and let counsel, by innuendoes, implicate others."

Martin expanded his not so subtle shot at Robinette when he added: "Talking about not hanging a dog on evidence of that nature, I suggest you would not even whip your dog on evidence such as this."

He said Evelyn Dick had played the "most successful game of any criminal in the annals of crime in this country. We know who killed this child. Although true, she escaped the supreme penalty.

"Bohozuk says he never started to go out with her before the fall of 1945. Has the Crown produced any witness to testify that they were seen together before October of 1945? Not one. Everything corroborates Bohozuk and the lie to that woman, Evelyn Dick."

The brevity of special prosecutor Rigney's summation to the jury signaled that he did not have a lot of confidence in his own case. He told the jury it was up to them to decide what weight to attach to Evelyn's statements.

Lebel was more blunt: "Since her story is before you, I think I should warn you that care should be taken in dealing with what is evidence of a circumstantial nature." He said that if Evelyn was an accomplice in the murder of her child, the jurors "should hesitate to accept her uncorroborated statement . . . There is not a tittle of evidence which corroborates it." Lebel said they were not to consider Bohozuk's moral conduct, "even though the actions of the two on one occasion [when they had sex] were reprehensible enough . . . You can see he has been exceedingly foolish to associate with a woman like Mrs. Dick." But the judge said there was nothing in the evidence to cause them to disbelieve Bohozuk's testimony.

It took the jury a mere twenty-three minutes to find Bohozuk not guilty of the murder of the baby. His jaw tightened, he fought off tears and lowered his head when he heard the verdict. He was acquitted on Saturday, March 29. On Monday he was back in court to face the charge of killing John Dick. A jury was quickly chosen and Timothy Rigney briefly outlined the Crown's case. There was a murmur in the courtroom when he called his first witness: Evelyn Dick.

"You are bound by law to submit to be sworn," said Mr. Justice Lebel when she took the witness stand, pale and determined. She refused to take the Bible put before her. "You refuse to be sworn?" asked Lebel.

"Yes."

"I order you to take the Bible and submit to being sworn in. You still refuse?"

"Yes."

"This is also, then, a separate offense you have committed," said Lebel, dismissing her.

Immediately, Rigney was on his feet. "In view of what has happened, and I refer of course to the refusal of Evelyn Dick to be sworn or give evidence, I feel it would be futile to attempt to proceed any further against Bohozuk. Her evidence is by far the most important and the only direct evidence of the crime charged. It is not my intention to call any further evidence against Bohozuk."

But the defense had even more going for it than Evelyn's refusal to testify. During the police interrogation of Bohozuk, he mentioned that, while John Dick was being killed, he was cruising the downtown and that senior rower Al Taylor, whom he knew casually from the Leander Boat Club, saw him chatting to little Frances, the ticket seller at the Palace Theatre. However, Frances couldn't confirm she had talked to him on that particular day, and Taylor denied seeing him.

When George Lawson heard the story at police headquarters, he remembered seeing Bohozuk and Frances together sometime in March. "And that's when I started to back check what I did on that particular day," recalls Lawson. "I went through the files to see when I was working. And we had diaries, you know, we keep them from day to day." He discovered that the day he saw Bohozuk and Frances was March 6—Ash Wednesday. "I put everything together and realized, my God, it was quite feasible that he wouldn't know Al Taylor that well, and he didn't know me that well. And I thought, jeez, it wasn't Taylor at all [who saw him], it was me."

Lawson took his information to the chief of police. "He says, 'By all means get over there and speak to Harvey McCulloch,' who was a crown. And I expected Harvey to throw papers around and bawl me out, but he didn't. He says, 'Thank you very much.' It was as if he was saying, 'This is just what we've been waiting for.' And of course Bohozuk's lawyers, William Schreiber and Arthur Martin, were really upset with me until I told them I would appear as a witness."

Of course, with Rigney telling Lebel he wasn't going to bring any evidence against Bohozuk, there was now no need to call Lawson.

Lebel turned to the jury and directed them to acquit Bohozuk immediately. He said there was no need even to go into the jury room; they just had to pick a foreman to stand up and announce the verdict. The jurors whispered among themselves for a few moments and, when called upon, announced their "not guilty" verdict.

Bohozuk and his supporters were joyous, but Lebel didn't dismiss him right away. "This has been a costly lesson to you," he said, "and should make you careful of the company you keep in the future. A man is known by the company he keeps."

After more than a year, Bohozuk's ordeal was over. In the witness room afterwards, Lawson spoke to him. "I went into the little holding room where Bohozuk was," he says. "We were familiar with each other but not buddy-buddies, but he was so happy to see me. 'George, I understand what you're here for,' he said. 'I thank you very much, because as God is my judge, I had nothing to do with it.' And I thought that was pretty good, because I felt a lot better, you know. Because I was still a little squirmish, you know, that there was a possibility he could have had something to do with it. But my times pinpointed it right down to the deal.

"The fatal mistake, I think, was her [Evelyn] pinpointing the time that Bohozuk was alleged to have committed the murder on the Mountain, when in fact he was sitting in his car on King Street in front of the Capitol Theatre there, talking to this little Frances who sold tickets at the Palace Theatre, which was only a block away."

Outside the courthouse Bohozuk said he was going to take a month-long holiday before getting back to rowing and returning to his job as first helper on an electric furnace at Dominion Foundry. He said Lebel's words were the same as "some of my mother's old advice, and I intend to follow it from now on."

With Bohozuk freed, there was only the forlorn figure of Donald MacLean left in the prisoners' box to face the charge of murdering John Dick. His trial began the moment Bohozuk left the courtroom. The Crown introduced evidence of all the items found at his Rosslyn Avenue home, but what it didn't have was direct evidence proving MacLean's participation in the actual killing of John Dick.

The next day a deal was struck. The Crown produced no further evidence against MacLean, and Lebel ordered the jury to find him not guilty for lack of evidence. Then MacLean pleaded guilty to a new charge—accessory after the fact. Before sentencing, a doctor told the court that MacLean was in poor physical and mental health.

Lebel sentenced him to five years in a penitentiary. Another five years, to run concurrently, was added later when he was found guilty of stealing from the Hamilton Street Railway. He was in his seventieth year when he headed off to Kingston Penitentiary, where he would serve four years before being released in 1951.

twenty one

Angel behind Bars

"I am glad to get away from Hamilton," said Evelyn Dick as she bade a thankful farewell to her guard and matron and left her Barton Street jail cell on July 16, 1947, to begin her life sentence at Kingston Penitentiary. The day before, her mother and daughter had visited her at the jail to say their goodbyes.

Before leaving Hamilton, Evelyn arranged to sell her house for $7,100, which was to be set aside for Heather's education and future. "I will have to move out by August 17," said Alexandra MacLean. "I can't go to an apartment because of Heather. I will have to buy another house. This one is too big for us now. I'd like to be all on one floor. The doctor said I must be careful."

She told newspaper reporters that her husband had wept bitterly before he went off to Kingston. "But Evelyn is anxious to go. She was very glad to see Heather when I took her down to say goodbye. Heather realizes that her mother is going away for a long time. She's a bright child. She will be a big girl when her mother comes home again."

Evelyn Dick's transfer to Kingston ended seventeen months at the dreary jail. It came a few days after J.J. Robinette wired Evelyn to tell her the Crown had lost its appeal of her acquittal of murdering John Dick. There would be a further appeal to the Supreme Court of Canada in August, but the court would refuse to hear it.

Evelyn's appeal of the life sentence for killing her infant son had also been dismissed. In late May the Ontario Court of Appeal rejected Robinette's suggestion that her sentence be reduced to five years.

Although the judges at Evelyn's various trials had instructed jurors not to make a decision based on her moral conduct, Chief Justice Robert Robertson appears to have done just that. "We are of the opinion we should not interfere with the judge who imposed the sentence he did," he said. "While the appellant has no previous criminal record or earlier conviction, she obviously had chosen an evil mode of life. This child was her third illegitimate child."

Robertson said the method used to dispose of the infant was utterly callous. "She has not the usual natural dislike of gruesome deeds that one would expect from a person of her years. Perhaps her upbringing is largely at fault.

"It may be that courts have usually treated infanticide as a less serious crime than the killing of an adult. But infanticide may in some circumstances indicate all the evil factors involved in the killing of a grown person." The maternal instinct, he said, should be the strongest of all the better qualities "which make a woman a proper member of a free society."

Robinette had complained to the court that Mr. Justice Lebel was "influenced by the suspicious circumstances surrounding the murder of John Dick, in which the accused [Evelyn] was acquitted after a fair and thorough trial."

Evelyn's trip to Kingston was made in the sheriff's car, which entered the jail grounds through the iron gates in the side yard at 6:15 a.m. The gates swung open fifteen minutes later and the jail's most infamous tenant was gone. The time of her departure was kept secret and she left almost unnoticed. The driver and another sheriff's officer were in the front seat, with Evelyn and a jail matron in the back.

"The quartet resembled a party going on a holiday," reported the *Star*. "The former glamour girl ate chocolate bars supplied by escorts and enjoyed the balmy weather and the scenery for the last time in many a long year."

It took almost seven hours to make the trip, "with the party ducking around corners in Belleville to throw any pursuing car off the track," said the report. "Lunch was eaten in Belleville in a private room in a restaurant."

At the Prison for Women in Kingston, Evelyn, wearing a rose wool suit, arrived with an armful of books and magazines. She entered without hesitation and was met by a uniformed matron.

A month later Alexandra MacLean was telling newspaper reporters that her husband and daughter were delighted with their Kingston accommodations. In a letter to his wife MacLean said, "Kingston is a thousand times better than Hamilton's Barton Street jail."

"My husband writes that the meals are delicious, that they are served cafeteria style and that there is plenty of sugar and butter," said Alexandra.

By all accounts Evelyn Dick made an amazing adjustment to penitentiary life.

"I think she accepted what was happening to her," says Faith Avis, who, as a volunteer with the Elizabeth Fry Society, often saw Evelyn in prison. "But I did get the feeling that by this very good behavior and by always trying to stay on the good side of the matron and the staff, she was from the very beginning hoping that she would eventually get out. And of course a lot of inmates lose hope, but she didn't. And she was quite popular with the matrons because she was very well behaved while she was here. She never caused any trouble or did anything to upset the matrons."

Avis, seventy-five, is a former public relations director for Kingston General Hospital and now a freelance writer and author. "Evelyn didn't know me well, but she knew me as a familiar face and she would always greet me," she says. "Elizabeth Fry of Kingston set up a Thursday night program where our people came in and they taught art and drama and first aid and all kinds of things, and the inmates could come and take part in that. And Evelyn often turned out for those. She was very polite, and a very good inmate. She was well spoken and she'd had a good education. She was popular with a small group of the prisoners but not with all of them, because she obviously felt that she was superior to them, and maybe was, in intellect."

Like others who knew Evelyn Dick, Avis strongly disagrees with the psychiatric assessment of her intelligence expressed in court. "I was absolutely astounded to read the report from the psychiatrist that they thought she had the intelligence of a thirteen-year-old. I would not have agreed with that at all, and I don't pretend to be anybody in psychiatry or psychology. But she was given this job of working in the front office with the matron, Lorraine Burke, and she did filing and some typing.

"I thought Evelyn was quite intelligent. I thought she used childishness as a tool to get people's sympathy. Whenever any man came in when she was around—it didn't matter if it was a maintenance man, or an RCMP officer, or somebody from over at the other prison—she would just turn on this girlish charm, very young girlish charm, even though she wasn't that young at the time. I think she may have fooled the psychiatrist."

One of Evelyn's biggest disappointments was probably the clothing the female inmates were forced to wear. As in her days at Hamilton's Loretto Academy, Evelyn was back to wearing uniforms, but they were nothing like the ones she wore in high school. Each inmate was issued two "dresses," which Avis says were similar to "mattress ticking—blue and white heavy canvas material. And that's what they wore. They were given two, and if you ruined one, if you stained it or ripped it, you almost had to get a lawyer to get a replacement. But Evelyn was always very well groomed. I think it's been documented that she gained a lot of weight while she was in prison, but even as a fairly plump lady she was very attractive, and she had glossy curly hair and great big eyes with long lashes, and whenever any man appeared, her whole demeanor would change. It was fascinating to watch her."

It is remarkable that Evelyn did so well, considering the bleak conditions at P4W, which finally led to its closing in the 1990s. "During the days when Evelyn was here, it was pretty tightly controlled," says Avis. "The very first time a film was shown to them on our E. Fry evening, a bell rang—a horrible clanging bell. And then the girls who wanted to come down and see this film—this, don't forget, was the very first time anybody had brought in anything in the recreational sense—they came down the stairs with a couple of matrons behind them and they each had to carry their own chair and a little bag with their personal whatever they might think they needed with them. And most of them smoked. And they had sardine cans that they carried along with them for ashtrays. So it was a very different atmosphere—much more tightly controlled than it has been in the last, well, almost forty years."

Conditions gradually improved during Evelyn's stay at P4W, and the Thursday Elizabeth Fry nights were a popular draw for inmates. "Until then they did nothing but smoke and play cards," says Avis. "There was absolutely nothing for them to do."

The Thursday sessions were held in an old dining room, with a low ceiling and exposed pipes. "They would be in these small, informal groups," says Avis. "Some of them talked art; others learned first aid from St. John's Ambulance; and some of us would just be there to help them write letters.

"And there were the famous, or infamous, Christmas concerts. They were hilarious. Some of them had incredible musical talent, but then you would get a skit or something that was just pathetic."

Evelyn Dick made the newspapers when she played an angel in her second Christmas at Kingston. The Toronto *Evening Telegram*'s Allen Kent reported that the star prisoner was making remarkable progress, "but even the most optimistic could hardly have hoped she would become so quickly an angel.[37] Her emergence as a white-clad angel, complete with wings, took place on Dec. 29, 1948, when the 'co-eds' at the women's penitentiary put on a Christmas program that included a tableau entitled 'The Christmas Story.'"

Prison officials identified only three other performers out of the two dozen inmates who took part. Two of them had also been sentenced to life terms, and the third, Scottish war bride Jean McAllister, was serving three years for killing her husband near Lindsay, Ontario. McAllister contributed a vocal solo: "Now is the Hour."

Lieutenant Colonel Wallace Bunton, the Salvation Army's territorial prison secretary, said Evelyn had shown a "marvelous improvement in her spiritual outlook since arriving at Kingston. She is full of regret—genuine regret for what she did, not just regret for getting caught—and she is determined to lead a better life from now on." Evelyn had another convert. "I wouldn't be afraid to let her out tomorrow," gushed Bunton. "I am quite certain she would go straight."

Whether because of her reputation or her personality, Evelyn kept to herself, but she seemed to be accepted by all levels of the inmate hierarchy and the prison staff. "I think she thought she was superior to most of them," says Avis. "Many of the staff members were not really trained. Some had minimal education, and they'd had no training in behavior control or how to manage difficult people. There was a group of the real streetwise drug users that I think many of the matrons were actually afraid of, and they certainly ran things in the prison. They were the top of the hierarchy. And of course there were a lot of lesbians, but that's inevitable in any prison.

"I did get the distinct feeling that Evelyn did try to make friends with the ones that she thought were in power or that could help her. She was careful to be polite and nice to Lorraine Burke, whom she helped in the office. I think she was manipulative, but not too obvious about it.

"Inmates both in the men's prisons and the women's prison are very innovative, and they do manage to create wonderful brews which they all get highly inebriated on—out of potato peelings and yeast and so on. I don't think Evelyn was ever deeply involved in that kind of thing. Again, I think she thought she was above it."

Avis says she "quite liked" Evelyn Dick. "I have to say, I found nothing objectionable about her. But I think her own well-being was her main concern—a lot of vanity . . . a lot of vanity. She had good self-esteem and never let herself look sloppy or her hair bedraggled or anything like that. I never saw her looking depressed or downhearted. But I don't think she ever showed her real personality, because she is an enigma—a born actress."

Former National Parole Board member Mary Louise Lynch, who knew Evelyn after she got out of the penitentiary, had access to her prison files, which she said paint a picture of Evelyn as a take-charge leader. "They respected her, and I think many of them were jealous," says Lynch. "The superintendent was this woman who was a registered nurse, who never went on the tier the whole time she was here. She was afraid of the inmates. Really, she let Evelyn run the place. She wouldn't go out where the inmates were. It's three or four levels, and they call that the tier, and in their recreation time they're wandering in the hall, they're not locked up. And she was nervous about that. She was hopeless.

"I've seen it in writing, that Evelyn was a good influence on the institution, that she sort of took charge. She told them they needed education—'You girls don't know anything, you need to go to school and learn something.'

"The teachers would be real teachers. Evelyn saw that the people who wanted it were being taught—how to read, how to write, and how to do simple arithmetic and all that sort of thing. She was a leader, yeah. She wouldn't stand for any nonsense."

Lynch says as a high school graduate Evelyn knew the importance of education, particularly for women. "At that time you could get a job with a high school education. Today it's not much help to you, but at that time it really was something. Not so many young people went to university then.

"There's no question, Evelyn had leadership qualities. She was a woman you'd respect, she really was."

Lynch says that Evelyn was "hard as nails. She didn't look hard, but she was a strong, strong woman." Citing the case of Lena Thibodeau, a beautiful young battered wife who was sentenced to hang for shooting her husband in a backwoods New Brunswick community, Lynch credits Evelyn with protecting and guiding her when they were in P4W together. Thibodeau, married at fourteen, had five children and was illiterate when she arrived at the prison.

"Evelyn takes one look at this beautiful girl and sees the butches eyeing her," says Lynch. "She said 'lay a hand on her and you answer to me.' So she took her under her wing and taught her English up to grade five or six level."

Thibodeau was released after seven-and-a-half years and later married a Queen's University professor. Lynch says

Thibodeau was one of the parole board's "great successes and Evelyn Dick was responsible for a great deal of that success."

The National Parole Board wasn't in existence when Evelyn Dick made her first application for a release under the "ticket-of-leave" program in 1955, the year her father died. Her request was denied. But three years later it was granted. She was released from the penitentiary on November 10, 1958, after serving eleven years and four months there, plus seventeen months in Barton Street jail—a total of almost thirteen years behind bars.

twenty two

Reborn

Evelyn's father, Donald MacLean, had never been much of a role model, but in Kingston she found a surrogate father figure who would have a profound influence on her future. He was Alex Edmison—lawyer, veteran penal reformer, and a director of the John Howard Society from 1946 to 1959. He was from Cheltenham, Ontario, and was a graduate of Queen's University and McGill Law School. For a time he was chief legal counsel for the Montreal Prisoner's Aid and Welfare Association, and from 1950 to 1959 assistant to the principal at Queen's University. He served on the National Parole Board from its founding in 1959 until his retirement in 1971.

Mary Louise Lynch, who served on the parole board with Edmison and remained friends with him until his death in 1979, says he was impressed with Evelyn when he met her at P4W and "saw the good work she was doing in there—making them go to school, and making them study and everything. And he wasn't too impressed with this warden that they had then, either. And then he got interested in her and thought she had been in there a long, long time and it was about time she got a ticket-of-leave."

Edmison realized early on that for Evelyn to survive outside prison she would need a new identity and a new place to live; it was the only way to avoid the media spotlight. "Alex worked the whole thing out and said she must have a completely new identity," says Lynch. "Nobody must ever know who she was. He was the architect of the whole thing. And Alex Edmison discussed it with Evelyn, and she immediately realized how important it [was] to have a new identity that would be completely secret and nobody would ever know about it."

Faith Avis was with the Kingston Elizabeth Fry Society when

the plan was being hatched for Evelyn's new life. "And they knew that as soon as the word got out that she was being released, she would be hounded by the media. They would want to know what was happening with the rest of her life." She says that, besides Alex Edmison, the only people in the prison who knew of Evelyn's new identity and the location where she would settle were the warden, the P4W matron, and, from the Elizabeth Fry Society, lawyer Vera Cartwright and social worker Rowan Patterson. "And those people were the only people who knew. And the rest of us did not want to know what her name was going to be or where she was going to be, because the fewer people who knew, the less likely it would become public knowledge.

"And so, in the middle of the night or early morning, two or three in the morning, they spirited her out of here and took her to her new identity and her new job. And actually, it's amazing, but to this day I have no idea where Evelyn is. I've heard rumors, but I don't know what town or city it was in and I don't know her name. And I don't want to know. But I would like to know whether she's still alive, and I don't know that either.

"I'm not sure whether her life would have been at risk, but I think they felt if she was going to have any chance of reha-bilitation, or of leading a normal life, that it was important that she not be followed all the time by her past. And I think that was the whole reason behind it."

Lynch says that keeping Evelyn's new life a secret was so important to Edmison, he didn't even share the information with his wife, Alice. "See, she could never have had a new life if she'd been Evelyn Dick—never in a million years—because she was infamous, really," says Lynch. "So it was very impor-tant that nobody know who she was."

When the National Parole Board came into existence in 1959, only seven weeks after Evelyn's release, the ticket-of-leave program was dissolved and inmates released under that provision now came under the jurisdiction of the board. That meant Evelyn's file ended up there. Including Edmison, it was a four-person board until Lynch, the only woman, was appointed in 1960.

Lynch has always known where Evelyn went to live, and her new identity, but has never divulged it. And today, at age ninety-one, she is proud of the parole board for keeping the secret for the last forty-plus years. "As far as I know, I'm the only one on the board that Evelyn ever saw, except for Alex, of course. I don't think she ever saw any of the others, and nobody on the board ever wanted it known who she was—never. It was a great, great secret. And I wouldn't want to be the one that would spoil her secret." She hasn't had contact with Evelyn for about fifteen years, and one thing she would like to know is whether or not she is still alive.

Evelyn's secret was buried deeper in 1985, when, at age sixty-five, she was granted a pardon under the Royal Prerogative of Mercy provisions of federal law. The pardon meant she no longer had to report to police or the parole board and her file was forever sealed. So restrictive is the law that, once the pardon is granted, the parole board is not permitted to acknowledge that the pardon was granted or that there is even a file on the individual concerned. Once a pardon is granted, says parole board senior officer Clarence Roussel, "a person can do what they want. They don't have to report any more—change of address or name or anything like that. She can completely disappear, as is the case with you and me, who have no records—she is free to do that."

Of Evelyn Dick, Roussel says: "We have no file or record or anything about her. We can't find out anything about her. All we know is that at some point she was one of those few who did get a Royal Prerogative of Mercy—a clemency under that provision of the law. But even if we had a file, we couldn't share its contents. Plus, the file would be sealed and not in our possession.

"Whenever a person is granted a pardon by any means, immediately all information about that offender, including the fact that a pardon was granted, become private knowledge. It's not available to the public. It's private—protected. So the reason for the pardon program is to enable the person to go back to being incognito, or to go back to being a free person, and not have people track them down."

twenty three

Sightings, Rumors and Hype

On March 18, 1987, an elderly couple was found dead in their home in Binbrook, a small farming community south of Hamilton. It's believed they were asphyxiated from a coal-burning stove and had been dead for two or three days. Police identified them as Etheli McLean, age seventy-three, and Lino Bartolotti, age seventy-five.

The *Hamilton Spectator* carried a story the next day: "Their deaths have fueled persistent speculation and rumors in the Binbrook area that the dead woman was Evelyn Dick, whose murder trial 40 years ago attracted international attention. Hamilton-Wentworth police say they are skeptical about these claims but confirmed they have sent the woman's fingerprints to Ottawa to compare them with Mrs. Dick's prints."

It didn't matter that the dead woman was seven years older than Evelyn, and that the woman's daughter, who lived in Deep River, Ontario, emphatically denied claims her mother was Evelyn Dick. For years some neighbors had been saying the couple, though pleasant, were secretive and the dead woman was a "hermit"; therefore she must be Evelyn Dick.

Of course she wasn't, but the story was typical of the rumors that have circulated in Hamilton and southwestern Ontario through the years.

That particular rumor was put to rest, but a week later the *Spectator* ran an item saying Evelyn Dick stories had been popping up for thirty years and would likely continue into the foreseeable future:

> *According to unconfirmed reports she has worked as a*
> *clerk at the Eastgate Mall, was a waitress at Gulliver's*
> *Restaurant until a few years ago, sold perfume at a local*

shop, and even underwent a period of therapy at Hamilton General Hospital.[38]

Last year, a garrulous cab driver told a Hamilton Spectator reporter that he knew Mrs. Dick well and drove her to bingo games every Wednesday night. Pressed for more information a few days later, the cabbie clammed up. "I don't know what I was talking about," he said.

Even if she appeared in person, Evelyn Dick might have trouble living up to her stories. They have become as deeply etched into the Steel City psyche as the smokestacks, Hamilton Mountain, and the Tiger Cats.

London, Ontario, was another favorite location for Evelyn Dick sightings. One report had her being admitted as a member of Metropolitan United Church in May 1958—a bit of a stretch since she wasn't released from the penitentiary until November of that year. There were also claims that Evelyn was living in the north section of London and that she visited a cottage on a small lake near Owen Sound.

Wilma Keeber, who went to Loretto Academy with Evelyn Dick, said she'd "heard or read that Evelyn had moved to California." When she was informed that wasn't true, she said: "Well, if she's still alive, she's in London, Ontario. Didn't she marry this minister I read about?"

Faith Reed, who with her brother and the Weaver boys first discovered the torso, says she heard that while in the penitentiary Evelyn was allowed out for shopping forays at exclusive stores whenever she pleased. "She bought nothing but the best clothing," says Reed. "Another report was she had a baby in the prison by one of the prison guards. There's so many of these rumors and stories that went around in Hamilton."

Jocko Thomas says there have been reports of Evelyn sightings for years. "One time I was told she was in St. Mary's, Ontario, but nobody could find her there. Stories go around that she's dead now. Someone told me she died down around the Vineland area. And one time the office got a tip that she was working in a restaurant in Windsor. I went down and spent a week there going to different restaurants but could never find her—nobody ever saw her. I know that media, not only the *Star* but also the *Telegram* and the *Globe*, tried to find her. Charlie Wood [of the OPP] told me about it, and I knew Charlie very well. He didn't know where she was either.

"The *Weekend* in Montreal and the *Star Weekly* both wanted to buy her story, and through lawyers they forwarded letters to Kingston Penitentiary, but she refused to have anything to do with it. She was let out secretly and nobody could find her."

Paul Wilson, who has been writing the *Hamilton Spectator*'s popular "Street Beat" column since 1988, says "she keeps resurfacing. It doesn't go away. Everybody in Hamilton claims to have a link to that murder, whether it's [through] their great aunt . . . or their piano teacher, and that continues to this day. To tell you the truth I'm starting to get a little sick of her. She's had her time. But it's tempting to keep doing them now and then, because people always respond. It was a grisly, terrible crime, but with the passage of half a century and more it's become glamorized."

Peter Preston says there have been rumors about Evelyn Dick "like there's rumors about Elvis Presley. He's here, he's there, he's everywhere—the Scarlet Pimpernel. And she's here, she's there, she's everywhere. She's in Vancouver, she's in London, she's just had a baby. Like Elvis Presley, she shows up but she's never there where they think she is. So nobody to my knowledge has ever been able to really pinpoint where she is. Some have said, 'Well, I know where she was, but not where she is.' I think she's been—not in the literal sense—effectively buried where nobody will find her. I think she's still alive, but effectively, to the public, she's buried."

Evelyn Dick may be metaphorically buried, but her story has been exhumed repeatedly. Besides all the newspaper coverage there was an early tabloid booklet by Fireside Publications of Toronto. Written by Keith Edgar and Richard Daniel, it was entitled *EVELYN DICK: The Tragic Story of an Emotional Degenerate* and was proudly illustrated with twenty-four photographs. An introductory "author's page" features only Keith Edgar, described as "internationally known for his fast-paced detective fiction." Now he was turning to factual writing "with this fascinating account of the most sensational criminal case in Canada's history."

Edgar tells the reader he is irritated because "had I written such a story in my fiction work, no editor would have accepted it, because it would be considered overdrawn [like his title perhaps], impossible and unbelievable. This is one case at least where fact puts the most lurid fiction to shame. There was so much detail, too sordid and gruesome to be published, that I doubt if the complete story of the Dick case will ever be told."

He dedicates his offering to "the superb Criminal Investigation Branch of the Ontario Provincial Police, and particularly to Inspector Charles Wood, whose brilliant work impressed me so much."

In 1974, Macmillan of Canada published the book *Torso* by crime writer Marjorie Freeman Campbell, and the story has appeared in several crime anthologies, including Max Haines's *Canadian Crimes*. In December 1982, CBC radio's *Scales of Justice* series, hosted by Toronto lawyer Edward Greenspan, aired a drama entitled *How Could You Mrs. Dick?* It was written by Doug Rodger, originally from Hamilton, who seven years later produced a successful play with the same title.

In her review of the play in the *Hamilton Spectator*, Tami Paikin Nolan said the following:

> *The title of the play sets the tone, glib with a capital "G". It is a play on words about the way Evelyn apparently tried to dispose of her husband's body. "You cut off his arms. You cut off his legs. You cut off his head. How could you miss his . . . ?" Little girls used to sing it as a skipping song.*
>
> *The drama does refer briefly to the theory that Evelyn Dick was sexually abused by her father as a child and that the murdered baby was most probably the product of that incestuous relationship. This would explain a lot of things about Evelyn's bizarre behavior and her precarious mental state.*

But Donald MacLean was not the father. Evelyn herself told Mary Louise Lynch that the father of the dead infant paid

Robinette's fees and "got the noose off my neck—so he doesn't owe me a thing."

The Hamilton-based punk band Forgotten Rebels put Evelyn's story to music with a two-minute cut called simply "Evelyn Dick" as part of its *Untitled* album, now available on CD.

In his novel *Blue Moon*, published in 2000 by Simon and Pierre, James King draws on Evelyn's story and imagines her life after her release from prison. He has her settling in Vancouver with a job as a bookstore sales clerk, undergoing therapy and becoming a successful author.

"It's never quieted down," says Faith Reed's brother, David. "The year before last, students from the University of Toronto came down to see me, and they wanted to interview me for something they were doing. And prior to that there were two students from Hamilton came down to my house. Every once in a while they talk about it on the radio still. So you keep hearing about it all the time."

Faith Reed says it "just keeps going, and going, and going. Every year, on the anniversary, they always put something in the paper about it."

The latest offerings on Evelyn Dick's story, in addition to this book, include the one-hour documentary *The Notorious Mrs. Dick*, produced by Anne Pick, and a made-for-TV movie called *Torso*, both aired on CTV in the fall of 2001. Kathleen Robertson, who plays Evelyn Dick in the movie, is originally from Hamilton, as is director Alex Chapple, now living in New York.

twenty four

Afterlife

Through his work with the John Howard Society, Alex Edmison knew a lot of like-minded prison reformers across the country. One of those was the wife of the mayor of a medium-sized city—outside Ontario—where Evelyn eventually ended up.

"Alex Edmison worked the whole thing out and said she must have a complete new identity and everything," says Mary Louise Lynch. "He was the architect—he and the wife of the mayor of this particular city who was a great, great friend of his. So they were the ones who thought up the plan and discussed it with Evelyn. And she realized how important it was if she was going to have a new identity that would be completely secret."

With the help of the mayor and his wife, Edmison was able to find Evelyn a job and a tasteful apartment in a pleasant neighborhood.

So, in November 1958, convicted baby-killer Evelyn Dick quietly slipped into her new city and her new life. "I'm almost certain the job was in real estate," says Lynch. "It was either real estate or manufacturing. It wasn't a financial business—a bank or trust company. They would scrutinize everything so carefully because they dealt with money. She went there under the sponsorship of the mayor's wife, so everything was smoothed out for her."

Picking up where she left off in prison, Evelyn excelled at her new job. "She was probably in marketing for this company," says Lynch. "She got to be head of a division or department and traveled quite a lot. I know she came at least twice to Ottawa on business."

At their luncheon at the Château Laurier, Evelyn told Lynch that she loved her job and the travel.

"She had a wonderful time," says Lynch, "because she was introduced to a group of very nice people. And Evelyn would fit in perfectly, in appearance and every other way, with these people. Evelyn never discussed this with me, but I know that from the very beginning she was fully accepted in this city. They just took her to their hearts. She was an attractive addition. And the local police never knew she was there. They didn't trust them. It was only the RCMP that she reported to, and they respected her privacy."

At thirty-eight Evelyn couldn't have imagined a better storybook ending or dream come true. She was suddenly dropped into the kind of life she'd always coveted. Alexandra MacLean would have been ecstatic, but she never got to share in her daughter's success. When she died in 1964, there was a lot of speculation around Hamilton that Evelyn would show up for the funeral.

"Evelyn told me she wouldn't dream of going to Hamilton—ever," says Lynch. "She said it was the last place in the world she would go. She said, 'Imagine, thinking I'd go for the funeral.' Her mother, you know, was really against her. She was a strict Christian. She didn't know the baby was there [in the suitcase in the attic]. Only Evelyn knew."

Mary Louise Lynch, before joining the parole board, had for fourteen years been newspaper baron Lord Beaverbrook's lawyer. Before taking up her post, she had a harsh view of criminals and thought they should be severely dealt with. Her attitudes quickly moderated when she began to meet inmates face to face. "It's a humbling job," she told a reporter in 1966, after five years with the board. "Seeing people who are in trouble, you realize the rotten chances they've had. You can't always judge people by your own standards."

Lynch was surprised when she learned that Evelyn Dick wanted to meet her on one of her business trips to Ottawa in the fall of 1962. By then Evelyn had been out of prison for almost four years, she was enjoying her new life and job, and she was brimming with confidence. When she knew she was going to Ottawa, Evelyn asked her parole board contact if he could arrange for her to meet Lynch.

"It was Evelyn Dick who made the contact," says Lynch. "I had read all about her, of course. And I knew about the baby, and John Dick being ground up in the driveway." For Lynch, who had only recently changed her view that "everybody should hang," it would prove to be an interesting meeting. They agreed on lunch at the Château Laurier.

"She had read about me and probably read all the things about our program," says Lynch. "She had seen pictures of me, because I was often in the newspaper. I went to every penitentiary in Canada. I was a household name for a long time. I even had a couple of cartoons about me.

"I had seen Evelyn's picture in the file, and in the newspapers, of course, many times. And I probably told her what I would be wearing. I saw her standing there, and I recognized her right away. And then Norman DePoe came along, and I knew Norman DePoe because he was quite a friend of my cousin, Charles Lynch, who was then chief of Southam News." When DePoe went off to the bar, Lynch walked over to Evelyn.

"Evelyn?" she asked.

"Oh yes, you're Miss Lynch. I recognized you."

Lynch says Evelyn was "elegantly but quietly" dressed. "There was nothing flashy about her. She was a beautifully groomed person, very good-looking, and spoke very well. Everything about her was completely *de rigueur*, it really was. She could take her place in almost any level of society."

After joking about Norman DePoe missing the story right under his nose, they went into the Canadian Grill for lunch, where John Turner came over for a short chat. "I didn't introduce her," says Lynch. "She just sat there."

It was near the end of the luncheon that Lynch mentioned Evelyn's dead baby. "I can still see Evelyn," she says. "And when I said, 'I think you're guilty,' she just sort of inhaled and blew the smoke out. Alex Edmison said that's the closest she'd ever come to admitting it."

A year or so after their initial meeting, Evelyn heard Mary Louise Lynch would be visiting her city and invited her to dinner at her apartment.

"She had a car," recalls Lynch, "but my memory is that I took a taxi and came back in a taxi. It wasn't a huge high-rise, I'd say at most seven or eight stories. It was a nice apartment and very nicely furnished. I think we had a cocktail first—sherry—and wine with our meal. I remember it was a delicious casserole; I don't know whether it was tuna or what, but it was a good one. And we had a very nice dessert. The table was set beautifully. Everything was as it would be if I'd gone to one of my friend's homes. She was a good house-keeper and a good cook.

"We had a very pleasant evening, but we never discussed her offenses at all. We just talked about various things and the parole board. And she wasn't keen on meeting any other members of the parole board—except for Alex Edmison. She was very grateful to him, always, you see. And I think probably every time he was in that area, he did go to see her, because there was a very close relationship."

Not long after her dinner with Evelyn, Lynch was visiting friends in St. John, New Brunswick. They were having a dinner party in her honor, and during the meal she told them about eating at Evelyn's apartment. "So I told them the story," says Lynch, chuckling. "And they said, 'What? You're lucky she didn't poison you.' And I said, oh no, that wasn't her modus operandi. She didn't poison people, she cut them up and ground them up in the driveway."

While Evelyn was enjoying her new life, her daughter, Heather, was growing up in Hamilton using her middle name, Maria. She was Maria MacLean until 1959, when at age seventeen she married a Hamilton factory worker, Robert Muirhead. A daughter, Cindy, was born in January 1960.

Heather hadn't seen her mother in years, but in July of 1965, Alex Edmison arranged for her and her daughter to meet Evelyn on one of her business trips to Ottawa. Once again Evelyn requested that Mary Louise Lynch join them.

"Alex arranged it because Heather never knew where [Evelyn] was, and she hadn't seen Evelyn for some years," says Lynch. "And he told me, 'Heather and her little girl are coming to spend the weekend, and they're going to be at the [Lord] Elgin Hotel. I've taken a suite for them.' And I have an idea they arrived Friday night, because we had lunch Saturday at the Roma Restaurant, a quite nice Italian restaurant in Ottawa. Heather wasn't the image of [Evelyn], but she was dark and she looked like her, except she was very tall and slim. I'd say Evelyn's not more than about five feet four or five. And Heather was very nice-looking, and the same coloring as Evelyn—dark hair and dark eyes. And the little girl was darling, she was about four or five, and she was in a very pretty little dress. You know, there was a family resemblance there, actually."

The reunion coincided with Heather's birthday, and Evelyn brought her a cultured pearl necklace and earrings to match. "And Heather said, 'You remembered!' Well, she said, 'Of course I remember.'"

Lynch says Heather was upset that Evelyn wouldn't divulge her new identity or tell her where she was living. "She said, 'Mother, you don't trust me.' And Evelyn said, 'No, I don't trust anybody about that, you know.' It was a very hard thing to get across to poor Heather. I can understand how she felt."

Lynch says Heather and Cindy left for home on Sunday, but Evelyn was staying over on business until Monday night, and they had lunch at the Lord Elgin. "Heather might have been living in Toronto by then," says Lynch, "but I have a feeling she was still in Hamilton. She had to leave to be at work on Monday."

"I felt so sorry for Heather because it was hard for me to explain to her," Evelyn told Lynch over lunch. "I was delighted to see her and to meet my dear little granddaughter, and I'm so thrilled about it. But you know, she doesn't know what this means to me. She told me I could trust her. But I said, 'No, suppose somebody offers you a hundred thousand dollars for my story, or to tell them where I am. I just can't take that chance, Heather. You'll have to trust me that I really am delighted about this meeting, and I'm very proud I have such an attractive daughter and dear little grandchild, but I just can't.'" Lynch says Evelyn told her it was "heartbreaking for Heather and heartbreaking for me too."

Lynch says she understood Evelyn's concern. While serving as acting chairman of the parole board, she received a call from a magazine—she thinks it was *Maclean's*—offering first $30,000 and then $50,000 for Evelyn's story. "They wanted her story and they asked me for her address," says Lynch. "Well, I said, 'I'm not giving you her address. It's one of our best-kept secrets. What I can do, I can get in touch with Mrs. Dick and ask her '"

"Miss Lynch," said Evelyn, "there's not enough money in the world for my story. I like what I'm doing. I have a very pleasant social life. I have nice friends and a very interesting job. So I'm not one bit interested in money for that."

"So that was that," says Lynch. "That was the only call I got like that, but there might have been others."

During their lunch at the Lord Elgin, Evelyn had an umbrella hooked over her chair, and at one point she accidentally bumped it to the floor. A former inmate of Kingston Penitentiary, who knew Lynch and recognized Evelyn from visits he had made to P4W on work duty, was sitting at a nearby table and saw the umbrella fall. "He was a very good-looking, charming Irishman," says Lynch. "He had the gift of the gab. I think his name was McCann. I think he served ten or twelve years for fraud and bank robbery."

When the umbrella fell, McCann came quickly to their table. "Miss Lynch, nice to see you," he said, picking up the umbrella. "Madam, you dropped your umbrella." He handed it to Evelyn, who rewarded him with a smile as he returned to his table.

"You know," said Evelyn after he left, "I'm lucky that it was a male inmate. A woman would never do that. She'd say, 'Oh, Evelyn, haven't seen you since we were in the Prison for Women together.'"

Evelyn had had another close call at a private club in her new city, when one of the food servers, a young woman from P4W, recognized her.

"Evelyn," she said.

Evelyn looked away.

"Oh, you're not speaking to me," said the server.

"Who on earth are you talking to?" said Evelyn.

"Oh yes, I know you," said the server, and she mentioned Palace Row, the nickname for one of the tiers in P4W.

"I don't know what you're talking about," Evelyn replied. The mayor of the city, standing nearby with his wife, quickly grasped the situation. He told the woman to quit bothering his friend or she would lose her job. She walked away immediately.

Relating that incident to Lynch led Evelyn to a discussion of how much more difficult it was for women to disguise themselves. "Men can grow beards and mustaches and do all sorts of things," she told Lynch. She said she had three moles in a triangle on her cheek and worried that they might give away her identity.

"And she thought, because not many people have that, it could be a problem," says Lynch. "So she went to a dermatologist and he said no, it's the kind of mole you shouldn't touch. And he suggested she just cover it. You would hardly have noticed it if she hadn't pointed it out. It wasn't a bit disfiguring—a little tiny black spot."

Lynch was in her early fifties the first time she saw Evelyn, and Evelyn admired the traces of white hair on her temples. "She had much darker hair—it was really black, and quite striking. But she liked my gray, and so she decided that she would just let hers go. So the last time I saw her she had black hair with little white wings—it was quite striking—three or four inches of white at the side."

Things were going so well in Evelyn's social life, she informed Alex Edmison, that she was planning to get married, but he advised against it. "And Alex said there are thousands of men on parole for life but I think only three women at [that] time, and it would be so easy to check it out," says Lynch. "So he said, oh no, don't do that."

Lynch says Evelyn took Edmison's advice but later married another man. "She wrote and told me she was going to marry him. And of course he didn't know about her past and she was never going to tell him. I think he was Jewish, a widower, from a prominent family, and he had two or three sisters who weren't pleased at all about the wedding. I know he was rich and, if I remember correctly, quite a bit older—like ten or twelve years. So if she is still alive, I think she's a widow." Lynch thinks the marriage was probably in the late sixties.

For years Evelyn sent letters and cards to Lynch, and sometimes they called each other. "I once got a postcard from a friend of mine who was married to a doctor in the government and they were on a luxury cruise in the Caribbean, and in the same mail I had a postcard from Evelyn, from the same place," she says. "And they were staying at the same hotel and everything. It was awfully funny. They might have sat at the same table, you never know.

"She knew my birthday and she always sent me cards— Easter, Christmas, and occasionally when she was traveling. I always got a Christmas card—a lovely one, too—usually a lovely Madonna or something. She had lovely handwriting, awfully good." Lynch guesses her last contact with Evelyn was about fifteen years ago.

In the end Lynch, who served on the parole board from 1960 until her retirement in 1975, at age sixty-six, considered Evelyn a friend. "I got to like her quite well. I think she was guilty as hell, but it was just one of those things.

"She certainly did some awful things, and she certainly was in on the Dick thing—it wasn't done without her. She's far from perfect, and no angel. But it's even more remarkable that she did lead such a good life. It shows you can be rehabilitated if you have it in yourself—even people who have done awful things. Now, I don't think a Bernardo or a Homolka or an Olson can be rehabilitated, because they're monsters, and she was not a monster, really.

"If you ever do find out if Evelyn is alive, will you let me know?"

twenty five

Whodunit

No one has ever been, or ever will be, convicted in the killing and butchering of John Dick. Donald MacLean, who spent a year in jail and four years in a penitentiary as an accessory after the fact, is the only one to serve any time at all. Many, including J.J. Robinette, believed MacLean was more than an accessory—that he was the murderer. But the evidence, and Evelyn Dick's own words, point to her as the killer, no doubt with her father's assistance and approval. Under the laws of the day, that would make him just as guilty.

To arrive at the conclusion that Evelyn Dick was the killer, Bill Bohozuk, the red herring in the two deaths Evelyn was charged with, must first be eliminated as a suspect. It took a jury twenty-six minutes to exonerate him on the one charge and, after a judge's direction, about two minutes on the other.

In the death of Evelyn's infant son, Peter David White, she said Bohozuk was the father and that, after leaving the hospital, she met him at the Royal Connaught Hotel, where he took the baby and killed it, returning it to her some months later encased in cement. This was a guy who didn't like roughhousing at the boat club and who wouldn't kill a rat with a shovel at the steel mill. How could he throttle a ten-day-old infant?

He couldn't and didn't. The baby was born in September 1944, so Bohozuk would have to have known and been intimate with Evelyn no later than December 1943. Bohozuk himself testified that the first time he even had a conversation with Evelyn was in the spring of 1945 and the first time they went out was in October of that year, thirteen months after Peter David White's birth. She didn't tell him she was a newlywed; she said she was the widow White, planning to go back soon to her maiden name—MacLean. Even Evelyn's mother, whom she shared a bed with before and after her marriage, didn't meet Bohozuk or hear his name mentioned until late summer or early fall of 1945. And police couldn't find a single witness to say the relationship started any earlier than Bohozuk claimed. And Evelyn herself, while in custody, said the first time she had sexual relations with Bohozuk was on October 9, 1945, five days after her marriage to John Dick. Bohozuk said that was the only time they had sex, and he stopped seeing her two days later, after being confronted by a tearful John Dick at Dominion Foundry.

Evelyn's statement to police was made before the discovery of the baby in the suitcase in her attic. It was only at that point that she changed her story to incriminate Bohozuk in the infant's death. By then she'd already conveniently implicated him in the murder of John Dick after police found his picture in her wallet and Detective Preston put the seed in her mind by asking if Bohozuk "was involved in this."

Although he never called Evelyn for another date, Bohozuk admitted driving her home after bumping into her at the liquor store one morning in November or December. And in late January 1946, when he was in debt and facing a repair bill for his damaged car, he took her up on an offer of financial help and borrowed $200, which he repaid out of a bank loan two weeks later. He had the bank records, canceled checks and repair receipts to back up his story. But Evelyn's story transformed the loan into an advance for a hit team that Bohozuk was supposedly hiring to kill John Dick. What professional gangster of any era would take on a murder contract to settle a *civilian's* personal squabble for a $200 advance, to be split four or five ways?

So how did Evelyn's baby die? It is useful to bear in mind that there was always some truth in the tales she told police. She said she took a taxi from the hospital ten days after the baby was delivered, but she didn't arrive at her parents' home until three hours later. She said she went to the Royal Connaught Hotel, where Bohozuk had a room. There is no record of him at the hotel on that day. Well, he was local and probably used a phony name, she said—that's what they do. Evelyn knew about matters like that. If you don't believe me, she said, check such-and-such a store, I bought a coat there after handing off the baby to Bohozuk. Sure enough, the store records show that she bought a coat that day.

In court the Crown contended that she probably took a taxi to her vacant Henson apartment on James Street South and killed the baby there. Another possibility is that she did take a taxi to the Royal Connaught, went into a washroom with her baby and her suitcase, and came out with a dead baby in a suitcase. Then she could simply check the suitcase or put it in a locker and go out and do a little shopping; a new coat would be nice.

It was pretty obvious that the cement used to encase the baby came from the bag in the basement of the Rosslyn house. The question remains: what role, if any, did Donald MacLean play? He's the one who said he didn't want another little bastard running around the house. It was his cement, and he was known to spend a lot of time alone in his basement, so he would probably have noticed if some of his cement was missing. Timothy Rigney's sexist assumption that only men mix good cement was probably true in Evelyn's case. Evidence showed she was an excellent housekeeper with a talent for entertaining men, but she had no practical work experience. Rigney's criticism of the cement was that no gravel was used in the mixture, making it difficult to set properly; a man would always have enough sense to use gravel, he said, so it had to be a woman—Evelyn. It was because the cement began to crumble that Evelyn wrapped her phony Red Cross skirt around it to hold it in place. She said she applied the skirt after Bohozuk brought the baby to her in February, but experts testified the skirt had so deteriorated that it must have been combined with the cement for several months.

Alexandra MacLean—who would rather incriminate her only daughter in a capital crime than tell a lie—said she definitely saw books in the beige suitcase in January. So the baby, in its layered packaging, was inserted sometime after that.

Until it was moved to the suitcase in the Carrick house, it was most likely kept in the burlap bag, in which it was found, in the basement of the Rosslyn house, probably with Donald MacLean's knowledge.

As for the death of John Dick, Mr. Justice Lebel put it best when he said there wasn't a "tittle of evidence" to back Evelyn's claim that Bill Bohozuk was involved. Corroborating Bohozuk's plea of innocence is the fact that, at the time of the murder, policeman George Lawson saw him downtown, flirting with the Palace Theatre ticket seller.

Considering his size and athletic ability, Bill Bohozuk was a pussycat. He had no history of violence. He liked his car, nice clothes and women—a "real ladies' man," says Lawson. In the vernacular of the day, Bohozuk was a lover not a fighter. He probably thought John Dick was quite deranged when he showed up so distraught at the foundry parking lot. And he must have wondered if all of Evelyn's oars were in the water, as she slept with him less than a week after her marriage.

John Dick, forty years old, totally smitten and out of his depth, was being shunned by his young wife, who seemed intent on making his life miserable. At first he blamed their problems on the cliché scapegoat—the busybody mother-in-law—and said as much to his best man a few weeks after the wedding. "Either she has to go, or I do," he told Dominic Pollice when he saw him on his streetcar.

Dick must have felt intimidated by Bohozuk's youth, size and good looks. And he was so obsessed and consumed with jealousy that he convinced himself the rower was continuing secretly to see his wife. It didn't help that two false sightings of Evelyn and Bohozuk together were reported to Dick. With his Mennonite upbringing Dick was probably as non-violent as his competitor, although he wasn't averse to verbal aggression, such as his threat to slit Evelyn's throat, overheard by Alexandra MacLean.

To deal with Bohozuk, Dick put out word that he was going to come after him with a shotgun. This bothered Bohozuk enough that he went to the home of a woman who said she had seen Evelyn in his car and told her it couldn't have been so, because his car was in for repairs. He told her Dick would be after him with a shotgun if she didn't tell him she had been mistaken. He even went to the Hamilton Street Railway to see Dick and explain, but he wasn't on shift. Bohozuk was worried enough that, to protect himself, he went out and purchased a revolver from a friend. However, he never attempted to fire the gun.

As for John Dick, he wasn't worried about Bill Bohozuk. At his grandmother's funeral a week before his own death, Dick told his mother and others that if anything ever happened to him, they should go after Evelyn and her parents for answers. And it was Donald MacLean whom Dick went to the police about, saying his father-in-law had threatened to shoot him and that he carried a gun.

In many ways this story is about money and greed, and John Dick wasn't a complete innocent, although he certainly didn't deserve the fate that befell him. He thought that, once married, Evelyn and her mother should bankroll him at will and that, as the husband, the Carrick house should rightly be in his name. That old-world patriarchal attitude didn't sit well with Evelyn, and even less so with her mother, who for years had been in combat with her heavy-drinking husband. At least she'd been able to wrestle some of the HSR's ill-gotten cash from the old bugger. She wasn't about to put up with a sponger—a foreigner to boot—who began hitting her up for cash even before the wedding.

Evelyn was so cash-conscious, she could tell police the cost—fifty-five cents—of the taxi she took from the Grafton Garage to her house after just witnessing her husband's torso being flipped over the brow of Hamilton Mountain. And although she wanted John Dick out of her life, in the divorce agreement she had drawn up but which he refused to sign, she was demanding a $10 monthly support payment.

Those were bothersome problems to Evelyn and her mother, but they were solvable—not worth killing him over. What probably sealed John Dick's fate was Evelyn telling him that her father had for years been stealing from the streetcar company. Donald MacLean was already furious at Evelyn for marrying Dick in the first place—so furious that he had cut off Evelyn's use of the Chrysler that sat in the garage at Rosslyn. (That was why Evelyn had to borrow Bohozuk's car for a day.) MacLean was further enraged when his daughter told Dick about the long-time, ongoing theft of cash and tickets. If management at the HSR found out about the theft, it would mean the end of MacLean's cash cow, and probably prison. It was when Dick blurted out that knowledge to MacLean that the Scotsman told him he had a gun and would shoot him if he ever spilled the beans to anyone. Significantly, when Dick went to the police, he told them about the threat but not about the stealing.

"John Dick no doubt was going to blow the whistle on Donald MacLean and that's why they wanted to get rid of him," says Jocko Thomas. "Otherwise, what had John Dick done? He'd lived a good life. He came from a good family. So I go along with what Inspector Wood believed—that Dick was going to blow the whistle and they decided they had to get rid of him. Because MacLean had a good thing going there."

In her stories to police Evelyn created Romanelli and the gang from Windsor, but she discarded that when she saw the police were skeptical. Then it became Bohozuk and his gang, and then, when she was most desperate, Bohozuk and her father. But even after Evelyn was sentenced to life for manslaughter, she refused to testify against Bohozuk— because he wasn't involved and she would look like a fool on the witness stand. She certainly had no reason to protect Bohozuk—one of her rich lovers, perhaps, but not Bohozuk, another spendthrift who borrowed money from her.

So, with Bohozuk removed from the equation, which he must be, only Evelyn and her father remain. Donald MacLean didn't like John Dick, and his lucrative scam was at risk. And when Evelyn found out that Dick had no family income, she felt duped. (Never mind that she had an illegitimate child and wasn't the widow she claimed to be.) And Dick's constant badgering of her and her mother for money was getting to her. He was a nuisance who wouldn't get out of her life.

John Dick would never have stepped into a car with Donald MacLean, gun pointed at him or not. He had already told his family, police and others that he feared for his life. And Evelyn's own words put MacLean in the tavern at Balmoral House "getting drunk" at the time John Dick was being murdered.

Donald MacLean already had the plan for cutting up and disposing of John Dick's body; it was in the article in the magazine found in his house. The method was simple enough: cut the body up and burn the pieces in the furnace. The gun used to kill John Dick belonged to Donald MacLean. It was an Ivor Johnson .32-caliber five-shot, and Evelyn said MacLean had given it to Bohozuk on Saturday, March 2, after he tested it in the Rosslyn basement. That becomes the starting point for what really happened.

It's Saturday, March 2. MacLean loads the gun with five bullets and fires two to test it. (Evelyn maybe fires one of the shots to get a feel for the gun.) Evelyn takes the gun.

The only one who can get John Dick into a car and out to the country is Evelyn. She borrows Bill Landeg's Packard on Monday, March 4, and drives downtown, where she finds Dick. But he's in a surly mood, asks her what the hell she's doing there and tells her to go away. This will take more effort than she expected. She telephones him the next day, Tuesday, and sweet-talks him on the phone. Maybe we can work things out, she says—or something to that effect. John Dick takes the bait. He's still smitten, and he knows Evelyn is rolling in dough.

Evelyn picks up the Packard around 2 p.m. on Ash Wednesday and then meets Dick after his fast late lunch at the Windsor. They drive into the countryside. She brings along some booze. Dick drinks enough to get intoxicated. Evelyn drinks ginger ale. She is looking for a secluded spot. He is worrying about getting to work on time—just after 4 p.m. When she turns away from Hamilton on an isolated, muddy, bumpy road and gets the car stuck, Dick becomes angry. She's purposely making him late so he'll lose his job. It's all a plot, he says. He rails on about going to a divorce lawyer the next day and naming Bohozuk as correspondent. Evelyn calms him down and they continue along the isolated road, so muddy with spring thaw that she has to use the windshield wipers. Finally she pulls over. They probably embrace. Then Evelyn casually reaches into her purse or fur coat pocket, pulls out the small revolver and fires a shot into the back of Dick's neck just below the hairline. The bullet goes upwards inside his skull, smashing blood vessels and causing blood to come out his right eye. Evelyn thinks the bullet has exited the eye. She fires again from almost the same spot. Dick slumps forward. Evelyn's adrenalin is pumping. She remembers smoke and blood, she tells police later. Getting out of the car, she goes around to the passenger side, reaches behind Dick and pulls the blanket covering the front seat over his head. She returns to the driver's side and as she is about to get behind the wheel, Dick moans. Standing back three or four feet, she fires into his body. The wound is to the chest, and superficial. The bullet stays in his clothing.

The .32 Ivor Johnson was once a police-issue revolver. Jack Webster, retired Metro Toronto police superintendent and former historian at the Toronto Police Museum, laughingly describes the gun as a "peashooter." It could kill at close range, as it did with John Dick, but its power could not compare to a .38 or a .45. It was because it was an Ivor Johnson that no trace of a bullet was found in the Packard; the bullets stayed in the body and the clothing.

Now Evelyn sees that there isn't as much blood as she thought there would be. There is none on the fur coat and only a drop on the skirt of her coral dress. She tells police later that it wasn't a problem because she had brought along a supply of handkerchiefs.

It is probably about 5 p.m. when Evelyn arrives at the Rosslyn house, where Donald MacLean is waiting. It's still daylight, but as Evelyn explains to police later, the driveway runs along the side of the house to the rear, where it is only a few steps to the cellar entrance. No doubt she stands watch as Donald MacLean, probably half drunk or worse in anticipation of his grisly chore, drags the blanket-covered body of

John Dick to the basement. There is a lot of blood as the butchery begins, but Evelyn doesn't wait around to watch. She has done her part and now takes the blanket and leaves. She is going to be late getting the car back, but she wants to clean it up. She picks up some "It" cleaning fluid at a drugstore and then heads for the garage at Carrick. Unable to get the Packard into the garage and fed up with her stubborn mother, she drives back to the Rosslyn house.

While she was gone, Donald MacLean has sawn off John Dick's head, legs and arms, but when he attempts to saw the torso in half, he cuts into the bowel, releasing a terrible odor that discourages him from further cutting. When Evelyn returns, he tells her there is a change of plans. He can't cut the torso into furnace-size pieces and they will have to dispose of it in the woods at the top of the Mountain. Evelyn is running late with the Packard and probably objects, but he insists. The torso is in a burlap sack when he drags it out to the Packard and lifts it into the front seat before flipping it over the seat to the rear, where it strikes the outboard motors lying on the floor. Pathologist William Deadman will later find marks on the torso consistent with striking the motors. And the palm-sized spot of blood on the front seat results from the sack resting there until MacLean flipped it over the seat. As Evelyn tells police in one of her many statements: ". . . where he had put the sack in the car the blood was coming out." The only other blood found later by police is on one door handle and on one of the outboard motors.

It's getting darker as Evelyn and her father set out for the Mountain with the torso in the sack behind the seat. MacLean is in a nasty mood and probably under the influence. "He said, 'Hurry up, drive faster,' and he kept putting his foot over top of mine because he didn't like the way I drove—I drove too slow," Evelyn says later of Romanelli. There was no Romanelli, it was her father.

At the Rosslyn house, MacLean removed John Dick's shoes and HSR jacket and trousers. He was probably thinking that in case the torso was found, it couldn't be identified if there was no clothing—especially clothing connecting it to the Hamilton Street Railway. And on the drive up the Mountain he tosses Dick's HSR cap out the passenger-side window, over the car and down the hillside.

When they are well along on Mountain Brow Road, heading towards Albion Falls, MacLean orders his daughter to pull over. They get out of the Packard and switch seats. He drives a few yards more and pulls off the road, stopping at a curve. MacLean opens the rear door and pulls the sack from the car. "Give me a hand with this," he orders, "it's heavy." Evelyn walks around the car just as MacLean is pulling the sack off the torso. She sees what's left of John Dick and vomits. Her father carries the torso across the road, removes the sweater, shirt and tie, and, according to Evelyn, "rolled him down the side." The torso comes to rest on a ledge twenty feet below, and there it will stay until Faith and David Reed and the Weaver boys discover it ten days later.

MacLean throws the clothing into the back seat and they drive down the Mountain, tossing out, at various points, the bloody shirt, the burlap sack and the front seat covers. MacLean, probably in somewhat of a panic, overlooks John Dick's sweater and the tie; they will be found later and produced as evidence. The shirt is found on Mountain Boulevard near Flock Road the next morning, and the cap a few days later. The sack and seat covers are never found. (It's also possible they were burned in MacLean's furnace.) Evelyn keeps the blanket and washes it at home, where police will later seize it.

The trip to the Mountain and the delays trying to get the Packard into the Carrick garage have put Evelyn well behind schedule, and after dropping off Donald MacLean and cleaning up any visible spots of blood, she returns the car about 7:30 p.m., leaving the note with the lie about her daughter bleeding and telling Landeg she will replace his front seat covers.

Some or all of John Dicks's limbs and his head were incinerated in Evelyn Dick's furnace. How and when they got there is open to speculation. MacLean probably cut them into smaller pieces in his basement and may have burned some of them in his own furnace. On Sunday night, four days after the murder, Evelyn again borrowed Landeg's Packard, this time for one hour. She probably picked up a bushelful of John Dick's remains and, under cover of darkness, locked them in the Carrick garage. They were probably burned on one of the days Evelyn encouraged her mother to take Heather out for a walk. The burning was completed by Wednesday, March 13, when Evelyn began hauling the ashes to the garage and dumping them in the muddy ruts in the laneway in front. It's certain that the head was among the remains burned by Evelyn because teeth and bits of skull bone were found in the ashes. Also, the bullet found later on the cinder floor of the garage had bits of bone attached. No bone was hit in the bullet to the chest, so it had to have fallen out of the severed head.

There can be no question about Donald MacLean's involvement. He had the gun, the how-to magazine article, the motive, the saw and the knives. Also, he was in and out of the Carrick house. Evelyn told police that John Dick's uniform was in a trunk in the attic. MacLean broke into a trunk before police got to it, and the uniform was never found. An HSR employee, Albert Tompkins, who often drove MacLean around in MacLean's Chrysler, said that on the evening of Evelyn's arrest he was asked to drive "Scotty" to 32 Carrick. "He said his daughter was in trouble," said Tompkins. And when they left Carrick to return to Rosslyn, "he had with him a burlap bag or potato sack." Tompkins said he didn't know what was in the bag, but it was half full and weighed about twenty pounds.

Also an indication of his guilt was MacLean's panic on March 16 when an HSR supervisor, worried that John Dick had gone missing, called MacLean into his office and told him he would have to send the police over to 32 Carrick, "the only address we had for him."

"For God's sake don't send the police down there," said MacLean. "I'll find out where he is." He telephoned at 1:30 p.m. the same day to say Dick was living at 225 Gertrude Street. He obviously didn't want the police snooping around the Carrick house.

That MacLean quickly accepted a plea of guilty to being

an accessory after the fact is further evidence of his deep involvement.

"There wasn't any doubt that her father was involved in it," says Jocko Thomas. "I don't think Evelyn Dick was capable of doing that by her lonesome, you know, down in the cellar by herself. She just concocted the craziest stories to try to cover it up.

"So when you analyze the whole thing, the murder of John Dick is still unsolved to this day, because nobody's been convicted of it. My experience with the police goes back fifty years, and I know there are many cases where people have been acquitted and they've certainly been guilty. But for the police records, of course—I don't know whether they still do this or not—if an indictment is returned against a person, even if they're acquitted, it's called case solved.

"If Evelyn Dick was cold-hearted enough to kill the child—and she did—she was certainly involved in the killing of her husband, although she wasn't convicted of it."

Probably the most pathetic figure in this story is Donald MacLean. There was no doubt that he hated John Dick, and looked down on him for being a foreigner, even though he himself was an immigrant to Canada.

"Your father looked on him [John Dick] as a foreigner, didn't he?" Evelyn was asked in court.

"Well, to be exact, a penniless foreigner," replied Evelyn.

In prison MacLean was looked upon as surly and uncooperative and his gall knew no bounds. Just before his release at the age of seventy-three in April, 1951, he wrote a long letter to Brigadier P.A.S. Todd, the general manager hired to clean up Hamilton Street Railway.

Former HSR general manager, Frank Cooke convulses with laughter as he relates the story: "MacLean writes to Todd on a piece of foolscap asking him if there's any chance of getting a job. Todd was a strict military man, and he couldn't believe it. You've got to have gall."

The request from MacLean, who may have stolen as much as a quarter of a million dollars from HSR, was of course turned down. HSR had sued to seize MacLean's bank accounts and got some of its money back, but rumors persisted that he had secretly stashed away thousands more.

"There were lots of rumors going around that I would have plenty to live on when I came out," MacLean told the reporter, "but this is not so."

Rejected by his estranged wife, Alexandra, he lived his last years in run-down rooming houses, living off his old-age pension, unemployment insurance and wages from occasional work such as a parking lot attendant.

MacLean was briefly back in the news in September, 1951 when he sued a former friend and benefactor for $41 he claimed was owed him from $240 worth of bonds he had given the man for safe-keeping. The suit was filed when the man refused to drive MacLean to Kingston to visit Evelyn.

The suit was tossed out when the man produced receipts proving that he had spent more than $500 helping MacLean since his release from prison five months earlier.

"I just wanted to see the extent of this man's ingratitude," said the defendant. "Through my efforts, he was able to get the old age pension. He has been roundly abusing me to his friends and to my friends and I permitted the case to proceed so that I would have an opportunity of clearing myself of his charges under oath."

"When he came out of jail he was nothing," says Ross Hough. "I was away then, but my parents got to know him. And people around the neighborhood who he'd been good to, gave him handouts and stuff like that."

MacLean died in hospital at age seventy-seven on May 3, 1955. There was speculation that Evelyn might be allowed to attend his funeral but Evelyn did not apply for funeral leave.

A few years after Evelyn Dick was released from prison, Mary Louise Lynch saw J.J. Robinette at a dinner in Fredericton. "He hadn't heard a word about Evelyn for years," she says. "So he was delighted when I told him how successful she was." "She was one of my favorite clients," said Robinette, "and I'm delighted that she's turned out so well."

Lynch later called Evelyn to tell her what Robinette had said. "She was very pleased. I think that was probably the last conversation I ever had with her."

Evelyn's daughter, Heather and granddaughter, Cindy, moved to Toronto after Heather divorced her husband, Robert Muirhead, in Hamilton in 1967. Muirhead committed suicide five years later. Alexandra Maclean died on July 7, 1964. She was buried in Woodlands Cemetery after a private ceremony. She left an estate, valued at $11,000, which went to Heather.

In an "In Memoriam" appearing in the *Spectator* two years later, Heather wrote: "Her love was true; her heart was kind. A better grandmother none could find."

Today Heather, who uses the first name, Maria, is fifty-nine and lives in Toronto's High Park area. She was contacted, through a friend, to be interviewed for this book but refused. Cindy is now forty-one. Her whereabouts are unknown.

William "Bill" Bohozuk died in Hamilton in November, 1996. He worked at Dofasco all his life and retired in a supervisory position. He remarried in 1952 and raised a son and a daughter. He kept his own name until after his marriage, but he was dogged by the rumors and publicity from the Evelyn Dick case and before his children were born changed his name to Burton.

At the time of his death his wife of forty-four years told Paul Wilson of the *Spectator*: "Bill never got an apology from anyone. He was persecuted all his life. If the people with the big mouths had a husband like mine, they'd have something better to talk about. He was a wonderful man."

Despite her twelve and a half years behind bars, Evelyn seems to have escaped with the least scars in this story. After prison, she went on to a successful career, married a wealthy man, and traveled in circles she most cherished in her youth. The details of that life are still being investigated. If she is alive she would be eighty-one on October 13, 2001.

notes

CHAPTER 3

[1]   Other accounts credit Jimmie Weaver with approaching the car.

[2]   *Toronto Evening Telegram*, March 27, 1946.

[3]   *Toronto Evening Telegram*, March 27, 1946.

CHAPTER 4

[4]   Mennonite Historical Society of Canada.

CHAPTER 5

[5]   *Hamilton Spectator*, Oct. 22, 1946.

[6]   Hamilton Street Railway archives.

[7]   *Hamilton Spectator*, June 11, 1998.

[8]   *Toronto Daily Star*, Oct. 17, 1946.

[9]   Marjorie Freeman Campbell, *Torso*, p. 25.

[10]   *Hamilton Spectator*, May 26, 1989.

[11]   Marjorie Earl, *Toronto Daily Star*, March 25, 1947.

CHAPTER 6

[12]   He was a member of Canada's rowing team in the 1936 Olympics in Berlin.

CHAPTER 7

[13]   *Toronto Evening Telegram*, March 7, 1947.

[14]   Evelyn's statement to police April 12, 1946.

[15]   Marjorie Earl, *Toronto Daily Star*, Feb. 25, 1947.

CHAPTER 10

[16] Val Sears, *Hello Sweetheart ... Get Me Re-Write*, p. 17.

CHAPTER 12

[17] *Hamilton Spectator*, March 23, 1946.

CHAPTER 13

[18] Jocko Thomas, *From Police Headquarters*, p. 89.

CHAPTER 14

[19] Marjorie Freeman Campbell, *Torso*, p. 72.

CHAPTER 15

[20] Jack Batten, *Robinette: The Dean of Canadian Lawyers*, p. 70.

CHAPTER 16

[21] The building was torn down in the 1950s and replaced with a non-descript brick, box-like structure.

[22] Brian Vallée, *Edwin Alonzo Boyd: The Story of the Notorious Boyd Gang*, p. 338.

[23] *Globe and Mail*, October 8, 1946.

[24] Jack Batten: *Robinette, The Dean of Canadian Lawyers*, p. 71.

[25] Marjorie Freeman Campbell, *Torso*, pp. 76–77.

[26] Marjorie Freeman Campbell, *Torso*, p. 112.

[27] Jocko Thomas, *From Police Headquarters*, p. 95.

[28] *Toronto Daily Star*, October 16, 1946.

[29] Marjorie Freeman Campbell, *Torso*, p. 123.

CHAPTER 17

[30] *Hamilton Spectator*, September 29, 1984.

[31] Jack Batten: *Robinette, The Dean of Canadian Lawyers*, p. 73.

[32] Jack Batten: *Robinette, The Dean of Canadian Lawyers*, pp. 76–77.

[33] *Canada Law Books Inc.*, 1999, p. 107.

CHAPTER 18

[34] Jack Batten, *Robinette: The Dean of Canadian Lawyers*, p. 82.

[35] Eva-Lis Wuorio, *Globe and Mail*, February 26, 1947.

CHAPTER 19

[36] Jack Batten, *Robinette: The Dean of Canadian Lawyers*, p. 91.

CHAPTER 21

[37] *Toronto Evening Telegram*, January 15, 1948.

CHAPTER 23

[38] *Hamilton Spectator*, March 28, 1987.

sources

The dialogue in this book was recreated as accurately as possible from statements to police, court transcripts, first-person recollections of those still alive, and newspaper accounts of events.

The newspapers themselves were, of course, a part of the story and coverage of the Evelyn Dick saga by the *Hamilton Spectator* and the three major Toronto papers of the day was rich in detail and captured the flavor of the time. I thank the dozens of editors and reporters, many of them now deceased, who brought the stories to life.

The photo of Evelyn Dick in a Red Cross uniform is from Ontario Archives Series RG 4-32. Attorney General Central Registry Files, File 1946 #284.

Other sources are listed in the notes.

index